TWO G
AND OTHER ESSAYS

TWO GIRLS
AND OTHER ESSAYS

ROBERTO SCHWARZ

Edited by Francis Mulhern

V

VERSO

London • New York

First published by Verso 2012
© Verso 2012
Introduction © Francis Mulhern 2012
Translation Chapter 1 © Nicholas Brown 2012
Translation Chapter 8 © Emilio Sauri 2012
Translation chapters 2 and 4 to 7 © John Gledson 2012

1 3 5 7 9 10 8 6 4 2

Verso
UK: 6 Meard Street, London W1F 0EG
US: 20 Jay Street, Suite 1010, Brooklyn, NY 11201
www.versobooks.com

Verso is the imprint of New Left Books

ISBN-13: 978-1-84467-965-2 (PBK)
ISBN-13: 978-1-84467-966-9 (HBK)

British Library Cataloguing in Publication Data
A catalogue record for this book is available from the British Library

Library of Congress Cataloging-in-Publication Data
Schwarz, Roberto.
Two girls : and other essays / Roberto Schwarz ; edited by Francis Mulhern.
p. cm.
Includes bibliographical references and index.
ISBN 978-1-84467-965-2 (pbk. : alk. paper) – ISBN
978-1-84467-966-9 (hardback : alk. paper)
1. Criticism. I. Mulhern, Francis. II. Title.
PQ9698.29.C44T96 2012
869.4'42– dc23
2012035738

Typeset in Fournier by Hewer Text UK Ltd, Edinburgh
Printed in the US by Maple Vail

Contents

Acknowledgements

Except where otherwise indicated below, the translations in this volume are by John Gledson. Their publication histories are as follows:

'Kafka's Family Man': first published as 'Tribulação de um pai de família', in *O Estado de São Paulo*, Suplemento literário, 12 March 1966, and reprinted in Roberto Schwarz, *O pai de família e outros estudos* (São Paulo: Paz e Terra, 1978), 21–6. The text printed here is based on the translation by Nicholas Brown, 'Worries of a Family Man' in *Mediations* 23:1 (2007), 21–5.

'Objective Form: Reflections on the Dialectic of Roguery': first published as 'Pressupostos, salvo engano, de "Dialética da malandragem"' in Celso Lafer, ed., *Esboço de figura* (São Paulo: Livraria Duas Cidades, 1979), and reprinted in Roberto Schwarz, *Que horas são?* (São Paulo: Companhia das Letras, 1987); here translated into English for the first time.

'Beyond Universalism and Localism: Machado's Breakthrough': written in English and first published as 'A Brazilian Breakthrough' in *New Left Review* 36 (November–December 2005).

'Capitu, the Bride of Dom Casmurro' and 'Another Capitu? Helena Morley's Diary' ('Two Girls'): first published as *Duas meninas* (São Paulo: Companhia das Letras, 1997); here translated into English for the first time.

'An Enormous Minimalism': first published as 'No país do *Elefante*' in *Folha de S. Paulo*, Mais!, 10 March 2002. This English translation was first published as 'In the Land of *Elefante*' in *New Left Review* 22 (July–August 2003), 93–118.

'City of God': first published as 'Cidade de Deus' in *Folha de S. Paulo*, Mais!, 7 September 1997. This English translation was first published under the same title in *New Left Review* 12 (November–December 2001).

'Brecht's Relevance – Highs and Lows': first published as 'Altos e baixos da atualidade de Brecht' in Roberto Schwarz, *Seqüências brasileiras* (São Paulo: Companhia des Letras, 1999). The English version was first published under the same title in *New Left Review* 57 (May–June 2009), 85–104, based on an original English translation by Emilio Sauri in *Mediations* 23:1 (2007).

Introduction
by Francis Mulhern

Roberto Schwarz is the foremost literary and cultural critic of his generation in Brazil and the most significant Marxist inheritor of the Frankfurt School tradition writing anywhere today. These joint distinctions are intimately associated in Schwarz's constitution as a thinker, which is complex. Frankfurt Critical Theory came to him as one element in the constellation of German Marxist aesthetic theory in the earlier and middle twentieth century. 'My work would be inconceivable', he has written, in a characteristically nuanced formulation, 'without the tradition – itself contradictory – formed by Lukács, Benjamin, Brecht and Adorno, and the inspiration of Marx'.[1] 'Equally' inconceivable, that is – to restore a missing word – for Schwarz preceded this statement with another acknowledging a debt to his teacher at the University of São Paulo, one of the outstanding intellectual personalities of the Left in Brazil, Antonio Candido.

The fundamental theoretical insight of the German tradition, for Schwarz's purposes as a literary critic, is the idea of the objectivity of form. Forms, whose substances are those of practical life, emerge as part of the historical social process, and may then be worked over

---

1 Roberto Schwarz, *Um mestre na periferia do capitalismo: Machado de Assis*, São Paulo, 1991, 13. The whole phrase reads: 'Meu trabalho seria impensável igualmente sem a tradição . . .'.

to create the 'structural reduction' that is the literary work itself, the proper object of an integrally dialectical criticism, in which form and social process are indissociable. Schwarz is emphatic in referring this dialectical formalism to the Hegelian-Marxist tradition and to Marx himself.[2] And yet, he insists none the less, its inspirational precedent in Brazil was precisely not Marxist: rather, it was the achievement of a socialist – Candido – who, with all his great international breadth of literary culture, was contrastingly 'national' in feeling and focus.[3] In this circumstance, there were the signs both of convergence and of possible crux. The Frankfurt School was preoccupied with 'the character and destiny of bourgeois civilization as a whole', Schwarz explained, in an interview given to mark Adorno's centenary in 2003; Candido's commitment, on the other hand, was to 'the peculiarity of the Brazilian experience, be it literary or social'. And what he concluded was that 'the categories of the countries that serve as our models are not convincing as universals, and their direct application in our case is a mistake'.[4] The transition from feudalism to capitalism, the spreading dominion of the commodity form, the great arc of bourgeois development and decline and the forward march of labour; these and the specifically literary-historical and cultural narratives they undergirded – the classic accounts of the historical novel, realism and naturalism, the competing evaluations of modernism, the transition from liberal to administered civilization, the steady permeation of the principle of exchange – were all vulnerable to critical check, and even rejection, as authoritative patterns for the world outside the heartlands of capital.

---

2 'Conversa sobre *Duas Meninas*', in Schwarz, *Seqüências brasileiras*, São Paulo, 1999, 236–7.
3 In English, see the selection of Antonio Candido's writings, trans. and ed. Howard S. Becker, *On Literature and Society*, Princeton, 1995.
4 Candido, quoted in Jorge de Almeida 'Pressupostos, salvo engano, dos pressupostos, salvo engano', Maria Elisa Cevasco and Milton Ohala, eds., *Um crítico na periferia do capitalismo: Reflexões sobre a obra de Roberto Schwarz*, São Paulo: Universidade de São Paulo, 2007, 49.

Candido had already studied the working of this antithesis in its most general terms as a conflict between universalism and localism in the Brazilian literature of the eighteenth and nineteenth centuries.[5] His preferred solution, in his own time, was to refuse the lure of polarization, instead upholding the value of spontaneous trans-migrations between the cultures of Brazil and the metropolitan centres, while taking a cautious view of the likely balance in the exchange, of what a country like Brazil might be expected to bring to the cultural ecumene or see embraced by its more prestigious members.[6] Schwarz was no less keenly aware of the incongruities of Brazil's dependent cultures. 'In the process of reproducing its social order', he wrote in his best-known essay, 'Misplaced Ideas', 'Brazil unceasingly affirms and reaffirms European ideas, always improperly'.[7] This was a rule of perversity from which Marxism was not automatically exempt, either in its official manifestations or, for that matter, in the leading forms of heterodoxy. Schwarz's solution, a subtle dialectical displacement of Candido's, was to pose 'the question of Brazil' (*a matéria brasileira*) as a problem internal to Marxism and to seek a satisfactory resolution in coherent historical-materialist terms. If Marxism appeared intellectually brittle in the face of the palpable realities of Brazil and the rest of the non-metro-politan world, the deficiency lay in its own underdevelopment, which it was necessary to put right. It was not that the country was simply aberrant in its relation to the canonical schemes of historical development, let alone essentially different in the sense of the cultural-nationalist picturesque. The secret of Brazil's uniqueness, Schwarz maintained, lay in its formation as part of the world system

---

5   Candido addresses this, above all, in his classic *Formação da literatura brasileira: momentos decisivos*, dealing with the period 1750–1880 (1959; 2 vols., Belo Horizonte, 1975).
6   See 'Literature and Underdevelopment', in *On Literature and Society*, 119–41.
7   'Misplaced Ideas: Literature and Society in Late-Nineteenth-Century Brazil', in Schwarz, *Misplaced Ideas: Essays on Brazilian Culture*, trans. and introd. John Gledson, London 1992, 29.

of capital, its *historical specificity* as a slave-owning economy structurally integrated with the liberal order of international trade.

In this lies the originality and significance of Schwarz's initiative
within his parent intellectual tradition. The compelling attraction of
Hegelian-Marxist cultural theory was also its notorious weakness:
its confident dialectical narratives offered to decipher bourgeois
society and culture as an integral, dynamic whole but seldom with
more than passing acknowledgement of the deep discrepancies of
history and situation that structure the world of actually existing
capitalism. This schematic historicism was troubling enough in the
metropolitan zone, where it did much to enhance the philosophical
counter-attraction of Louis Althusser and his co-thinkers in the
later 1960s and after. In more dramatically contrasted conditions,
such as those in Brazil at the end of the 1950s, it provoked a concentrated critical initiative, at once highly specific and – for just that
reason – quite general in implication. Assimilating the theoretical
resources of his direct inheritance from the culture of the German
Left and bringing them to bear on the question of Brazil, in the
formative environment of the legendary *Capital* seminar at the
University of São Paulo, Schwarz began to develop a variety of
Marxist critical practice that was unmistakably Lukácsian and
Frankfurtian in its bold dialectical ambition, yet rigorous, as a
matter of principle, in its fidelity to the distinct shapes of Brazilian
history and culture, which were now seen as specific local forms of
an articulated world order of capital.[8] Here, to paraphrase one of the

---

8   Schwarz was born to leftist Jewish intellectual parents in Vienna in 1938 and
brought to São Paulo in flight from Nazism as a baby. He speaks at length about
his intellectual relationship with Lukács, from his student days onwards, in an
interview given in Eva L. Corredor, *Lukács After Communism: Interviews with
Contemporary Intellectuals* (Durham, NC and London, 1997), 174–98. For the
Capital seminar, see Schwarz's retrospect, ,'Um seminário de Marx' in *Seqüências
brasileiras*; and for more anecdotal recollections, two contributions in Cevasco
and Ohata, *Um crítico na periferia do capitalismo*: Michael Löwy, 'Ad Roberto
Schwarz' and Fernando Henrique Cardoso, 'Roberto Schwarz, seminarista'.

presiding spirits of the seminar, Jean-Paul Sartre, was a Marxism willing and able to find out something new.[9]

The character, logic and significance of that practice are the substance of this volume of essays, which will speak persuasively on their own account. Here, we may simply pick out its most important defining characteristics. At the heart of Schwarz's critical achievement are his studies of Joaquim Maria Machado de Assis, Brazil's greatest novelist. Extending across three books and numerous short texts, these develop a sustained account of Machado's historical intelligibility as a student of his own society in the later nineteenth century and make a strong case for his historic originality in the international culture of the novel as well as his continuing actuality as a critical force in Brazilian culture.[10] Given this central concern and the fact of his commitment to artistic realism, it is tempting to identify Schwarz as a Lukácsian of a kind. This would be misleading. Machado's narratives are very remote from Lukács's canons for realistic writing – which indeed have no counterpart of any kind in Schwarz's work. His realism is much closer to Brecht's in spirit, evaluating novels and plays according to their yield of illumination, without prior judgement of artistic means, always centrally engrossed in questions of form but not in the manner of Lukács's formal academicism.[11] The difference is important, and the more so because Schwarz's Brechtian commitment to realism goes together with his

---

9   Both Schwarz (93) and Cardoso (330) cite Sartre's *Question de méthode* (first published in 1960) as a key text for the group; Georg Lukács's *History and Class Consciousness* was another.

10   The books are *Ao vencedor as batatas* (São Paulo, 1977; partly translated in *Misplaced Ideas*, which also contains several short studies of Machado); *Um mestre na periferia do capitalismo: Machado de Assis* (1990; trans. John Gledson, *A Master on the Periphery of Capitalism: Machado de Assis*, Durham, NC, 2002); and *Duas meninas* (São Paulo, 1997), now translated here.

11   See Bertolt Brecht, 'On the Formalistic Character of the Theory of Realism', in Adorno et al., *Aesthetics and Politics*, London, 1977, 70–6; cf. in the same volume Lukács's critique of Ernst Bloch's defence of German Expressionism, 'Realism in the Balance'.

conviction, which he voices with all possible clarity, that literature is capable of discovering new knowledge. This is not the old Romantic claim of privilege for poetry: here capability is not an unambiguous guarantee of outcomes, and there is no suggestion that the knowledge is of a special order. But it is far bolder than the conventional proposition that artistic realism can aspire to present, in its own way, what theory always already knows – the effective limit of Lukács's acknowledgement. Manuel Antônio de Almeida, in the form of his novel *Memoirs of a Militia Sergeant*, discovered a dialectic of order and disorder that made possible the reinterpretation of an existing body of knowledge of Brazilian society; Candido had demonstrated as much. What Machado knew about Brazil he knew before anyone else working in any other mode, and the articulation of his discovery was a formal innovation – the device of the 'unreliable' or tendentious, 'narrator'.[12] This is the meaning of Schwarz's declaration that 'a good novel is a genuine event for theory'.[13]

The emancipating possibilities of such events are inseparable from the responsibility they presuppose. Schwarz's general critical position implies an ethics of reading. If the experience of literature is to lead to the discovery that may be there to be made, it behoves us to read well, with due care and patience. 'Close reading' has long been upheld as the special virtue of Anglo-American traditions in literary criticism, with 'dialectical' interpretation featuring as perhaps the outstanding case of its sorry opposite. Schwarz outplays this received dichotomy, combining his dialectical commitment to totality with tireless, micro-fine attention to the detail of the texts he reads, be they Machado's novels or the tiny poems of Chico Alvim or the adolescent Helena Morley's diary. 'Daring' comes high on his list of the virtues, as readers of *Two Girls* will learn, and it is a

---

12 'Narrador parcial' is Schwarz's phrase. The English equivalent has been conventional since Wayne C. Booth's *The Rhetoric of Fiction* (Chicago: University of Chicago Press, 1961).

13 See ch. 2, 'Objective Form: On the Dialectic of Roguery', below, 22.

conspicuous feature of his own analyses, as he opens out the data of story and language to disclose the lines of a whole characterology of Brazilian society, the most general matters of the historical social order in the smallest inflections of a text.

Schwarz's preferred critical form is the essay (much of his work, including half the contents of this book, has been produced for non-academic venues, such as newspaper supplements), and he intends this choice in a sense he takes from Adorno: the essay as a kind of text that finds its occasions in 'culturally pre-formed objects', moving somewhere between science and art, though always in the medium of concepts, and not intending to illustrate a received theoretical system, let alone elaborate a new one.[14] His disdain for elaborate methodological prospectuses is of long standing,[15] and it is in keeping that his own most focused statement of theory and method, 'Objective Form: Reflections on the Dialectic of Roguery', should be a nuanced reflection on the work of someone else, an essay mostly devoted to another essay that moves from structuralist diagramming at one end of its rhetorical range to paraliterary merging with rural folklore at the other. (His title, in the Portuguese, is itself a mime of sorts, though also a summons to theoretical self-examination.)[16] Above all, with its embrace of provisionality and hesitation, and its magpie curiosity, the essay is a critical mode especially well suited to the purposes of a Marxist criticism morally committed to the value of being surprised.

The contents of *Two Girls and Other Essays* have been designed to make manifest the overall logic and significance of this body of work. A few introductory sentences may be useful as signposts.

---

14 Theodor Adorno, 'The Essay as Form', in *Notes to Literature*, vol. 1, ed. Rolf Tiedemann, trans., Shierry Weber Nicholsen, New York, 1991, 3.
15 See Schwarz's satirical '19 princípios para a crítica literária', in *O pai de família e outros estudos* (1976), São Paulo, 2008.
16 In literal translation, it is 'Presuppositions, if I am not mistaken, of the "Dialectic of Roguery"'.

The collection opens with the early study of Franz Kafka's 'Worries of a Family Man', a text already emblematic in the Frankfurt tradition, and, in Schwarz's treatment, the occasion for a first exploration of some defining preoccupations of these essays and his work as a whole: tendentious narrators, the logic of commodities and its relation to patriarchal social forms, intimations of a liberated existence.

Then follows a pair of essays, the first of which, 'Objective Form: Reflections on the Dialectic of Roguery', discusses Antonio Candido's innovations in the study of literature, and, in doing so, marks key coordinates of theory and procedure for Schwarz's own critical practice. The second, 'Beyond Universalism and Localism: Machado's Breakthrough', is a concentrated statement of the principal historical and literary-critical theses of his work on Machado de Assis.

Introduced and framed in this way, the heart of the volume is Schwarz's *Two Girls*, a book in itself in the original, and a companion to his full-length studies of Machado. The first essay returns to Machado, to the brilliantly deceptive novel *Dom Casmurro*, the second to another, more recent classic of Brazilian literature, *The Diary of 'Helena Morley'*, with the central purpose of establishing, by this unlikely comparison of two young women's lives, rendered from mutually remote orders of cultural production, the tangible historical reality of objective form. The vicissitudes of the impulse to enlightenment form the ethical core of these contrasting narratives, one a personal recollection in which the widowed Dom Casmurro confines and traduces his wife, the free-minded Capitu, the other a diary giving uninhibited voice to her spiritual sister, Helena, in the beguiling utopian circumstances of a diamond-mining region on the slide.

A final group of three essays illustrates the wider range of Schwarz's work. A long study of Alvim's poetry brings Schwarz's recurring concern with modernism to the fore and extends the consideration of popular language begun in 'Two Girls', while the next essay, 'City of God', discusses Paulo Lins's innovatory expansion of the apparatus of novelistic realism – at the same time returning to the thematic of Candido's dialectic of roguery in the setting of Rio de Janeiro today.[17] The closing essay on Brecht, referring in particular to *Saint Joan of the Stockyards*, reviews the currency of epic theatre in historical perspective, from the 1920s onwards, including in particular a discussion of his place in the political ferment of Brazil in the 1960s, and moves finally to ask what in his work remains actual today.

It is a token of Robert Schwarz's standing in his own country that key phrases from his writings have for years circulated in semi–self-contained form as high-speed versions of his theses; 'misplaced ideas' is one such phrase, 'objective form' is another. It is a further token, this time of gratitude and esteem, that he should at length have been given the mantle he wove for Machado: *un mestre na periferia do capitalismo*.[18] This is a warm compliment but not a simple one, as Antonio Candido had already explained, as if by way of premonition, in an essay on literature and underdevelopment in Brazil. 'We always recognize our inevitable dependence as natural', he wrote. 'Besides, seen thus it is no longer dependency, but a way of participating in a cultural universe to which we belong, which crosses the boundaries of nations and continents, allowing the exchange of experiences and the circulation of values. And when we in turn influence the Europeans through the works we do (not through the thematic suggestions our continent presents to them to elaborate in their own form of exoticism), at such moments what we give back are not inventions but a refining of received instruments.'[19] What, then, is a master on the periphery? Candido's words are a counsel of caution, and many would be guided by them. Rights of audience in the prevailing global cultural order are brutally differentiated. But Schwarz has empha-

---

17 Francisco Alvim, *Elefante*, São Paulo, 2000.
18 This phrase was a recurring motif in the conference proceedings published in Cevasco and Ohata, *Um crítico na periferia do capitalismo*.
19 'Literature and Underdevelopment', in Becker, *On Literature and Society*, 130.

sized the value of daring, and it may be that a little of it is in order here. For, if what he has accomplished in and for his inherited tradition of German Marxism is valid on its own national ground, then it implies a general lesson that cannot be passed off as a mere refinement. It is not simply that the general schemes of Hegelian-Marxist cultural history had to be modified, more or less dramatically, to accommodate hard cases such as Brazil; the logical implication of Schwarz's turn to a rigorously historical practice of dialectical criticism is that they were in some way wanting even on their own metropolitan ground – the concatenation of nation-states from which the master-narratives of capitalism and the bourgeoisie were elicited and projected onto the screen of world history.[20] What is called for, then, is not refinement but correction or reconstruction, and that is a task for which we have a commanding model in the pioneering work of Roberto Schwarz. As they say, rightly, a master.

---

20   Neil Larsen makes a similar suggestion, referring particularly to the United States: 'Por que ninguém consegue entender Roberto Schwarz nos Estados Unidos', in Cevasco and Ohata, *Um crítico na periferia do capitalismo*, 20–1.

I

1

Kafka's Family Man

Here, to begin with, is my own translation of Franz Kafka's story *Die Sorge des Hausvaters*, or 'Worries of a Family Man'.[1] A commentary follows.

Some say the word *odradek* comes from the Slavonic and look for the word's derivation on that basis. Others think it comes from the German, only being influenced by the Slavonic. The uncertainty of both interpretations permits one to conclude that neither applies, particularly since neither leads to a meaning for the word.

Naturally nobody would occupy himself with such study if there were not actually a being called odradek. It looks at first like a flat, star-shaped spool, and, in fact, it does appear to be wound with thread; which, to be sure, is really only ragged, old, knotted-together or simply tangled pieces of string of mixed colour and description. But it is not only a spool, since a small crossbar emerges

---

1   The English version of 'Worries of a Family Man' presented here hews as closely as possible to Kafka's German while following, where feasible, the stylistic choices represented by Roberto Schwarz's Portuguese translation. The English version, 'The Cares of a Family Man' in *Franz Kafka: The Complete Stories*, edited by Nahum N. Glatzer and translated by Willa and Edwin Muir (New York, 1971, 427–9), is more elegant than my own but differs from Schwarz's, which is closer to Kafka's language in several respects. [*Tr.*]

from the middle of the star and another bar joins the first at a right angle. With the aid of this second bar on one side and one of the points of the star on the other side, the whole thing can stand upright, as though on two legs.

One is tempted to believe that this entity once had some purposive form and is now simply broken. Despite appearances, this is not the case. At least, no evidence can be seen for it; one cannot find a mark of incompletion or rupture that would suggest anything like that. The whole thing looks senseless enough but in its own way complete. At any rate, nothing more precise can be said since Odradek is exceedingly agile and not to be caught.

He hangs around in the attic, on the stairway, in the hallways , in the entryway by turns. Sometimes he is not to be seen for a month at a time, having probably moved on to other houses; but he never fails to return to our house. Sometimes, if one steps out the door and he is leaning against the stair rail just below, one feels inclined to speak to him. Naturally one doesn't ask him difficult questions, handling him rather – his smallness makes it hard not to – like a child. 'What's your name then?' one asks. 'Odradek', he says. 'And where do you live?' 'No fixed abode', he laughs; but it is the kind of laugh only someone without lungs would produce. It sounds something like the rustling of fallen leaves. Generally that's the end of the conversation. Incidentally, even these answers are not always forthcoming; often he is silent for long periods, as wooden as he looks.

To no avail, I ask myself what will become of him. Can he even die? Everything that dies must previously have had some kind of purpose, some kind of activity which has exhausted itself; this doesn't apply to Odradek. Is he then always to be at the feet of my children and my children's children, tumbling down the stairs with thread fibres dragging after? He evidently harms nobody, but the idea that he is furthermore to outlive me I find almost painful.

'Worries of a Family Man' is a minor masterpiece. Slight and delicate, it is nonetheless violent and touches the nerve of an entire culture. The story does not explain bourgeois life but implies it with such deadly felicity that it emerges from this simple – although fantastic – domestic scene quite worn down. For Kafka, the key to the world is made of tin and can be found on the outskirts of towns. Had he been a revolutionary, he would have made suppositories instead of bombs.

The German and Slavonic camps argue over the word *odradek*. They argue over it, but do not know what it means. This implies that they are idiots, quite unlike the family man who makes the observation and triumphs in these first lines. The family man consolidates his triumph, saying 'actually', 'naturally', 'at first', 'in fact' and 'to be sure', phrases which suppose, and in presupposing establish, a community of good sense. He is so prudent and objective, not to mention droll, that he does not say 'I' or 'we' until near the end. Meanwhile, however, he does not come to exist as a character; he is simply a narrative voice. The source of his affirmations is like the grammatical subject 'one', which indicates the anonymous, indisputable and happy consensus of men of good judgement.

The reasonable man doesn't want to be a bore. Mindful of his hopes for general approval, the family man gives a comic description of Odradek, which he presents as some old thing whose use has been forgotten. A being in the form of a spool that is not a spool is ridiculous, all the more so if it is covered in tangled thread. The smile before the useless and obsolete thing is one of superiority. To the superiority of a practical man is here added that of a humorous fellow with his head screwed on. Then comes the superiority of an adult, created by the bonhomie with which he speaks of little Odradek. The procedure is always the same: entice the reader, establish the tacit agreement among adults, whites, civilized men.

Suddenly, a detail that is not a detail: the strange thing can stand upright, it is alive. The fact is mentioned as though it were one more piece of thread on the spool. But it is not, and this changes every-thing – as the translation indicates in shifting the initial *o* of the name from lower case to capital. Why describe a living being as inert? It is like saying: more rounded than angular, yellow, slightly creased, and Arthur Johnson's cousin. With this detail, the physical description of Odradek – as a thingamajig – changes meaning: if among useful objects, the thingamajig is always negative, among the living, its gratuitousness can change polarity, as we shall see. The narrative then begins to seem intentional; there is a strategy in its sensible, descriptive gesture. The procedure might just be humorous, but the next paragraph already shows that it is not. The anonymity of the voice is false. It allows us to discern, little by little, the family man's anxiety, and it falls apart in the final lines, where the natural pronoun of anxiety – that is, 'I' – prevails. In a parallel movement, the family man recognizes the person of Odradek: he refers to him by the personal pronoun 'he' (*er*), not the impersonal 'it' (*es*), as at the beginning. This twin recognition – of the existence of Odradek and of the subjective unhappiness hidden only unsuc-cessfully by the reasonable public face – is what needs to be explicated.

Just as he withheld life from Odradek, the family man supposes for a paragraph that he is 'simply broken' – even though the narra-tor soon recognizes, and repeats three times, that he is not. Quite to the contrary, Odradek is 'in his own way complete'. If we re-read the story, we note, behind the objective posture – or better, in it – the impalpable but sustained defamation of Odradek: in the choice of words, in the careful reticence of the narrator. Why?

Odradek is mobile, colourful, irresponsible, free from the system of obligations that bind the man to the family. More radically put: Odradek, as a construction, is the impossible of the bourgeois order. If, in a capitalist society, production for the market permeates the social order as a whole, then concrete forms of activity cease to have their justifications in themselves. Their end is external; their partic-ular forms inessential. Odradek has no purpose (that is, no external end), but he is in his own way complete; he embodies his end (without which we could not speak of his being complete) in himself. Odradek, therefore, is the precise and logical construction of the negation of bourgeois life. Not that he is simply in a negative relation to it; he is rather the very schema of its negation, and this schematism is essential to the literary quality of the story. This is what guarantees the details of this trivial and matter-of-fact prose their extraordinary reach and power: referring to Odradek, they become options facing culture.

On a modest scale, Odradek's utopian existence is subversive: it is the family man's temptation. Gratuitous existence catalyzes the contradictions of bourgeois vocabulary, which values, but does not value, freedom. This is how we are to understand the mixture of disdain and envy that Odradek awakens, and therefore the defamatory strategy of the narrator. And there is yet another meaning in Odradek's seductive gratuitousness: its properly pecuniary, or better yet anti-pecuniary, side. Odradek is made of leftovers, of disreputable materials without name or price, which have been eliminated from social circulation. He is the extreme image of liberty amid the effort required by propriety; a perfection neglected but perfectly safe, since he is made of parts that nobody wants; a lumpen proletariat without hunger and without fear of the police. The dismissive gesture of the prose – a class gesture, emphasizing Odradek's sorry threads – is a tacit admission of the power implicit in the narrator's finer cloth, and of the risk of losing it. The social place of a reconciled life cannot be named on the map of bourgeois society; it is trash.[2]

Because he is the image of the absence of worry, Odradek worries the family man. The story owes its literary violence, however, to an astonishing phrase that frames the entire story. Odradek, after

---

2   According to Marx, 'The product of an individual capital . . . may have any natural form whatsoever. The only condition is that it really should have a use form, a use-value, that stamps it as a member of the commodity world capable of circulation.' *Capital: A Critique of Political Economy* vol. 2, *The Process of Circulation of Capital*, Harmondsworth, 1978, 508.

saying that he has no permanent home, laughs; the narrator comments: 'but it is the kind of laugh only someone without lungs would produce.' The sentence is clearly different from the others. It has greater weight, since it is written with an awareness of the body. To describe Odradek's laugh, the family man abandons the visual, 'objective' posture, whose object is by nature indifferent and external, and looks for an image of internal feeling: what separates him from Odradek's happiness are his lungs. Because it is unintelligible without reference to our own body, the sentence does not allow us the distanced reading that the narrator invites. Its terror is in the 'verification' it compels, which is entirely personal: to experience it and Odradek's prodigious laugh is to catch oneself in the act of the ambiguous laughter to which the narrator leads us. Bodily feeling, a limitation contrasting with Odradek's inorganic lightness, gives a new tension to the description, even in retrospect. This is what stings: the restored truth of the gossipy prose.

Odradek's charm is inhuman, and human life is dreary. It appears that there has been a displacement of the problem: the bourgeois order, which is not a biological fact, can be transcended, but the lungs in question cannot. A metaphysical reading presents itself, according to which Kafka is not speaking of a particular society but of mortality in general, of the anguish of having entrails. According to this school of thought, what hurts is not being a family man but being mortal. To me, the choice between the two readings does not appear free: were mortality the problem, the eternalization of a humdrum life of obligations would be the formula for paradise – God help us. The suspension of bourgeois obligations that is figured in Odradek, on the other hand, sustains his air of happiness in spite of the permanence of death. A laugh 'only someone without lungs would produce': unhappiness has become embedded in the body itself. What separates the family man from life is not death but present life turned into an irremediable body.

From this perspective, the paradox and the sinister force of the final lines can be explained. At first sight, it appears that the narrator is jealous of Odradek's immortality. But we have already seen that immortality would not make sense to him. Also, the positioning of 'furthermore' in the following sentence relegates survival to secondary consideration: 'but the idea that he is furthermore to outlive me I find almost painful'. The family man does not want to live forever, he wants to outlive Odradek: in other words, he wants Odradek to die first. Naturally he is too urbane to wish death upon a being who does harm to nobody, who is in his own way complete; but his urbanity does not prevent the existence of such a being from causing him pain. Respectable in every regard, the family man is the unacknowledged partisan of destruction.

2

Objective Form:
Reflections on the Dialectic of Roguery

The defining concern of Marxist criticism of literature is the dialectic of literary form and social process. This watchword is easily uttered but difficult to act upon. It was very widespread in Brazil before the military coup of 1964, yet the critical yield was almost negligible. If we discount the vocabulary, which, in the enthusiasm of the period, became more and more social, the interpretation of Brazilian literature, whether as a whole or simply in the form of its most important representatives, hardly changed. It was only in 1970 – when the repression and intellectual fashion had already greatly reduced the numbers of those sympathetic to this tendency – that there appeared, for the first time in Brazil, a genuinely dialectical literary study. Forgoing boasts about method or terminology, giving structuralism a wide berth and keeping a distance, too, from the concepts of Marxism (which was, however, its basic inspiration), Antonio Candido published a cogent and startling explication of Manuel Antonio de Almeida's novel *Memoirs of a Militia Sergeant*.[1]

---

1   Antonio Candido, 'Dialética da malandragem', *Revista do Instituto de Estudos Brasileiros*, 8, São Paulo, 1970; trans. Howard S. Becker, 'The Dialectic of Malandroism', in Antonio Candido, *On Literature and Society*, Princeton, NJ. Manuel Antonio de Almeida's novel was first published in the *Correio Mercantil*

Reflecting on the form of *Memoirs*, Candido discerned, behind the ups and downs of the narrative surfaces, a complex plot organization with far-reaching implications. This plot, he argued, evokes a general aspect of Brazilian society, which it transposes artistically and whose importance – hardly mentioned by critics, least of all those on the Left – the formal consistency of the novel itself indicates. Uniting formal analysis and sociological reconstruction, procedures shown to be mutually complementary, he opened up a perspective that allowed the identification, naming and analysis of a powerful strain in Brazilian literature, one that theory had never seen. This is the strain of *malandragem*, or 'roguery', which goes back to colonial times.[2] Appearing in the guise of the hero of folklore Pedro Malazarte, in the poetry of Gregório de Matos, in popular humour, in the comic and satirical press of the Regency period,[3] it culminated in the twentieth century, with novels such as Mario de Andrade's *Macunaíma* and Oswald de Andrade's *Serafim Ponte-Grande*, where it is stylized and raised to the status of a symbol.[4]

1852–53, and in book form in 1854. See the bilingual Portuguese/English edition, *Memórias de um sargento de milícias – Memoirs of a Militia Sergeant*, trans. Mark Carlyon, Rio de Janeiro, 2010.

2   Candido's Princeton editors decline to translate *malandragem* – roughly 'roguery', but no English-language term is quite adequate – which refers to the specifically Brazilian figure of the *malandro*, a layabout and trickster living on the edge of legality. 'Malandroism' is a coinage based on a borrowing from the Portuguese, morphologically English but not a translation in any fuller sense. (The figure is often portrayed as Zé Pelintra, or Joe the Rogue – a black man, whose skin colour denotes poverty but who wears a natty white suit, two-tone shoes and a slouch hat.) In this essay, *malandro/malandragem* has strictly conceptual status and is rendered as 'rogue' or 'roguery', or left untranslated. Elsewhere in the volume, a range of near equivalents have been called upon as translations of the term from one occurrence to the next. [*Ed.*]

3   Pedro Malazarte, often known in Spanish as Pedro Urdemales, exists in the traditional folklore of the Iberian peninsula and Latin America: he is the unscrupulous trickster, always up to mischief; Gregório de Matos (b. 1636–d. 1696) was a satirical poet who lived in Salvador, Bahia. [*Tr.*]

4   Mário de Andrade, *Macunaíma* (1928; translated as *Macunaíma: The Hero Without a Character*, New York, 1984). Mário de Andrade (b.1893–d.1945) is the

Here, genuinely put into practice, without dependence on ritual formulae, the dialectical programme displays its analytical power. In Candido's study, the critical act (the rational justification for literary judgement) contains: first, an analysis of the novel's composition, which allows a new reading and gives it an extraordinary importance; second, an original synthesis of scattered elements of knowledge about Brazil, reached in the heuristic light of the book's artistic unity; third, the identification of an important vein that had not hitherto had a place in Brazil's literary historiography, whose shape is modified by this essay; and finally, an exploration of the contemporary scene, based on the social configuration outlined in *Memórias*.

I

Candido's argument goes as follows. Critics have valued *Memoirs* as belonging to one or the other of two traditions, either as an heir of the picaresque novel or – thanks to its documentary fidelity – as a predecessor of the realist novel. Careful comparison with the picaresque reveals more differences than similarities, which discounts that inheritance as a decisive critical element. Something similar is true in relation to the documentary novel. While not denying this dimension of the book, Candido observes that the moments when it dominates are weak, and that the novel is strong only when it is subordinated to another impulse, that of the action, which remains to be defined. In his counter-proposal, the hero, Leonardo *filho*, is seen not as a *pícaro* (that is, as an example of a figure and a form

---

leading figure of Brazilian modernism; the novel recounts the adventures of its lazy, playful, absurd hero, who represents the typical Brazilian (for further discussion, see ch. 5). Oswald de Andrade, *Serafim Ponte Grande* (1926); translated as *Seraphim Grosse Pointe* (1979). Oswald de Andrade (b. 1890–d.1954), no relation to Mário. *Seraphim Grosse Pointe* is an experimental novel in 203 fragments and a violent satire on Brazilian bourgeois society. For further discussion, see chs 5 and 6. [*Tr.*]

consecrated in European literary tradition, which would resolve the critical problem) but as a *malandro*, a historically original figure, who brings together: (a) a folkloric, pre-modern dimension – that of the trickster; (b) a specific comic climate – that of the satirical production of the Regency period; and (c) a profound intuition concerning the movement of Brazilian society. As this combination implies, the specifically documentary aspect of the novel cannot be decisive here since it is only one among others, and not the principal one. Moreover, since it turns on the figure of the *malandro*, the novel does not deal with slaves or with the ruling classes, which however were the basic social classes of the time – an omission that from a strictly documentary point of view would be unpardonable. In short, the veridical realism of *Memoirs*, if it exists, is not of a documentary order. It has a different modality, which Candido calls representative and later goes on to explain. It is linked to the intuition and figuring of a sustained historical dynamic.

This dynamic is made manifest in the literary form and above all in the oscillations of the plot. Accompanying the movements of the characters, Candido notes that they move to and fro between the social spheres of order and disorder and that Almeida's novel contemplates these comings and goings with impartiality; that is to say, without subscribing to a distribution of positive and negative value, which the camp of order usually insists on for itself and its opposite. The same alternation presides over the construction of the sentence, in which there is always room for both sides of any question, and this means the suspension of moral judgement and the class viewpoint it conveys. At crucial moments, this dialectic of order and disorder finds its symbolic equivalents in certain images: in the Chief of Police Major Vidigal, who wears a frock coat but also his rough clogs, which he has forgotten to take off, or in the master of ceremonies, caught in his skullcap and slippers in his gypsy lady friend's bedroom. In Candido's terms, this form is at once the skeleton that supports the novel and the *structural reduction* of a social situation, external to literature, belonging to history. It is the *aesthetic formalization* of a generalized rhythm in Brazilian society in the first half of the nineteenth century.

Paradoxically, the apprehension of this rhythm is linked to the novel's limitations as a document. For by omitting slaves, the novelist was in effect omitting most of the labour performed at the time; and by omitting the ruling classes, he was omitting the mechanisms of control. What remained was an intermediate and anomic sector of society, whose characteristics are nevertheless decisive in its general ideology. It is a sector in which order was imposed and kept with difficulty, 'surrounded on every side by a lively disorder, which opposed twenty situations of concubinage to every marriage and a thousand chance unions to every situation of concubinage . . . What was left was the playful atmosphere of this flickering, feeble organization fissured by anomie, translated by the dance of the characters between legality and its opposite, in such a way that we cannot say which is one and which the other, because, in the end, they all circulate from one to the other with a naturalness that recalls the way families, prestige, fortunes and reputations were formed in urban Brazil in the first half of the nineteenth century'.[5] This is the historical reality of which the dialectic of order and disorder is the formal correlative.

What does this formal correlative consist in, and what is its status? The reply to this question encompasses the main constituents of Candido's methodological position. In his words, the dialectic of order and disorder is a *principle of generalization* that at a deep level organizes both the data of reality and those of the fiction (whether or not they are documentary in nature) and makes them intelligible. It is a *generality* that participates in reality and in the fiction; it is there in both, and in it they encounter their common dimension. Thus, the fictional data do not come directly from the real data, nor does the sense of reality in the fiction depend on them, even while presupposing them. It depends on mediating principles,

---

5   Translation modified; cf. Becker, ed., 'Dialectic of Malandroism', 95. [*Tr.*]

which are generally hidden and which structure the work, and it is thanks to them that the two orders, the real and the fictional, cohere.

However, in *Memoirs* the intuition of a historical movement is not everything. It alternates with another kind of stylization, one that draws from folkloric archetypes of cunning. The tension between the two is the characteristic that truly constitutes the dialectic of roguery: the suspension of determinate historical conflicts through a general expertise in the art of survival, which does not internalize these conflicts and has no knowledge of moral convictions or remorse. Almeida's narrative constellation generates the image, half-fabulous, half-real, of a *world without guilt*. Candido's observations on this topic are numerous, and suggestive. For now, we may mention three. First, he suggests that *Memoirs* is unique in Brazilian nineteenth-century fiction in not embodying a ruling-class point of view. Second, he claims that the novel conveys a very Brazilian attitude, one of 'corrosive tolerance', which has persisted from colonial times into the present, as a marked element of the national culture. Finally, he thinks that although its accommodating spirit, which is central to the dialectic of roguery, may seem inferior to the puritan values on which capitalist society nourishes itself, the novel would facilitate a possible future integration into a more open society.

2

Candido's point of departure is the arguments established by Brazilian critics of *Memoirs*, arguments he disagrees with and attempts to refute. There are other contrastive reference points, too – sociologism, or vulgar Marxism, and structuralism – against which his methodological originality stands out, as it develops its own notion of form and its relation to social process, although these go unmentioned in the essay. We may best approach this general issue via some further consideration of Candido's relation to Brazilian critical tradition, above all nationalism.

In querying the affiliation of *Memoirs* to the picaresque and suggesting that the novel is sui generis in its form, moulded by the kinds of social interaction and satirical journalism of the Regency, Candido repeats the argument of nationalist criticism since its beginnings: Brazilian literature is not a repeat of forms created in Europe but rather something new. However, there is a difference, for in Candido the question is treated factually and not as a matter of national amour propre, as in Romantic patriotism. His argument questioning the picaresque affiliation is examined without prejudice, for there is nothing, in principle, against the cultivation in Brazil of a form not peculiar to the country. In today's jargon, the choice between an endogenous and exogenous dynamic, which worries Brazilian historiography in all its branches, gets the only possible dialectical reply: it depends . . . Thus, in Candido, the emphasis on the *national* character of literary originality, which in different ways has been the ideological and aesthetic banner of Romantics, modernists and others, undergoes a change of meaning. It corresponds to a *recognition of historical fact*, linked moreover to aspects of reality that are themselves relatively original, yet nothing to be proud of, such as the social anomic accompanying slavery. Having been an unquestioned patriotic value demanding recognition and assent, national uniqueness is now a fact of life, calling for critical treatment.

The same spirit animates the arguments Candido opposes to the thesis of the novel as documentary. This thesis was enshrined by criticism of a naturalist leaning and is founded on the descriptions of customs, which are indeed numerous in *Memoirs*. The trouble, according to Candido , is that these descriptions do not account for the artistic quality of the novel, for as it progresses and improves, they are brought under the command of the plot, no longer simply informational – referring to something external – but now elements of the composition, whose reference is internal. Even here, he considers the question as one of fact, not of principle. If *Memoirs* is read as a dynamic whole, and not as a succession of veridical reports, that is, if it is read *aesthetically*, it is because it inhabits this dimension, which does not exclude the documentary, though the latter is subordinated to it.

This does not imply an opposition between the *aesthetic* and the *social*. Quite the reverse, for the form is considered as a profound synthesis of the movement of history, as opposed to the relative superficiality of documentary representation. In this sense, the emphasis on the mimetic value of the *composition*, as against the descriptive value of the parts, implies a more complex consideration of reality, which cannot be grasped in the immediacy of events. A composition is only an imitation if it refers to something organized – which, we may say, indicates that an aesthetic reading has more affinity with a wide-ranging social interpretation than a reading limited to authenticity of detail. Aesthetic reading and historical totalization are related. Both suspend the facts in a complex whole without suppressing them.

So, the originality attributed to Brazil, implied in the form of the *Memoirs* and explored in 'The Dialectic of Roguery', is of a structural order. Here, a historical structure is imitated by a literary structure. Of course, the country alluded to by the form of a novel is not the same as that alluded to by a text with a documentary aim. *Memoirs* belongs to Brazilian Romanticism, which, with its abundant local colour, participated in the patriotic effort to consolidate a national identity and literature, something, moreover, which the documentary intention also contributes to. The picturesque details offer the reader an easy, congenial identification with the nation, something that could operate as an end in itself. This function is more ideological than artistic, and is responsible for a note of provincial complicity, present in all the novels of this phase. They are books written in the certainty of drawing the applause owed to the well-meaning fellow citizen who has given our everyday life a literary fragrance.[6] Thus, to relegate local colour to a secondary

---

6   Candido himself formulates and discusses these questions in *Formação da literatura brasileira*, Belo Horizonte, 1975.

position means leaving behind this identity-affirming Brazil of Romantic nationalism (and perhaps of naturalist criticism too). And to insist on literary construction is to bring forward the Brazil of modern consciousness, with its historical social process in which no unanimity is possible. This objective crux forces Almeida's hand, as the novel's initial balance of local descriptions and integral form progressively shifts to the advantage of the latter. Properly understood, this one-sidedness is a decisive achievement, because it sees more where there seemed to be less, and gives the work a reach it perhaps had no desire to achieve, but which – once the essay has been read – it in fact possesses. For all its air of simplicity, *Memoirs* can be treated as a serious realist novel, in which the meaning of contemporary life is in play. In other words, we are passing from a criticism of national edification to an aesthetic criticism; from a criticism whose functions are purely local to one that explores the contemporary world; from a criticism in which national qualities are celebrated to one where they are historicized. Contrary to what the nationalists say, dialectical understanding depends on formal analysis, and its referent is not the country in our hearts but the real country of social classes.

3

How are the Brazilian social process and the literary form of *Memoirs* linked? Here, Candido leaves the company of Brazilian criticism and competes with contemporary tendencies anywhere. However, to get to this simple question, he had first to deal with local interpretations in which: (a) the problem did not exist, since the form is European and (b) national reality can be found on the indisputable, contingent level of the *subject matter*, which is Brazilian because it is Brazilian. These, as it happens, are versions of the two formative strains of Brazilian literature, universalism and localism. The synthesis, according to which the country's national originality (a) exists and (b) exists as a process and a part of the contemporary scene, and not as a question of national honour, a provincial compendium of picturesque details or as a tautology – this is the synthesis that Candido's essay attempts to achieve.[7]

The thesis that *Memoirs* is original and profoundly representative of Brazil is by no means obvious. Candido takes several steps here, of which three are most important. In the first, he characterizes the central character as a *malandro*, a figure conjoining the legendary trickster, the historic satirical style of the Regency and a movement in which is transposed a historical dynamic of national significance (the comings and goings between the hemispheres of social order and disorder). In the second step, he presents a detailed survey of the evolution of the characters that shows how this alternation between order and disorder constitutes the novel's form, the internal law of its plot. And, in the third step, he offers this formula – the dialectic of order and disorder – as defining the rule of life of a crucial sector of Brazilian society: that of free men, neither slaves nor owners, who live in an intermediate, anomic social space, in which it is impossible either to do without order or to live within it.

In what does this procedure consist? In the first step, the relationships between fiction and reality are of the order of common sense. The *malandro* figure exists on two levels, and the extra-literary features that define him also define the literary space set up around

---

7 The alternation of universalism and localism – and their basic complementarity – is one of the governing themes of *Formação da literatura brasileira*, ibid. Candido is following a famous predecessor here, steering in the wake of Machado de Assis's crucial essay on 'the instinct for nationality' ('Instinto de nacionalidade', 1873), which opposed a 'certain intimate feeling' to the deliberately picturesque topics of Romantic nationalism. This feeling, according to Machado, allows the artist to be of his time and country while talking of other places and epochs. Machado's formulation lends itself to several commentaries and can also be applied to 'Dialectic of Roguery', which attempts on the literary-critical level what the novelist was proposing on the level of fiction. Machado's primary intention is to free writers of the patriotic duty to be picturesque. He also affirms their right to every kind of topic. However, this is not universalism; it is a different view of what is 'national' in literature. See ch. 3 below.

him. (Thus, its coordinates are enough to differentiate *Memoirs* from the picaresque novel.) The situation becomes more complex when, in contrast with the case of a typical character, the term common to reality and fiction cannot be identified at first sight. Or, worse, when an ability to identify similarities between the two is not enough, because the related terms do not appear – either in everyday life or in the stock of available theories – in the form necessary for their articulation. This is true of steps two and three, which are correlative. Here, it was necessary to *discover* (to intuit and then explain), among the innumerable formal aspects of the novel, the one that, as a transposition of a significant aspect of the historical process, colours the others with historical relevance. The search for form in this case is not governed by the repertoire of normative aesthetics, whose forms it is considered that the work should repeat. On the contrary, the literary form in this emancipated sense may be any and every nexus that subordinates others in the text – including the fixed forms themselves. Once the parameters of tradition have been laid to one side, the historical dynamic of meanings comes properly into play, and the real referent of the form becomes *contemporary historical reality*. Thus, though strictly occurring on its own level, the search for form happens in the light of extra-literary knowledge and reflection on that knowledge, which plays its part in the definition of the result. Conversely, such knowledge is also reconsidered and reshaped in the light of the problem posed by the formal unity of the novel, which represents the possibility of a totality discovered by the novelist and which, in the very nature of what modern literary works aim for, escapes common sense. Thus, in the case of *Memoirs*, it is necessary to locate the element of the social whole whose movement is synthesized by the book's form. However, this element had never been identified in theory or in general awareness as possessing its own set of problems. In reading 'Dialectic of Roguery', then, we are present at the first conceptual crystallization and historical foregrounding of a socially distinctive point of view: we witness the passage of a varied body of knowledge about the lives of free, poor men in Brazil towards a concept which unites them under a certain aspect, formalized in *Memoirs*, that Candido calls a dialectic of order and disorder.

In other words, what has to be done is to read the novel against its real background and study reality against the background of the novel – more on a formal level than in relation to its content, and in a creative way. That is to say, not according to the received forms, which are precisely those that the emancipation of the form – and its move towards the magnetic field of contemporary history – has caused to be put on one side, but through a bold exploration of aesthetic experience and available knowledge: reading one through the other, literature and reality, until the mediating terms are found. However, we have already seen that 'finding' is not the right word, for the novel and the reality are not available to us in the same degree, nor is the way of studying them the same. In literature, in the nature of things, even the most secret, unconscious and intellectualized form has to be graspable by the imagination: otherwise it ceases to exist. But on the plane of reality, which for the person writing is made up of practical life, knowledge and the existing writing on the topic, it may not exist in a form that is available in a literary way, though it may be intuited. In such cases, the critic has to *construct* the social process in theory, keeping in mind that he must create the conceptual generality capable of giving unity to the novelistic universe he is studying, a generality that the novelist has already understood and transformed into a principle of artistic construction. This work, if it is worthy of the delicacy of its object, will produce new knowledge. What happens, then, is that we arrive at a structure of structures, or rather, a structure composed of two others: the form of the work articulated with the social process, which has to be constructed in such a way as to bring out and make intelligible the coherence and the organizing force of the literary work, which is the point of departure of the reflection itself.

As for the method, in the back-and-forth movement between fiction and reality, it is the literary form that takes precedence, posing the problem that the critic's studies and varied knowledge help to interpret. And the more subtle and complex the formal apprehension, the more interesting its formulation and explanation will be, if they are successful. From this viewpoint, which places emphatic (though not exclusive) value on the cognitive dimension of fiction, a good novel is a genuine event for theory. What is more, for someone with an open mind, there is nothing exceptional about this, for the advantages of letting oneself be enlightened by a good book and by the qualities of a good writer are plain enough. However, this attitude, almost simple good sense (were it not that 'good sense' is on the side of content), is rarely put into practice. In fact, you could count on your fingers those works in which formal observation – which in this perspective can also be called aesthetic experience or confidence in the power of art as an instrument of knowledge – is the real guide in the discovery of new aspects of reality. These are the rare, truly illuminating works. In this sense, 'The Dialectic of Roguery' has no precedents in Brazil and is in the best possible company in the wider world.

Thus, the junction between novel and society happens through the form, the latter being understood as a mediating principle, which organizes the elements of fiction and of reality at a profound level, and is part of both. Without ignoring the role played by invention, which of course exists, reality is present here in a strong sense, much stricter than literary theories usually suggest. In sum, before it is intuited and made objective by the novelist, the form the critic studies has been produced by the social process, even if no one is aware of its existence. This is an emphatic theory of literary realism and of social reality *as something formed*. In this conception, the dominant form of the novel includes, among other elements, the incorporation of a form of real life, which is put into action in the field of the imagination. It is not a realism of simple mirroring, for a form is not the whole of reality and moreover can combine with elements that are historically uncharacteristic – for example, the folkloric element of *Memoirs*, which pulls the novel towards the fabulous.

Since Antonio Candido is discreet in his theoretical statements, we should not press the implications too far. Let us stay with what is plainest. In this view, the notion of form can be applied beyond the literary sphere, for reality is seen in the same light, or, we may say, in a Marxist sense: social forms are objective; that is, created by the process of social reproduction, independent of individual consciousness. For example, the reproduction of the slave-owning order creates in the sphere occupied by free men, who are not property owners and have to live as parasites, the dialectic of order and disorder. It is worth insisting on this point to highlight the *practical-historical* foundations of the articulation of the aesthetic and social spheres; this explains the difference from structuralism, which also searches for forms in several different spheres. Within Marxism, too, we must make a distinction: although the vocabulary is different, we are in the German tradition and specifically that of Lukács, whose aesthetic constructions depend, precisely, on the objectivity and historicity of social forms (this, in contrast with the Althusserian view, for which the form is a scientific construction with no reality of its own). These affinities and differences have to be accepted with a certain reserve, for Candido's reticence in the face of sharply defined ideological or scientific terminologies is intentional. Is it above all a response to the fetishism prevailing in these spheres? Or an expression of his fundamental differences with them?

4

The aesthetic formalization of social conditions; the structural reduction of external facts; the function of historical reality in constituting the structure of a work: these are differently angled formulations of what interests Candido here. They designate the moment in which a real form – one posited by practical life – is transmuted into a literary form; that is, into a basis for the construction of an imaginary world. In other words, these are expressions that mark the way in which aesthetic dynamics is bound to social dynamics, to the exclusion of other ways. Thus, the unification of the novelistic sphere with that of reality comes about through their almost total separation, and the dialectic of the two works through their precise articulation, and not, as usually happens, through some kind of conflation. The contents of novels are not real contents, and to look at them aesthetically is to see them in the context of the form, which in its turn resumes (by elaborating or reproducing) a social form, understood in terms of the movement of society as a whole.

The advantage of this general construction is that it exactly defines the relation between the novel and reality, and allows us to speak without impropriety of the social material of the literary form and of the virtualities of the reality it explores – which, after all, is to bring an age-old subject of polemic into full understanding. To put this in another way, it is a procedure that tries to overcome the disjunction between what we call *internal* and *external* studies of the work of fiction. This disjunction is emphasized by the defenders of aesthetic reading; that is, of reading that focuses on the effects of the form – effects ignored by so-called external reading, which relates the work to its milieu through its contents. Now, once we have found that real nexus, whose logic has become an element of the structuring of the novel, the link between internal and external domains has been made. Where once there was a choice between simple confusion of the two spheres and their disjunction, we now have an articulation. Much of what can be said about that real nexus will deepen our understanding of fiction, which, at the same time, will be understood not merely as an imaginary world but as an imaginary world constructed according to the logic of a reality, which represents a particular time and place in the social totality, and is itself an object of discussion. The place of reality in fiction and the place of fiction in reality are both determined. If the connections between literature and society are an old topic, the articulation of their structures is not. It is a new theoretical object, offering new knowledge.

Thus, the formal principle of *Memoirs*, the dialectic of order and disorder, gives general relevance to the experience of one sector of society, the intermediate one, which lacks regular work, does not accumulate wealth or issue orders and which in this sense seems the least essential of all. Why give precedence to it? Cândido not only does this but associates it with a great Brazilian literary tradition, the dialectic of roguery, which runs from colonial times to the masterpieces of modernism, thus magnifying the interest of the question. Why interpret Brazil through this relationship? Situating the dialectic of order and disorder in the anomic space created by slavery, he makes it into a structural feature of Brazilian society and thus comprehensively explains the *national* character of the novel's form, which does not refer to any single process to be encountered here or there in the country but to an indispensable, though only complementary, aspect of the social construction of the country as a whole.

5

Such insights apart, the originality of 'The Dialectic of Roguery' does not lie in the desire to link literature and society, which is after all common enough. It lies in the resolution with which Candido gives priority to formal judgement, whether in discriminating among the novel's components and setting out its organization or in looking for its social correlative, which will be constructed *to explain the form*. If criticism of a sociological bent ignores the literary form and uses the fictional data as if they were documents concerning reality (formal questions are make-believe, according to the anti-aesthetic bias of the positivist spirit), this is its diametrical opposite. However, the opposite idea, that the writer's work has great cognitive value, even though the 'facts' of fiction are not simply real and must be considered in their own context, is not uncommon. Why then are studies that act on it so rare?

It frequently happens in literary studies that in attempts to relate fiction to something external to it (human psychology, social and economic worlds), only one of the two juxtaposed entities has a structure. In consequence, internal necessity will exist only on one side – either that of art or that of reality – while the other side is treated as a source of interesting information supporting its logic. This procedure does not produce new knowledge, for the unstructured side will necessarily say what is said on the structured and thus end up simply illustrating it. If both sides are structured, however, this merely illustrative function loses its rationale, and the perspectives opened up by the particular forms of articulation now take priority. And here, an aggravating material difficulty arises from the way knowledge is institutionalized nowadays, in the university above all. Recognition of a problem depends less on its intrinsic interest than on the position it occupies in the context of some prestigious discipline. From this point of view, there is no less promising point of departure for such reflections than the artistic labour of an independent writer. For the same reasons, taking a literary form seriously as an effort to achieve knowledge or as a basis for identifying problems makes the worst-possible impression, unless it is as an illustration of some linguistic law. At the same time, the academic division of labour makes us all – historians of literature, linguists, psychoanalysts, sociologists, philosophers – uncomfortable in our neighbours' disciplines. And if, by chance, there are those who move with ease in several specialities, even then they will not feel safe from the problems of interdisciplinary collaboration: inwardly, they will be all fingers and thumbs, for compartmentalization and the insistence on the specific domain of each discipline (that is, on the lack of communication between them) are part of their scientific status, and to ignore this is to be a dilettante. In all, you'd be better off respecting the division between different kinds of expertise and forgetting the unclassified interest that, in an evil hour, a novel awoke in you. Doing otherwise presupposes, beyond being conversant with several disciplines (something difficult to achieve in its own right), an independence of judgement in relation to them, and a certain relativization, in the name of the primary experience itself and the theoretical whole to be constructed, which to a certain extent makes the science itself, which, after all, is our protection and the means of our livelihood, look ideological. Finally, even if we leave the system of university interests on one side – though it has enormous weight – dialectical thinking is in a difficult position. The separation of different spheres is not just ideological; it is the very structure of the real process. Thus, aiming at the process in its integrity is much more than a methodological position; it is a lifelong struggle not to resign oneself to the compartmentalization that the process itself imposes. It is also more than a critical position, for it depends – really and truly – on observing and assimilating what is happening in other compartments, in the academic field, and, above all, in society itself.[8]

6

However, it is true that in 'Dialectic of Roguery', the literary form gets a more structured treatment than does the social reality. I have not paused over this so far, wishing rather to highlight the play between literary and historical structures, which is the centre of the essay. The emphasis, among Candido's several observations on Brazilian social history, has fallen on the main thing: the construction of the dialectic of order and disorder out of the situation of poor, free men inside the slave-owning order. However, in the body of the study, this argument is one among others, even if it is dominant and others are mentioned: the precariousness of marriage, for example, and the characteristically dubious legality

---

8   See Theodor Adorno, 'The Essay as Form', in *Notes to Literature*, vol. 1, 1991.

of the forms of social advancement in the urban Brazil of the earlier nineteenth century. Here, we have an ensemble of observations organized by its *affinity* with the alternation of order and disorder, and so with the form of *Memoirs*, but not a *totality*. Candido is strict about the critical construction of literary form and in his description of its social pertinence, but on the historical level he prefers a looser construction. Whether out of theoretical conviction, a didactic or an aesthetic concern, he opts for a light touch, for apt sociological detail rather than a complete schematization.

It remains true, however, that as a common denominator of insights into society, the dialectic of order and disorder turns into a *cultural constant.*[9] Summing it up, we can say that the arguments pull now in the direction of the historical, now in the direction of a cultural ethos, terms that are not inimical to each other, but refer to different dimensions of reality. Thus, the dialectic is initially constructed as the experience and perspective of a specific social sector, within the framework of a historically determined class antagonism; while at another moment it appears as a *Brazilian mode of existence*, a cultural trait by which we can compare ourselves to other countries, and which in favourable historical circumstances may come to our aid.

The transformation of a class-specific mode of existence into a national one is the basic operation of ideology, with the peculiarity, in this case, that what is being generalized is not the ideology of the rulers, as is usual, but that of an oppressed class. Candido identifies the dialectic of order and disorder as a mode of existence of the popular classes. Later, he generalizes it to the whole country,

---

9   In this respect Candido's line of inquiry resembles that of the classic works *Raízes do Brasil* (Rio de Janeiro, 1936) by Sérgio Buarque de Holanda, Gilberto Freyre's *Casa grande e senzala* (1933) and *The Masters and the Slaves: A Study in the Development of Brazilian Civilization* (trans. Samuel Putman, ed. David H. P. Maybury-Lewis, Berkeley, 1956), each in its way putting forward a view of Brazilian national character.

underlines the drawbacks (racism and religious fanaticism) that it spares us, and speculates on its affinities with a less unfavourable world order, which judging by its context would be post-bourgeois. Thus, he maintains, the matrix of some of the best aspects of Brazilian society lies in the kind of social relations developed by the poor, and it may be that the future will give them a chance. In other words, as well as identifying these resources and attributing value to them, Candido sets them among the wider options of contemporary history.[10] This is the position, and – why not say it? – the ideological originality of this essay.

However, we still have to understand its special colouring. Having explained the historical component of *Memoirs*, Candido returns to its folkloric dimension and argues that the mutual tension and inter-contamination between the two constitute the work's peculiarity: the non-specific universality of popular wisdom volatilizes much of the book's realism, which in turn lends social concreteness to the very general patterns of folklore. This is a brilliant critical characterization, but for our purposes, we can see that this form – which dominates the novel – in which the historical and the ahistorical are balanced, will not itself be treated historically. In other words, history, here, is not the primary ground of *everything*, on whose basis everything should be interpreted, even what tries to escape it. Following Almeida's example, the essay puts history and popular wisdom on the same footing, imitating the novel and participating in its 'gently fabulous' realism, in Candido's happy phrase. Obeying the form of the fiction, going along with its sense of life, the conceptual movement of the essay enters into a mimetic relationship with it, which translates itself into a certain attenuation of the dominance of contemporary reality. This makes itself felt in the fluctuations

---

10   The same social sympathy animates Candido's wonderful studies in the culture of the old Brazilian interior, *Os parceiros do Rio Bonito: estudo sobre o caipira paulista e a transformação dos seus meios de vida*, São Paulo, 1964).

of the final part of the essay, dedicated to the 'world without guilt', where the dialectic of order and disorder is here a contingent feature of an oppressed class and there a positive national characteristic, and above all is where the 'world without guilt' itself shifts between magical idealization and social reality. These are delicate movements, hard to formulate with precision, linked to the intimacy between the critical prose and its object and to the beauty of the essay itself. In the terms we used above, we can say that the reading of the fiction against its real background, and vice versa, finds its own limit, in reality, in Candido's fellow feeling for the universe he is studying. With the impartiality of Almeida himself, he prefers not to choose between a popular form of consciousness and historical consciousness proper, thus protesting against the oppression suffered by the former and distancing himself from the truth of the latter.

Outside the circle given aesthetic shape by mimetic fidelity to the novel, the social perspectives of 'Dialectic of Roguery' suffer from the pitiless commentary of present-day reality. It is worthwhile making this commentary explicit, for it is the dialectical opposite of the enchanted atmosphere of the final part of the essay. In this context, we may consider the moment when the world without guilt of *Memoirs* is compared to the harshness that dominates in Hawthorne's *The Scarlet Letter*. As Candido says, in Hawthorne's work the primacy of law ensures inside society the cohesion and identity of the group, while permitting unlimited brutality outside it. Taken as ways of life that are historically formed, one in Brazil, the other in the United States, the two are compared, with advantages and disadvantages on either side, and the advantage on the Brazilian side is assigned in an unprejudiced fashion to the relatively weak interiorization of order. We should note also the moment in which the Brazilian way of life is defended in opposition to the puritan values that nourish capitalist societies, and presented as a trump card at the hypothetical moment when we integrate into a more open world – a socialist one, perhaps?

But what is the historical space implied here? As far as I can see, the comparison between ways of life presupposes separate national histories, in the context of a concert of independent nations, whose differences, it is implied, are part of humanity's cultural wealth. The historiography that corresponds to this would, in this case, be national, though not nationalistic. The trouble is that this concert of nations nowadays seems unreal, and this retrospectively casts doubts on whether it existed previously. Faced by the extraordinary unification of the contemporary world under the aegis of capital, this community of nations is a concept removed from the available historical experience, a dialectical dead zone. Would it not be more plausible to look for the terms of a common history – which currently looks more like an open-ended sentence of sorts – a history in which both *Memoirs* and *The Scarlet Letter*, Brazil and the United States would participate, and which both would illuminate? The social process to be understood is not national, even though nations do exist.

There is a great distance between the culturalist and Marxist approaches. It suffices to remember that representatives of the former do not concern themselves much with capital, and, where they do, it is as a type of culture, thus provoking vociferous objections from the adepts of the latter. In these circumstances, it seems arbitrary to bring together, as we have done, 'Dialectic of Roguery' and Marx without any indication from Antonio Candido to this effect, and still more arbitrary to go on to inspect the differences between them. It happens that the historically created conflicts between Marxism, communism, dialectics, the love of truth, university research and so on have been fierce, shaping a world of mutual substitutions which have fundamentally affected the intellectual life of the Left, where the process of thought, if advancing at all, has done so amid confusion. The divorce between the spirit and letter could hardly be more complete. Thus, it is natural that the best instance of Brazilian critical dialectics – in which for the first time the dialectic of literary form and social process is no longer a dead letter – should be cast in a terminology, and even in notions, of another order. For Marxists who remember that a good part of latter-day historical materialism has been in fact functionalist, when it was not state ideology or religion, this is not a cause for shock and horror, but for celebration.

3

Beyond Universalism and Localism: Machado's Breakthrough

At the age of forty, Joaquim Maria Machado de Assis invented a narrative device that transformed him from a provincial, rather conventional writer into a world-class novelist. This leap is usually explained biographically and psychologically. Critics like to say that Machado, who nearly went blind, lost his illusions and passed from Romanticism to realism – and so on. Explanations of this sort, however, are beside the point, since anyone can contract an illness, shed illusions or accept a new literary doctrine without becoming a great writer. But if we consider the change as one of literary form, the terms of the argument alter. Machado's innovation then appears as an aesthetic solution to objective problems lodged within his own earlier fiction, but also in the development of the Brazilian novel and indeed of Brazilian culture at large – perhaps even of ex-colonial societies in general.

Textbooks usually classify Machado de Assis as a realist writer, situated after the Romantics, whose illusions he methodically undoes, and before the naturalists, whose unspiritual materialism he rejects as an artistic error. Yet such a classification is open to obvious objections, for not everything that stands between Romanticism and naturalism is realistic. Machado's narrative style was in a way old-fashioned for its time, owing much to a strand of digressiveness and comic rhetoric found in English and French writing of the eighteenth century. Nothing could be further from the realist ideal of an unobtrusive prose, strictly dictated by the subject. Machado's unconventional sense of motive, on the other hand, was not behind but ahead of the times. Anticipating the philosophy of the unconscious, it explored a kind of materialism that outdid both realism and naturalism, prefiguring Freud and twentieth-century experiments. Machado ostensibly shied away from the naturalist preference for the lower sides of life, but in fact only plunged further down, substituting temper and heredity for the servitudes of physiology and climate, the former being the much more debasing servitudes of the mind in society. There was a definite element of rivalry between Machado and the naturalists that left their bravado, with its penchant for scabrous subject matter, looking rather naïve and even quite wholesome.

By most conventional criteria, then, it would seem more reasonable to call Machado an anti-realist. Yet if we think of the distinctive spirit of realism as the ambition to capture contemporary society in motion, he can indeed be considered a great realist. But it would be truer to his complexity to call him a realist who works with apparently anti-realist devices. Of course, we need to ask why. My argument will be that this paradox, in effect a deliberate mismatch between a set of aesthetic devices and the life they depict, raises the question of what happens to realism in a peripheral country where the sequences of European social and literary history do not strictly apply, thus losing their inner necessity – or to put it more generally, how modern forms fare in regions that do not replicate the social conditions they originated in and still in some sense presume.

For literary forms may not mean the same in the core and at the periphery of our world. Time can become so uneven, when it is stretched far across space, that artistic forms which are already dead in the first may still be alive in the second. Such contrasts can be viewed with regret or satisfaction. Progress may be lamented in the name of older forms of life, richer in colour and meaning, or backwardness deplored as a refusal to cast off outworn garments and catch the air of the times; or both can be dismissed as two sides of the same coin. Brecht, who did not want to lag behind his epoch, said it was futile for a realist to stare at workers trudging through the gates of Krupp in the morning. Once reality has migrated into abstract economic functions, it can no longer be read in human faces. Observation of life in a former colony, where social divisions remain stark, might then seem more rewarding. But such concreteness is suspect too since the abstractions of the world market are never far away and belie the fullness of spontaneous perception at every moment.

Be that as it may, the aesthetic and social field I want to consider is at once international and unbalanced, bending literary forms to circumstances that are often far from aesthetic, although rarely in any predictable way. We may well think that questions to do with literary realism cannot be answered by looking simply at formal labels as such, without reference to individual works or their quality. Today, after all, superficial features of realism are omnipresent in rich and poor countries alike – in soap operas, second-rate novels, movies, advertisements. Yet these are debased versions of the original, reducing the credibility and complexity of classic realism to the repetitions and moral simplicities of melodrama and commercial inducement. What seems to have disappeared, as modernist writers and critics pointed out a century ago, is what was once realism's capacity to grasp what is new and be true to it. Or, conversely, what has vanished is the kind of society and social dynamics that realism in its heyday captured. It is a part of this change that later critics denied any such grasp ever existed, or was even an artistic ambition.

I

One particular side of this situation is less well known. In Brazil, literary historians outside the mainstream have shown that when this former colony became an independent nation, its peculiar and in many ways untenable morphology – invalidated by a progress that remains out of reach – imposed on European-inspired literary schools new tasks that involuntarily altered them. Some of these changes have been carefully studied in Candido's classic *Formação da literatura brasileira.*[1]

The first of these formative moments, neoclassical in style, occurred in the last fifty years of Brazil's colonial period. It was followed by Romanticism in the fifty years after independence in 1822. Mainstream historiography, nationalist from the cradle, has it that neoclassicism, with its stylized imagery of shepherds and nymphs and its universalist spirit, represented the alienation imposed by the metropolis on its colony, while Romanticism, with its motifs of chivalrous Indians and lively depictions of local contexts, stood for the attitudes of independence. Candido, who wrote not as a nationalist but as a socialist studying the formation of a national literature, took a different view. The thesis he develops in *Formação da literatura brasileira* is that, notwithstanding the sharp artistic and intellectual contrasts between them, these two long literary moments were both under the spell of Independence-in-the-making, which put them to its own uses, and, in doing so, unified them to some degree. This offers us a much more interesting picture, one that allows us to sense, if we will, the pull of world history and the variations it generates. Here, the shepherds and nymphs of the neoclassical school articulate the Enlightenment, with its principles of reason and public duty, its sense of educational and civic responsibilities, self-interest and self-government, which

1   Antonio Candido, *Formação da literatura brasileira: momentos decisivos* (1959), 2 vols., Belo Horizonte, 1975.

take on an anti-colonial coloration and inform the first conspiracies for national independence. Even Arcadian conventions acquire new meaning, as they blend with the local environment to produce tangled loyalties: Brazilian poets attached at once to the bare and anonymous backwardness of their native surroundings and to the illustrious landscapes of classical mythology, a strange combination of period rusticities that often tore them asunder. Thus, one of the most universalist, timeless and theatrical conventions could convey a quite specific, concrete historical situation in a way that was poetic in its own fashion and free of the restrictions of an exotic localism.

Romanticism too underwent a kind of inversion: As members of Brazil's small educated minority, Romantics tended to occupy positions close to power, finding themselves forced by tasks of national construction into adopting a rather responsible, managerial air and idiom with strong neoclassical continuities. At the same time, the effusive displays of localism – which were Romantic par excellence – that accompanied independence can be said to have reflected a degree of submission to European expectations of tropical countries: the very opposite of what they were supposed to signify. There is an irony and unintentional originality in these reversals that is characteristic of the Brazilian experience and deserves further consideration.

2

The discovery – and it was a discovery – of the unifying and modifying twist that national independence gave two successive and opposite literary schools established a historical object in its own right: the formation of a national Brazilian literary system, as a constituent of decolonization. For Candido this was a relatively compressed and willed process, with its own logic, its own aims and its own comedy, which defy any simple chronological sequence and conventional literary-historical narrative. The formative stage comes to an end when the main contemporary schools of the West have been mastered and the whole of society, including all the country's regions, has been transposed into literature. This made it possible for an organic Brazilian imagination to develop, capable of self-reference and a certain degree of autonomy. The value of such an internally grounded and less passive way of confronting contemporary experience, which went beyond literature, is self-evident.

All this may sound rather formalistic and programmatic, yet it has proved to be a remarkably accurate representation of the development of Brazilian cultural life, giving intellectual visibility to some of its hitherto unacknowledged realities. Two examples will suffice: we have seen that the sequence of neoclassical universalism and Romantic localism, a familiar pattern of European cultural history, turned out to be functional for the requirements of the newborn nation and former colony. Yet these requirements belonged to a field of forces of quite another order, which could not be subsumed into this sequence of cultural styles. Instead, in an unexpected way, universalism and localism corresponded to the need of a small cultured minority to participate as equal and capable citizens in the general civilization of the West, escaping colonial seclusion, and at the same time to play a distinctive part in the concert of nations, with an identity of its own. This has meant that alternation between the universal and the local is a permanent law of motion of the country's cultural life, quite independent of its first appearance under the sign of the struggle between neoclassicism and Romanticism. Another previously unacknowledged and original feature of Brazilian cultural reality is that the newly independent country summoned its educated men and women to perform the national duty of providing it as promptly as possible with the equipment of civilization that it lacked, from museums to philosophical theories, from new fashions to the latest literary forms. What this amounted to, as Candido put it, was a peculiar kind of *engagement* on the part of intellectuals who were required to participate in the building – rather than the critique – of the national culture. This special bond would allow, for example, a student writing a Parnassian sonnet to feel like a hero on a patriotic mission.

When it was published in 1959, *Formação da literatura brasileira* was a materialist retort to *A literatura no Brasil,* a collective project begun three years earlier and organized by the critic Afrânio Coutinho, who found his inspiration in René Wellek and Austin Warren's *Theory of Literature.*[2] Coutinho prided himself on being scientific, by which he meant that his categories of periodization were exclusively literary, that is, relating only to questions of style, as if these were universal forms with no admixture of historical circumstance. In his view, the baroque was baroque no matter where; the neoclassical, neoclassical; the Romantic, Romantic; and so on, in that order and under all conditions. The general weaknesses of this approach should be obvious enough, but they become especially pronounced when we consider former colonies, where the difficulty or impossibility of repeating the development of the core countries is the primary social, economic and cultural experience. Discerning the silver lining in our relations with these core forms, a Brazilian wit once spoke of 'our creative inability to copy'.[3] In more recent decades, rigid periodization of styles has again become fashionable, taking its cue this time from Foucault's sequence of self-enclosed *epistemes.*

But *Formação* was also an alternative to vulgar Marxism. The patriotic task of assimilating the basic elements of European civilization, of catching up with new developments abroad, of making up for what the country lacked, in awareness of its grave shortcomings as a modern nation, amounted to a powerful ideology. The pressure was real and exerted its own authority and attraction. It also lent a

---

2   Afrânio Coutinho (b.1911–d. 2000) , Austin Warren (b. 1899–d. 1986), René Wellek (b. 1903–d. 1995). The classic *Theory of Literature* (1949) defended the irreducible objectivity of the poetic datum, synthesizing the thinking of US New Criticism and Russian and Czech Formalism. [*Ed.*]

3   Paulo Emílio Salles Gomes, *Cinema: Trajetória no subdesenvolvimento*, Rio de Janeiro, 1980, 77.

certain legitimacy to the elites, who felt themselves to be a civilizing force, invested with a national mission. The imperatives were objective enough, yet when Candido was writing there were no terms for them in the contemporary Marxist lexicon, which spoke only of imperialism and internal class relations. The desire in Brazil to share in what was new in the world, a substantial historical appetite, went unnoticed or was viewed with suspicion by Marxists, remaining a conceptual blind spot for them.

In effect, there was no way either to escape from the terms that European developments imposed on Brazil or to live up to them. The result was a culture continually off balance. But this did not mean only local goucheness. It could lead to insight into the fatal, often grotesque imbalances of the entire historical process, once core and periphery were seen as correlative realities.

3

How, then, does realism fare in such conditions? Matter-of-factness and critical awareness of circumstance are of its essence. Yet to Brazilians, and perhaps to all peoples of the periphery in the mid-nineteenth century, the realist novel was also something else. It was one of those new and prestigious European developments that had to be taken over if the nation was to catch up with modernity. Let us suppose, then, that in peripheral countries realism was both a critical commitment to modern reality and a flattering token of belonging to its most fashionable – advanced and enlightened – expressions. The two aspects were separable and did not carry equal weight. Indeed, for realism to operate as a sign of up-to-dateness, which at first may have been the principal reason for its adoption, it was sufficient for a critical commitment merely to posture as such, in underlying indifference to the actual circumstances at hand. But in any case, matter-of-factness and attention to circumstance are less straightforward notions than one might think, since the facts and circumstances that will count are not simply given in advance and can vary from society to society. The opposition between the core and the periphery of capitalism would have no substance were this not so. Literary history can be instructive on this point.

The first Brazilian writer to make a serious attempt at realism was José de Alencar, a reader of Balzac.[4] His best achievement in this vein was a novel called *Senhora* (1872). The main characters, the atmosphere and the type of plot and conflict are all direct or indirect borrowings from Balzac. The cast of secondary characters and motives derives from Romantic chronicles of everyday urban life, revelling in local colours, tones and usages – as much a foreign import as Balzac, although an earlier one, which time and habit had rendered native. Schematically, what does the novel tell us?

The story revolves around a young beauty, born poor, who inherits a fortune. Once rich, she becomes outraged at the servility her wealth creates around her, especially in the fashionable young men who hope to marry her. Among these is a penniless dandy who jilted her when she was poor, but whom she nevertheless continues to love. He needs to provide a dowry for his little sister, but is up to his neck in debt. To punish him, herself and the whole of society for the immorality of money, the heroine devises a plot to lure her dandy into a marriage, celebrated in the dark, in exchange for the sum he desperately needs. He walks straight into her trap. The nuptial hour arrives and he discovers that not only has he got the cash he needed but also the woman he loves. Then his new wife presents him with a contract, explaining the terms on which he has sold himself. The humiliation is complete. He decides to retaliate by behaving strictly as her property, with no will of his own, until the inhumanity of the situation becomes unbearable for her too and she is forced to invite him back into love and a happy conjugal life. The novel is divided into four parts, entitled 'Price', 'Quittance',

---

4   For José de Alencar (b. 1829–d. 1877), see further Roberto Schwarz, 'The Importing of the Novel to Brazil and Its Contradictions in the Work of Alencar', in *Misplaced Ideas*, trans. John Gledson, London and New York, 1992. [*Ed.*]

'Possession' and 'Ransom', to underline the pitiless priority of mercenary calculations over human feelings. The whole thing is rather childish, but Alencar carries it off with ingenuity and vivacity.

For our purposes, the main points are these. A contemporary tension – love match vs. marriage of convenience, or, more simply, love vs. money – is taken to dramatic extremes by characters who turn it, at no matter what cost, into the abstract issue on which they stake their lives. This kind of device, halfway between content and form, comes from Balzac and depends on a blueprint of modern society in which individualism knows no bounds, such as only the French Revolution could have brought about. It has major literary consequences. What happens when it is applied in a peripheral country and topped up with local subject matter, without which realism would not be realism?

The fashionable young people who occupy centre stage in the novel behave according to this shrill Balzacian formula, with its extreme social choices. But the secondary characters, drawn from nature or adapted from the topical press, in a style at once comic and local, live with a much more relaxed tone, in which abstract principles do not count. They belong to the world of patron–client relationships, of paternalism – a less dynamic domain – where love is no absolute, money is not meretricious, though it may be scarce, and the individual is supposed to respect, if not obey, the many ties that bind him. In other words, the substance and the form of the central conflict are alien to the crowd of lesser characters, who are nevertheless in charge of assuring a local feel to the book and of conveying the tenor of the society. One of the great effects of Balzac's novels – the substantial unity between the principal conflict and secondary anecdotes – does not come off.

How is one to understand this relative failure of *Senhora*? Why is it that modern conflict à la Balzac is at odds with characters who carry the local tone? What is the content of this dissonance? The answer can only be historical. Brazilian independence was a conservative process that did not bring about a restructuring of society. The colonial heritage of landownership, slavery, traffic in human beings, extended family and generalized clientelism went almost untouched. Brazil's insertion in the modern world proceeded by way of a social *confirmation* of the colonial ancien régime, not its supersession. This made for a disconcerting kind of progress, in which pre-modern inequalities were simply replicated in one new context after another, rather than being eradicated. This pattern may be a key to the peculiarities of Brazilian culture, with its penchant for both radical modernism and unending compromise. What is one to think of the strange lack of tension between the ultra-modern and the indefensibly pre-modern? The terms make for a harsh contrast, yet they keep good company, and together make for a colourful and rather amiable national emblem of uneven development. The inner motor of modernization appears to falter.

Alencar's novel shows us just how half-hearted such oppositions may be. Evocations of local society and its paternalist relations, though secondary to the main plot, nevertheless have a feel of reality powerful enough to give the lie to the high-minded individualism of the main characters, which is supposed to strike a truly realist and modern note in the novel. This reversal is not the outcome of antagonism between the old and new ways, which do not compete with each other at all in the book: it is rather that the antagonism itself is phony and the realist boldness of the heroes and the narrator something of a juvenile sham, even a fashion statement – more self-congratulation than social criticism. Such discrepancies of register and proportion are characteristic of Brazilian novels of this period: expressions of the desire to be up-to-date without renouncing the basic relations of local society, which are less than modern. With a little artistic twist, which became the specialty of Machado de Assis, this deep-rooted ambivalence could become the stuff of great literature, capable of that awareness of circumstances that realism demands.

4

Ten years younger than Alencar, Machado understood what was weak and unreal in his realism. His own early novels reversed the priorities and proportions established by his predecessor. Patron–client relations, with their peculiar set of intricacies and issues linked to personal fidelity, moral indebtedness and humiliation came to the fore; while fashionable debates about individualism were reduced to a minimum, functioning merely as conventional signs of modernity, along with cigars, waistcoats, canes, speaking French and playing the piano. What had been local colour now became the core theme, and what had been core became outward signs of the times.

The oddities of the national situation that Machado sought to capture came from the unexpected, meandering ways in which clientelism, slavery and modernity concatenated in Brazil. The massive presence of slaves created a precarious labour market, forcing poor free men to seek the protection of landowners and the well-to-do, on whose favours their livelihood depended – naturally, in exchange for all kinds of personal services. Hence, the ubiquity of a very diversified layer of social dependants, ranging from rural bullies and tame voters to *agregados* – men or women attached to a family as permanent adjuncts, who could be put to any and every task at hand. In these dislocated conditions, the typical position of the poor remained below the water line of modern liberties. As for the wealthy, who renounced neither the colonial privileges they inherited nor the liberal image to which they felt entitled as the country's civilizing elite, they entertained, inevitably, an extravagant idea of themselves.

Once Machado had sensed some of this, the way was open to a searching analysis of paternalist authority and personal dependence, and the deadlocks they produced. In his early novels, like *A mão e a luva* (1874), *Helena* (1876) or *Yayá Garcia* (1878), a poor but worthy young woman – a kind of *agregada*[5] – is a victim of these deadlocks: in each instance, she tries to circumvent the narrow demands of people of property, and at some crucial moment the grotesque arbitrariness of the possessors is devastatingly exposed. The struggle of the dependent party for acceptance and dignity, or against humiliation, is fought in a spirit that differs from novel to novel. The heroine is by turns artless, cynical, disillusioned, pious or severe, each disposition representing a different possible response to the whimsical authority of the powerful.

The conclusion Machado drew from his quite systematic exploration of the field was that the nub of the problem was not psychological. It was not to be found in the personal caprice of the patriarchs and matriarchs of propertied families but in their dual and ever-shifting social role. They were men or women of property; but they were also the heads or heirs of Brazilian extended families, to whom their social dependants – and actual slaves – owed obedience and fidelity. Since these roles would alternate according to the momentary convenience of the rich, their dependants were continually at a loss to know with whom they were dealing. There was no way for them to foresee whether they were paying respect to a godfather and sponsor who would reciprocate; to a figure of authority who would brutalize them; or to a modern person of property, to whom inferiors were perfectly indifferent, to be treated like strangers.

In other words, paternalism could be humane and enlightened or it could take a vicious and backward form, in which the poor as a colonial rabble fared little better than slaves; or it might choose to be modern, forgetting its paternal role altogether, and treating its dependants as free, autonomous persons to whom nothing was due. The degree of uncertainty was extreme. The social molecule, composed of property and slavery and poor dependants without

---

5   For the term *agregada/agregado*, which roughly translates as 'dependant', see ch. 4, n. 11. [*Ed.*]

rights, had a logic of its own that did not match the liberal norms to which the country officially subscribed. Machado's literary achievement in capturing some of this was far more substantial than Alencar's frivolous seriousness about liberal catchwords. Yet nobody would say that these first novels are great literature. For in focusing on the universe of paternalism as the more real world, they paid a high price: they did not belong to the present of the world at large. They undeniably represented an advance in the development of a local realism. Yet were it not for Machado's later work, which offered a completely different solution to the problems posed by their subject matter, they would barely deserve to be read today.

5

In 1880, Machado published *The Posthumous Memoirs of Brás Cubas*, the first world-class Brazilian novel.[6] The 'memoirs' are written by a dead man, with the candour that only death allows. All the grand concepts of life are debunked, from Love, Poetry and Philosophy to Politics, Science and Enterprise. His cadaverous jokes about these subjects furnish a metaphysical stage set for allegories of human frailty. But on closer inspection, the aloofness of the deceased turns out to be a facetious device for allowing the narrator a spectacularly shameless display of the meaner motives of the living – at the reader's expense. The narrator is less a disinterested wraith than a distinct social and national type: his memories show him to be a wealthy *fainéant*, steeped in slavery and clientelism, and full of claims to modernity. Once these dimensions of the character emerge and command due attention, they expose his chatter from beyond the grave as the language of the casually brutal upper classes. Thus, the resounding nothingness in which the novel ends has more to do with Brazilian circumstances than with metaphysics. Behind a

---

6   Translated as *Epitaph of a Small Winner* (1952). [*Ed.*]

travesty of the human condition, there lies the nothingness of a ruling-class experience.

What had changed with this novel? Its stroke of genius was to move the narrative point of view to the upper-class position. Hitherto, the narrators in Machado's novels had always sympathized with those in a precarious, socially dependent situation, fretting over the arbitrary and unreliable behaviour of those who called the shots, as if to ask how such dependants could persuade their overlords to behave in a civilized manner, to make society more just and liveable for all. At some point, however, Machado must have decided the task was hopeless – an important historical judgement – and dropped this formula. The replacement he hit upon was unexpected and extraordinary. Instead of a narrator siding with the weak, whose pleas led nowhere, he contrived one who not only sides with social injustice and its beneficiaries but brazenly relishes being of their party.

This turncoat departure may seem odious, but it is more duplicitous than at first appears. For what, with high artistry, it achieved was a complete, intimate exposure of the very viewpoint it ostensibly adopted. Instead of bewailing the fickleness of a liberal, slave-owning and paternalistic propertied class, Machado took to imitating it in the first person singular, so as to provide plentiful and compelling natural illustrations of all the misdeeds of which its social dependants would accuse it, were they in a position to do so. For his narrator, Brás Cubas, is programmed to enact, at their most vicious and opportunistic, the continual lurches from paternalist concern to bourgeois indifference, from a cultivated, well-intentioned liberalism to the unfettered authority of godfather/slave owner and back again, that the rich made the dependent classes endure. What had hitherto been the central problem of his fiction as content, the amazing class substance of the shifts, becomes in *The Posthumous Memoirs* its form, the inner rhythm of the narrative. To enlarge the scope of this to-and-fro, and render it universal, Machado endowed his narrator with an encyclopaedic stock of knowledge and rhetorical tropes, and in so doing held up a kind of mock synthesis of the Western tradition to the mirror of Brazilian class relations. Not only the poor but also the West – if I may put it like this – are made to get the feel of this kind of rule. If we were to extract an artistic maxim from these moves, we might say that the procedure consisted in joining the upper class at its most self-satisfied, as if to praise it, but in fact to lay it open at its most unguarded.[7]

The young Machado had been right to give priority to the old, familiar issue of paternalism over the brand-new, burning questions of liberal Romanticism that so engaged Alencar, and to reduce these last to the role of scenery. Yet his great move only came now, as he reintroduced this atmosphere of individualism and modern civilization on a grand scale – in the form of recent philosophical theories, newly invented gadgets, parliamentary debates, financial ventures and so on – through the words and deeds of an upper-class narrator unafraid to subordinate the whole world to the immediate convenience, or inconvenience, of the indefensible class to which he belongs.

The disconnection between the spheres of paternalism and individual self-interest, which had unbalanced *Senhora* and Machado's first novels, is overcome. Machado's new narrator shuttles nonchalantly from one to the other, without choosing between them, taking it for granted that they complement each other. The least edifying possible combination of these worlds is thus staged: paternalist authority is retained, its responsibilities refused; private interest is pursued with due diligence – we are all rational individuals in the end – while one's fellows are treated according to the rights of those who own property over those who have none. Some would say the upshot is not modern, since it is infected by a patriarchal personalism; others that it is an effective figure of progress.

*   *   *

---

7   The strategy has affinities with the anti-bourgeois aesthetic of Heine, Flaubert and Baudelaire. See Dolf Oehler, *Ein Höllensturz der Alten Welt: Zur selbsterforschung der moderne nach dem Juni 1848*, Frankfurt am Main, 1988.

This narrator is an invention that breaks new ground. Technically, we have a pastiche of whimsical narratives of the eighteenth century – in his preface to *The Memoirs*, Machado famously refers to Sterne and Maistre as his rhetorical models. He might have mentioned Diderot as well, especially *Jacques le fataliste*. But, of course, imitation of outstanding writers of a former century rarely produces good literature. Machado, however, adapted, with outstanding artistic intelligence, eighteenth-century explorations of human spontaneity to his nineteenth-century exploration of the irresponsibility and self-indulgence granted to Brazilian elites by their ownership of slaves, along with its attendant set of more or less enforced relations of personal subjection. In effect, he redirected the rather playful effronteries of the unreliable narrator of the eighteenth century to the grim realities of class relations in a former colony of the nineteenth. The dissonance of the combination points to the inadequacy not only of a *national* history that falls so short of contemporary ideals of progress, but also, at a deeper level, of the ideals themselves, which lend themselves so easily to this sort of arrangement.

The literary trappings of the novel are antiquarian – an eccentric, even snobbish, display of bookish learning, ostensibly alien to modern reality; and yet they relate to the harsh form of contemporary class society, much as they do in the case of nineteenth-century realism. There is a similar mixture of period and temper in the narrator, when we consider him as a character among other characters. At first sight, he is a poetaster, an enlightened gentleman of old-fashioned tastes who always has a fine quotation to hand from Augustine, Shakespeare, the Bible, Erasmus, Pascal or other classics. Yet once we see through him the world of semi-colonial oppression, of which he is a prosperous and remorseless beneficiary, the innermost meaning of this display of civility is altered. Enlightened talk becomes uncivil and a perpetuator of unenlightened forms of society. This reversal is more modern than the moderns, and is just the kind of effect that realism should aim to achieve.

In other words, Machado's unreliable narrator has a distinctly nineteenth-century class substance, and this is its secret as a device. Brás Cubas is a social type, as partial and as situated as his characters, whose world he inhabits. His rhetorical manoeuvres do not belong primarily to the general repertoire of humanism, where they were nevertheless picked up. They answer, and owe their depth, to his well-to-do position in a specific society; a morally indicted part of the contemporary world. The narrative somersaults of this highly 'civilized' slave-owning gentleman of the nineteenth century are not the same as anyone else's. They are not variations on a classic tradition of authors teasing their readers, but the indirect rendering of a real, unavowed aspect of modern history. In *The Posthumous Memoirs*, Machado strips narrative procedures of their innocent neutrality and authority, giving the lie to the very idea of an abstract narrative function capable of floating above historical time. What we get is not only an awareness of narrative in the making, but something more radical and unprecedented: a narrative that performs at a highly cultivated and artistic level, yet fashions the world according to a particular and indefensible interest, into which we must look if we are to understand what is going on. I cannot think of a writer who accomplishes this decisive exposure with greater daring and thoroughness. By the same token, readers of *The Posthumous Memoirs* are obliged to read against the grain, refusing the narrator's support, since it is self-serving, and if they are up to the task, proceeding against it, with the help of all the scepticism and critical spirit they can muster. Rather than looking for the author's intention, they need to decipher the meaning of the whole form, of which intentions are only an element. Once the authority of the narrator is questioned, it is up to us to interpret what we hear and see when we read. We must become self-reliant readers, secluded, active and judicious, such as a truly modern literature seeks to create as a sort of historical threshold.

7

To conclude, let us recapitulate some of the steps that led from the provincial fiction of a former colony to the very advanced writing of Machado. What were the obstacles that had to be overcome? First, there were peculiarities and anomalies of a newly independent nation, inheriting from its colonial past international marginality and the rightless condition of the poor. In such circumstances, the import of modern ideas and cultural forms to close the gap with the advanced world was a patriotic task of sorts. Yet since the world of local relations was of an order that differed from that of the advanced world, such importation created special difficulties in its turn, as contemporary ideas and forms were put to unforeseen uses and tests. We have seen, for example, that Alencar's attempt at a realist novel was not realist in its motives. It had more to do with displaying a familiarity with metropolitan fashions, with catching up with the societies that were our models, than with a critical revision of present or former social relations. On the other hand, of course, straight imitation would cause realism to lose its clear sight and critical edge, blinding the artist to what was decisive in Brazilian society.

Machado, who was younger and sharper than Alencar, would try to repair the damage. He dropped the standard themes of realism, issues derived from significant moments in recent European history, and focused instead on the unfashionable subject of the social relations dominant in Brazil. An unintended consequence of his effort to get closer to local reality was that his writing in this period lost touch with the contemporary world at large. It was less naïve and more complex than Alencar's, but not less provincial, and even more remote from a wider idea of the present.

Four novels and eight years later, Machado would achieve synthesis. He kept to the social discoveries of his youth but took a less charitable view of them. He now considered that good counsel given by friendly novelists would not improve the ways of our privileged classes. Their way of handling the unprivileged would determine the country's lot for a long time to come. No less disturbing, this way extended beyond its immediate, practical ends to the field of culture as well, indeed to the whole of the Western tradition, which lost its binding power and was forced to accommodate itself to Brazilian-style class bullying. By this point, Machado had given up trying to change what ought to be, but would not be changed. He would try instead to draw out as fully as he could the consequences of his society's failure to change. In the early novels, the arbitrary authority of the propertied was something capable of reform, featuring as a regrettable and occasional flaw that furnished the dramatic pivot of the plot. In *The Posthumous Memoirs*, Machado moves it to a much more significant position, making it the governing law of the narrator's conduct. He has the narrator of the book mimic and stylize it throughout, rendering it the perpetual, all-pervading negative ambience of national life.

This volatile and unreliable narrator, with his endless Shandean somersaults, is vehemently modern. Brás Cubas is a literary device that turns the crucial content of the Brazilian novel before *The Posthumous Memoirs* into form. As such, it was a truly dialectical supersession – a breakthrough that put the conception of literature in Brazil on a par with its advanced counterparts elsewhere. Machado was a contemporary of Henry James, to whom he should be compared. Like James, he did not believe in a reality that was not mediated by a point of view. In his writing, such mediation has a conflictual class character, beyond questions of individual psychology. The unreliable voice is undoubtedly a social one, a tendentious voice because it is part and parcel of a social question, falling into line with realism in unexpected ways. The same overly cultured narrator also mediates between civilization at large and this limited and semi-segregated sphere with its colonial imprint, a sort of backyard of the modern world.

Inevitably, given its class character, this mediation is not benign. To put it another way, the narrator is quite content with the abyss that separates the cultivated from the benighted characters he tells us about, and who form his world. The manifest comedy stages an elite that betrays its dependants and is not unhappy at their dejection. The novel's less obvious and more modern effect is to force us to acknowledge the adaptability of civilization to purposes that are contrary to its very idea. If we consider that these were the great days of imperialism, we may find that Machado's satire on the shameless use of civilization's finest resources strikes a chord that reverberates beyond its local setting. Whether because there was no visible means of overcoming such conditions locally, or because the global drift of the time remained obscure, with this novel Brazilian literature had built a vantage point from which to think about the world's present.

I I
TWO GIRLS

4

Capitu, the Bride of Dom Casmurro

For Gilda de Mello e Sousa

Machado de Assis's novel *Dom Casmurro*[1] (1899) makes a good vantage point from which to appreciate the author's advance over his fellow Brazilians. The book is a trap of sorts, and administers a sharp critical lesson – if, that is, the trap is recognized for what it is. From the beginning, there are jarring notes, obscure moments and disturbing emphases, which set up a puzzle, an enigma. The solution, while not exactly hard to find, comes at a great cost for anyone of a conformist frame of mind because it leaves one of the elite types most dear to Brazilian ideology in a parlous state. Accidentally or not, it was only sixty years after the novel had been published and republished many times that an American academic (because she was a woman? because she was a foreigner? maybe she was a Protestant?) began to look at the figure of Bento Santiago – the Casmurro of the title[2] – with the necessary mistrust. It is as if, for

---

1   Machado de Assis, *Dom Casmurro*, trans. John Gledson, London, 1997. All references to the novel are to this edition, and are indicated in the main text by the relevant chapter number as styled there, thus: (XXV).

2   The 'Casmurro' of *Dom Casmurro* has two possible meanings, one of which the narrator admits to: 'a quiet person who keeps himself to himself'. The other more embarrassing meaning, which the narrator only refers to indirectly (telling the reader not to look it up in the dictionary), is a person who is 'stubborn',

the Brazilian reader, the sordid implications of certain kinds of authority had been less visible.

Dom Casmurro, the narrator of the novel, recounts the idyll of his adolescence, culminating in his marriage to the beloved Capitu, and then her deception and eventual exile, together with her son, who he suspects is not his. He concludes with a question: did the sweetheart he adored when he was fifteen already carry within her the deceitful woman who would later betray him with his best friend? Prompted to review the evidence, we are led to remember dozens of cases of calculation and dissimulation in the girl's behaviour. However, on further reflection, we also see that these same indications have been scattered through the text by the narrator himself: this changes everything and forces us to reverse the direction of our mistrust. In place of the nostalgic evocation of the past, the sincere, emotional memoir that seemed to deserve all the credit in the world now appears as a disguised defamation of Capitu and a tortuous self-justification on the part of Dom Casmurro as, possessed by jealousy, he sends his wife into exile. The book, then, asks for three successive readings: the first, a romantic one, in which we accompany the growth and decay of a love affair; the second, one that is carried out in an inquisitorial patriarchal spirit, looking for advance signs and evidences of an adultery that is a given and as such is unquestionable; and the third, a reading against the grain of the narration, in which the suspect and later the accused is Bento Santiago himself, in his urge to convince himself and the reader of his wife's guilt.

This narrative set-up, though intricate, is clear enough and ought to turn the accuser into the accused. If the critical about-turn does not occur to readers, this is because they have allowed themselves

---

'gloomy' or 'morose'. In this text, then, Bento Santiago and Dom Casmurro are one and the same person (though seen under somewhat different aspects), as is Bentinho, the diminutive form of Bento, used above all in the first part of the novel. [*Tr.*]

to be seduced by the social and literary prestige of the figure who
has the floor, so to speak. How can we withhold our sympathy from
this distinguished, tender-hearted gentleman who is admirably
well-spoken and a little clumsy when it comes to practical matters,
above all when they involve money; who is always wrapped up in
memories of his childhood, the house where he was born, the back
garden, the well, the old toys and the street cries; and who is a
tearful worshipper of his mother and obsessed with his first sweetheart? And so, in spite of the decisive evidence against it, the
conformist reading has prevailed. As an example of the attendant
tone, which even notably subtle critics would adopt, here is a
passage taken from the first appreciation of Machado's work as a
whole, published in 1917:

> Let us come to *Dom Casmurro*. It is a cruel book. Bento Santiago, an
> innocent, good soul, submissive and confiding, made for sacrifice
> and tenderness, has since childhood loved his delightful neighbour,
> Capitolina – Capitu, as she is called at home. This Capitu is one of
> Machado de Assis's most beautiful, strongest creations. She carries
> treachery and perfidy in her eyes, full of seduction and charm. Sly
> by nature, cunning is for her, so to speak, instinctive and perhaps
> unconscious. Bento Santiago, whom his mother wanted to be a
> priest, succeeds in escaping from the fate that has been prepared for
> him, graduates in law and marries his childhood companion. Capitu
> betrays him with his best friend, and Bento Santiago realizes that
> the son he thought was born of the marriage is not his. His wife's
> deception makes him sceptical, and even malevolent.[3]

The critic's identification with the point of view being questioned
could not be more complete.

In 1960, Helen Caldwell, who thought Bentinho's allegations
against Capitu unfounded and dictated by jealousy, published *The*

---

3   Alfredo Pujol, *Machado de Assis*, São Paulo, 1917, 240.

Brazilian Othello of Machado de Assis, in which she uncovered the basic device of the novel, whereby Othello is given the role and credibility of the narrator and allowed to tell the story of Desdemona's deserved punishment. So began the work of deciphering Machado's puzzle. The next advance was also the work of a critic from outside Brazil, John Gledson, in a perceptive study imbued with a democratic spirit. Gledson returned to Caldwell's thesis – that the point of view of Bento Santiago, the only one allowed to speak, is specious – but now finding more complex reasons for his lack of objectivity. Behind the emotional ups and downs that dominate the foreground of the novel, Gledson identifies the presence of strictly social factors linked to the structure of a paternalist order and its crisis. Instead of the new Othello, who out of jealousy destroys and defames the love of his life, there appears a rich young man, from a declining family, a mummy's boy, for whom the energy and free opinions of a more modern girl (who is also the daughter of a poor neighbour) are in the end intolerable. In this sense, the jealousy signifies a broad, historically specific social predicament and represents the convulsions of a patriarchal society in crisis.[4]

Thus, after delighting several generations, Casmurro's lyricism begins to disclose an aspect that is questionable if not downright hateful – much to the advantage of the novel. Born of an antipathy towards the husband's prerogatives – he being the property owner and the owner of the words themselves – this about-turn in the reading of the novel gives eloquent meaning to the book's opaque passages, which the conventional interpretation had no option but to ignore. Examined at the proper distance, these moments change their aspect and are revealed as crucial, as clues and also as symptoms: interrupted arguments, elucidations that might seem superfluous, incongruous interpretations, an

---

4   John Gledson, *The Deceptive Realism of Machado de Assis: A Dissenting Interpretation of Dom Casmurro*, Liverpool, 1984.

excess of clichéd formulae and arbitrary artistic stratagems all stand out in a new relief, offering unexpected testimony concerning the narrator. In the same way, the mannered simplicity of tone, favoured by school anthologies, begins to suggest the height of duplicity. In these respects, *Dom Casmurro* manifests its association with the detective novel and psychoanalysis, which were then coming into existence.

Its hidden structural demand for reading against the grain is among the essential traits of the most advanced fiction of the time. Like his contemporary Henry James, Machado invented *narrative situations*, or *narrators placed inside a given fictional circumstance*, creating fables whose drama is only complete when we take into account the interested nature, the active partiality of the storyteller himself. The narrator's authority, his superior, exceptional status, is undermined in a universe wholly shared with the other characters; he becomes one of them, with his own aspect, individual, problematic and above all unavowable.[5] There is no doubt that this is a step forward from the objectivism of the realists and naturalists: the arbiter of the novel is also an interested party, and must be held suspect as such. But, as Gledson rightly says, in refuting the conventional viewpoint, the deceitful behaviour of the author-protagonist does not suspend the operation of social conflict, nor of history – quite the contrary.[6] Dramatized within the narrative method itself, the clash between different interests comes centre stage, where its nature as a conflictual social relationship is fully, objectively operative, even if critics have usually overlooked it.

By adopting an unreliable narrator, and making him the axis on which his literary form turns, Machado placed himself among the

---

5   Henry James speaks numerous times of his preference for the combination of an interesting anecdote and a limited angle of observation, whose personal component may be explicit but need not be. See, for example, 'Preface to "The Golden Bowl"' and 'Preface to "The Ambassadors"', in Henry James, *The Art of the Novel*, ed. Richard P. Blackmur (New York and London, 1934).

6   Gledson, *The Deceptive Realism of Machado de Assis*, introductory chapter.

innovative novelists of Europe and alongside advanced thinkers who knew that every representation carries within itself an element of will or of interest: this is the hidden truth to be examined, the sign of the crisis of bourgeois civilization. In the local sphere too, the consequences of the new technique were striking. Our citizen above suspicion – the eminently cultured lawyer, the adoring son, the jealous husband, the well-to-do man of property with no head for business who supports his poor relations, the young man with a good Catholic education, the cultured man with a feeling for the past – is now himself under suspicion, deserving all the mistrust he may awaken. Finally, from the viewpoint of Brazilian artistic ideology, this narrator well provided with credentials but stripped of credibility produced an unprecedented situation, hard to accept, and in marked contrast to the previous one. The edifying certainties characteristic of the period in which the nation was being formed were overtaken; in the earlier perspective, being artistically up-to-date and acquiring literary proficiency were unimpeachable services rendered to the nation by its dedicated men of letters.[7] With Machado de Assis, for the first time in the history of Brazilian literature, the understanding of form and modern ideas appears free of provincial pettiness and gaucherie and thus no longer has the same spirit of mission. The notable intellectual resources exemplified in Bento Santiago do not represent a further contribution to Brazil's civilization – rather, a cultural disguise for class oppression. Far from being a solution, the intellectual refinement of the elite now emerges as one aspect – itself with positive and negative elements – of the social configuration that the novel recalls with nostalgia, or disenchantedly strips bare.

---

7 Antonio Candido, 'Uma literatura empenhada' , in *Formação da literatura brasileira*, vol. 1, Belo Horizonte, 1975.

I

Seen in broad outline, *Dom Casmurro* falls into two very different parts, with the first dominated by Capitu, the second by Bento; or, in other words, the first is under the sign of enlightenment, the second under the sign of obscurantism.

In the first part, the young lovers fight against superstition and social prejudice. The superstition is that of Dona Glória, Bento's mother, who had promised her son to the Church, from fear of losing him at birth. The prejudice is due to the difference in their situations: Capitu is the daughter of poor neighbours, half dependent on Dona Glória, while Bentinho belongs to an upper-class family, the head of which had been a plantation owner and a deputy in parliament, leaving property when he died. Capitu directs the young couple's campaign with splendid lucidity, understanding and determination – qualities completely lacking in her friend. Her manoeuvres reach a happy ending, with their love triumphing in marriage, thus overcoming class considerations. The conflict that seemed imminent never arrives, for the girl astutely forestalls it, by winning her future mother-in-law's favour and soothing her religious scruples. Naturally, the reader whose heart is in the right place takes the side of the lovers, against the seminary and family intrigue – the side of enlightenment against myths and injustice.

The second part begins with chapters of marital bliss. The old house on Matacavalos Street, where Bento passed his childhood, has been exchanged for a new one, in Glória. The only cloud is the absence of children, who refuse to appear. But even this is resolved after a time, with the birth of Ezequiel. Their son is clever and likes to imitate others, among them the couple's best friend, Escobar, whom he begins to resemble. Then, Escobar, a keen swimmer, drowns. At the wake, men and women are crying. Suddenly, Bento stops crying, seeing tears in Capitu's eyes as she looks at the dead man. His habitual jealousy now surges so strongly that he cannot read out the words of farewell he has written for the cemetery.

Appearances deceive, and what the mourners see are signs of grief: one example of a possible misreading, just as Capitu's tears – and there are not so many – might suggest adulterous feeling where there was none and just as the resemblance between Ezequiel and Escobar might be an accident.

The fact is that Bento finds his son looking more and more like the dead man. He withdraws from Capitu and becomes Casmurro. He wants to kill his wife, his son and himself. At one point, to distract himself, he goes to the theatre to see *Othello*. But instead of drawing the lesson that jealousy is not a wise counsellor and that impressions can deceive, he reasons, rather strangely, that if the Moor strangles Desdemona because of a handkerchief when she was innocent, what should he not do to Capitu, who is guilty! The hint could hardly be clearer: the character-narrator distorts what he sees and draws false conclusions. There is no reason to accept his version of events.

This is the *tendentious* protagonist, who on the final page formulates his famous question about the overall meaning of the novel: 'What remains is to know if the Capitu of Glória beach was already in the girl of Matacavalos, or if the latter had been changed into the former because of some intervening incident' (CXLVIII). In other words, all we have to decide is whether Capitu was always deceitful or became so only after her marriage. Ostensibly, we should examine the purity of the first love: was it impure too, in spite of its poetry? But the tacit effect of the question is to vindicate the narrator, for it concerns only the moment when the guilt began, leaving no room for the hypothesis that she might be innocent. The same trap is sprung again in the next sentence, this time with biblical support: Bento remembers the good advice of Jesus, son of Sirach, who commands us not to give way to jealousy, lest his wife 'deceive [him] with arts she learned of [him]' (CXLVIII).[8] Here, too, the

---

8   The biblical quotation is from *Ecclesiasticus*, or *The Wisdom of Jesus, Son of Sirach*, one of the books of the *Apocrypha*. [*Tr.*]

appearance of uncertainty serves as a cover for the rights of the stronger party, for accusation without the right of reply: the nub of the matter is whether Capitu's infidelity – certain and beyond dispute – was the effect of the husband's recurrent mistrust or whether it was already there, in the girl, 'like the fruit inside its rind'. This false finale, in the form of a sophism backed up by Holy Scripture, by the narrator's suffering, by his emotional and literary disposition and also by the conclusive value that we usually attribute to a novel's last words gives us the measure of Machado's artistic daring.

A balanced conclusion might be as follows: it is impossible to decide whether Ezequiel is Escobar's son or not since the likeness between the two, recognized by Capitu, proves little in a book deliberately full of physical similarities and coincidences of every sort – all of them warnings against drawing hurried conclusions, and only the more urgent since one of *Dom Casmurro*'s distinctively modern topics is the conscious or unconscious impact of repressed interests on the formation of judgement, or, more precisely, on the way similarities are or are not noticed. (Two years later, Thomas Mann would publish *Buddenbrooks*, whose irony also consists, at least in part, in the psychological relativization of naturalist certainties about heredity.) In sum, there is no way of being certain of Capitu's guilt, nor of her innocence – which is hardly exceptional, since there is no such thing as certain, assured virtue. On the other hand, there is no doubt that Bento writes and organizes his book with the aim of condemning his wife. The enigma we have to decipher is not in her but in her husband.[9]

---

9   According to Silviano Santiago, 'In sum: the critics were interested in searching for the truth about Capitu, or the impossibility of reaching the truth about Capitu, when the only truth to be looked for is the truth about Dom Casmurro' ('Retórica da verossimilhança', in *Uma literatura nos trópicos: Ensaios sobre dependência cultural*, São Paulo, 1978, 32). Santiago detects the resources of the ex-seminarian and the professional lawyer in Casmurro's narrative technique and the Brazilian nature of that combination.

What is the meaning of this shift? In the first half of the book, love, intelligence and mutual confidence win out, both over a promise made to heaven and over class prejudice. The victory is short-lived, however, for in the second half the traditional world will reappear and impose its will, this time within the marriage. The husband-narrator creates a unique atmosphere of poisoned poetry, which is sentimental, domineering and out of control, literally reactionary, and whose portrayal is one of the novel's most notable achievements. In the light of Bento's incurable suspicions, Capitu's lucidity and clear resolve are traduced as proofs of a selfish, cunning character, while the admiration with which he himself has obeyed her instructions makes him look like a ridiculous simpleton. The mocking, sinister slander on the qualities prized by the Enlightenment, and indispensable to any individual's self-realization, has begun.

Once the evidential value of the likenesses and coincidences on which the narrator's specious advocacy are based are seen in proper perspective, what stands out are his suspicious tendencies themselves, which are no longer effect but cause. Now what attracts the reader's attention are the jealous paroxysms to which Bento has always been subject. When still a teenager, he had the urge to sink his nails into Capitu's neck, judge her and then maybe forgive her for crimes which he had invented according to his own psychic needs (see LXXV). There are several episodes of this kind, and once linked, they redefine the character of the 'owner' of the words, and so the value of the words themselves, completely altering the terms of conflict. If the reader does not follow this road at first, it is because Dom Casmurro's literary art points our mistrust in another direction and also because he describes his jealous crises randomly, as facts of differing kinds and not as an abiding inclination. He treats them as psychological curiosities, anecdotes from school, sporadic accidents, examples of an impulsive, naïve nature struggling with female wiles and cold reason. Thus, the belated identification as executioner of the person we thought was the

victim and the unmasking of the obscurantist, misogynistic opinions that led to the mistake itself result from the basic structure of
the work. We have seen that there is no valid reply to the final question about the moment when Capitu's character took shape. In the
narrator's case, however, there is no possible doubt: the same
jealous man who lives in Glória was already a finished article in the
child of Matacavalos, with one difference, as we will see. This said,
the turnaround in the interpretation has wider implications than the
rather limited fascination of *did she or didn't she?* and of the family
setting in which the conflict seems to be confined. To appreciate
this, it is necessary to bring the social composition of the characters
into the foreground and thereby to reveal an order and a historical
destiny in operation. The characters form a rigorous social system,
with an internal necessity, far from the sentimental, picturesque –
that is, the Romantic – reasons which move Casmurro to remember
them with such notable precision.

2

The characters of *Dom Casmurro* make up an extended family, one
of the great social building blocks of traditional Brazil. At its heart
is a wealthy property owner – at the beginning, Dona Glória –
surrounded by relatives, dependants and other hangers-on and
slaves, all more or less bound to her will and favours. Domination
takes the form of paternal authority, and subordination that of filial
respect, both tinged with religious devotion, since the best example
is the relationship with God the Father. The overall dominance of
Catholic-familistic motives displaces strictly individual and
economic reasoning into a decorous clandestinity but does not
prevent it from existing, in the same form in which nineteenth-
century capitalism and liberalism had created it. Confronting such
interests, modern but submerged, the world of paternalist expressions, ties and reasonings looks ridiculous, an anachronism with a
provincial taint. The opposite view is also given voice, the

traditional values showing up bourgeois rationality as suspect of materialism, egotism, calculation and so on. From yet another point of view, we can say that arbitrary authority and direct personal dependence, its complement, exclude freedom of conduct, a desire for which is, however, indispensable to the dignity of the advanced citizen – in the middle of the nineteenth century and in a country which explicitly aspires to civilization and progress. To define the historical nature of this question, which goes beyond psychology, we should remind ourselves that this complex of ideas cannot be understood without reference to the social 'anomaly' of slavery. In the very terms accepted at this time, slavery lent property itself a note of barbarism, and, in another sphere, both limited the opportunities for paid work and stripped it of respectability, forcing a large number of poor Brazilians to seek protection and subsistence in clientelistic relations.[10] How, then, were they to reconcile dependency, which was inevitable, with autonomy, which was de rigueur? Or, again, how could they be modern and civilized in the conditions generated by a slave owning economy? The question and the impasses it implies have evident grounds in the social world set up in the novel, which, in decisive aspects, is a miniature of Brazilian society. We will see that the imaginary solutions to this true squaring of the circle are specialities of Brazilian self-understanding and of Machado's fiction.

José Dias is the *agregado* of the Santiago family – a person who, owning nothing himself, lives *by favour* in a rich family, where he provides all kinds of services.[11] The fifty-year old with his respect-

---

10   'Some greedy, barbarous landowners in the interior of the country didn't understand how to deal with free men, and didn't want to carry out their stipulated obligations faithfully', Aureliano Cândido Tavares Bastos, *Os males do presente e as esperanças do futuro: estudos brasileiros*, 2nd ed., São Paulo, 1976, 86; originally published in 1861. I owe this quotation to Walquíria G. Domingues Leão Rego, 'Um liberal tardio' (PhD thesis in political science, University of São Paulo, 1989, 88).

11   In my version of the novel, I use the word 'dependant' as a translation for *agregado*. It is the best available translation (the only other possible one is

able air, his civic and rhetorical baggage, who sounds like a privy counsellor but in reality is nothing more than a message boy, admirably concentrates the tensions of the time in his position and status. Machado studies this character and, above all, the bogus way he manages to combine relationships of favour with aspirations to independence and citizenship with scientific precision, joining the Romantic sense of local and historical particularity with the greatest possible analytical demands, schooled in French classicism. The internal logic of this social type is rigorously constructed, as is the logic of the other types and the dominant social divisions, which then cohere into a kind of architecture.

On his first appearance, José Dias announces 'a great difficulty' to Dona Glória (III). Before he explains – it is Bentinho and Capitu's courtship – he prudently goes to the door to make sure the boy is not listening. The comedy lies in the contrast between the Victorian gravity of the character and the humiliating subterfuges he is driven to. Here we have the model of the distinguished *agregado*, who speaks, gives his opinion and shows off or mistreats the neighbours with the authority of a member of the family, within which, however, his situation is completely uncertain, always dependent on more or less humiliating concessions. Machado is a virtuoso in the observation or invention of personal traits illuminating the complexity of this position. Thus, when asked what he thinks, the *agregado* made sure he *'didn't overdo it, and knew how to give his opinion submissively'* (my emphasis). In the same way, the narrator describes how 'he laughed aloud, whenever necessary: a forced but somehow infectious laugh, in which his cheeks, teeth, eyes, his whole face, his whole person, the whole world seemed to laugh with him. At serious moments, he was extremely serious' (V). Indeed, who is he to laugh on his own initiative, not to laugh aloud 'whenever necessary', or to laugh 'at serious moments'? This

---

'retainer'). Here, since the original Portuguese word is explained and is more exact in its social context, I have decided to keep it. [*Tr.*]

is an acute description of an authoritarian and submissive laugh, the thickness of whose details, however, fits without any excess, and with complete economy, into the general sociological scheme. More cruelly, his excess of zeal at one moment changes the poor man's sex, as he attends Bentinho 'with a mother's affection and a serv-ant's attentiveness' (XXIV). The most ingenious characterization of all is perhaps José Dias's dual tempo, at one moment 'slow and stiff', then 'in a flurry of gestures', 'as natural in one mode as in the other' (V). This two-speed figure unites the representative and subservient functions of the agregado as well as the constant activ-ity of a person living by his wits.[12]

In all these examples, we are observing the conjunction of personal dependency with a certain spectacle of dignity, which alludes to the status of the free individual in the modern bourgeois order. The two elements, even though incompatible, are indispen-sable to the character's composition, but the first carries more weight, of material necessity. The pretence involved is obvious and has to be carefully controlled to prevent any adverse reaction. When dealing with his superiors, the *agregado* lays the adulation on thick because if they fall out of sympathy with him, they might not grant recognition to the momentary whims of a free man, which thus take on a false, comic air. When he deals with his fellow men ('equals' being a notion absent from his universe), he puts the great-est possible emphasis on dignity, which is turned into its own farcical, authoritarian opposite, since it rests on the social prestige of the family that protects him. The satirical side of this characteri-zation, centred on the emptiness of his respectability, needs no commentary. However, as we come to understand its social neces-sity as well as the lack of real profit the man himself gets out of it – for with all his diplomacy he gains nothing – his impostures begin to

---

12   The reader can judge if we go too far in imagining that the same structure moves the dancers in a samba school, slow and princely from the waist up, while the feet are given over to a speedy, varied set of little jumps.

seem less 'reprehensible', more sympathetic, for they are a way of surviving in adverse conditions. In any case – this is one of the more daring suggestions of the novel – they seem truer than their counterpart, the equally empty respectability of the rich, disguised as tact, delicacy and poetry.

José Dias cultivates grammar, prosody, clean ties, law, belleslettres, the history of the Brazilian nation: the respectable side of order, in other words. He also loves superlatives, which give 'an impressive aspect to his ideas' (IV), and rolls his eyes with pleasure when he creates an expression meriting the applause, let us say, of a teacher of theology (LXI). He evinces the affected air of the humble creature so possessed by the culture of the rich that he literally forgets his place. There is an abject side to this attachment, for the delights it provides, which imaginarily compensate for real social worthlessness, exclude rebellion, the formation of one's own values or any reflection on them. But there is also a cunning side, since visceral identification with the possessing class provides a relative advantage, above all in competition with the other candidates for protection, over whom José Dias methodically asserts the superiority of his speech and manners. In another perspective, the *agregado*'s ignorant love for the things of the mind ends up extending discredit to these very things themselves. Quite innocently, he sees them as an ornament for upper-class people and reduces them to a façade. This reduction is an achievement too, in its way, since it reflects the functioning of nineteenth-century culture in a society that separates a large proportion of its members from civilization, when not keeping them in slave huts, while another large section, although free and anxious to participate, lacks the personal independence necessary for opinions of its own. In this sense, the satire on José Dias's sententious emptiness is aimed at a specifically Brazilian social configuration, and at the nostalgia-ridden ideas of history entertained by Casmurro himself, which are also the adornments of property and the established order. The complementarity of the vices of masters and slaves, noted by Joaquim Nabuco in

Abolitionism,[13] can be extended to the relationship between masters and those dependent on them. On the other hand, this local truth, which the satire conveys, and which is interesting in its own right, is not the limit of its reach. It is as if the Brazilian setting refined and stressed a kind of privilege that in European societies, where there is free labour and rights to citizenship are less precarious, might seem inessential, outdated and a fit subject for an operetta. And yet, this frock-coated, anti-democratic aspect of dignity still exists everywhere and brings us back to the original link between freedom and bourgeois property ownership (something that speaks to José Dias's heart). The *agregado* takes his love of formalities to its ultimate conclusion, which is disbelief in the forms themselves. He jumps from one to the other as it suits him, with no embarrassment, with no need for consistency, with dizzying mockery of the dignity he worships, and this gives him a kind of freedom of movement vis-à-vis his masters. It is worth mentioning the lack of self-respect (he is a Brazilian soldier Schweyk) with which, so as not to obey an order, he admits he is a charlatan; all this without for a moment pausing from his highfalutin manner: 'I was a charlatan . . . No, don't deny it . . . I lied in the service of truth; but it's time to set the record straight' (V).[14]

The gamut of relations of paternalist dependency in the novel is varied and carefully chosen. As well as the owner and the *agregado*, the figures include slaves, neighbours who owe favours, people who cadge meals, poor relations of differing degrees, acquaintances who hope for protection and people who simply know of the importance or the wealth of the family, which is enough to inspire a

---

13   Joaquim Nabuco (b. 1849-d. 1910), author of *Abolitionism* (1883), an acute diagnosis of the social evils caused by slavery. [*Tr.*]
14   Compare Cf. Jaroslav Hašek's *The Good Soldier Švejk and His Fortunes in the World War* (1920), whose hero survives thanks to a magnificent lack of amour propre. The character was taken up again in a play by Bertolt Brecht, *Schweyk in the Second World War.*

certain reverence. It is a loose unit, with numerous members, typi-
fying what Gilberto Freyre, in *The Mansions and the Shanties*,[15]
describes as the persistence of the large rural family of the colonial
period in the urban, Europeanized conditions of the nineteenth
century. All these types are worth attentive study and have something interesting and individual to teach us on this subject, as well
as establishing, as a group, the substratum they all share. For the
aims of this discussion, we will limit ourselves to the principal poles.

In the dependants' camp, José Dias's opposite is Capitu. The
difference, associated with modern demands for personal autonomy
and objective judgement, or, in other words, with the clash between
paternalist and bourgeois norms, has a conspicuous moral meaning.
For all his wiliness, the *agregado* does not really think of himself as
an individual, separate from the family he serves, with whom in his
imagination he merges, and whose importance gives him the sense
of his own worth. His subjection to Dona Glória's husband, then to
the widow and finally to the son is not an external contingency but
something in the pattern of his spirit, which never manifests itself
outside the immediate necessity of pleasing and shedding lustre on
his betters. Capitu, on the other hand, satisfies the requirements for
individuality. She knows the difference between reality and imaginary substitutes for it, and has no time for the latter. (In a country
so sentimental, and never more so than when it comes to young
girls, Machado's decision to study the beauty, the adventure and the
tension proper to the use of reason is most unusual.) Thus, when
Bento's saintly mother decides to fulfil a promise and send her son
to a seminary, putting at risk the conjugal plans of the poor neighbour, Capitu explodes in a rare spectacle of independent spirit and
intelligence. It is Bento who brings her the news, at which she turns
pale and unseeing, 'as if she were made of wood', for just enough
time to take stock of the situation; then she breaks out in the

---

15   Gilberto Freyre, *The Mansions and the Shanties: The Making of Modern
Brazil*, Berkeley, 1986.

unexpected: 'The sanctimonious so-and-so! Always at the altar rail! Never away from mass!'[16] Capitu not only has her own aims, which she always takes into account; she has a well-formed and critical opinion of her protectors, and even of their religion. Then, she reflects; shuts her eyes; wants to know the circumstances, the replies, the gestures, the words and the way they were spoken; gives her attention to Dona Glória's tears; she 'can't convince herself she's understood them' (XVIII). As Bento later puts it, 'She gave it all her minute attention. She seemed to ruminate on everything, the story itself and the dialogue. Or you could say that she was comparing, labelling and, as it were, pinning my account up in her memory' (XXXI). Exact details, checking them over in her mind and a certain critical recapitulation of the situation go together, pointing to a nexus between mental freedom and objectivity; this is a real, methodical effort of thinking. The clarity of her decision presupposes a distance from the system of subjections, obligations and imaginary merging of interests characteristic of paternalism.

Capitu shines also in comparison with the other dependants. José Dias compensates for his precarious situation as an *agregado* with superlatives and double-dealing. Cousin Justina, a poor relation of the family, boosts her self-esteem by speaking ill of people who are not present and vicariously sharing the budding love of the son and heir as a curious onlooker, another way of consoling herself for her meagre existence. The most interesting comparison of all is with Bento himself, who while still unmarried should be included among Dona Glória's subjects. When he tries to tell his mother that he cannot become a priest after all, because he wants to marry Capitu, something in him falters, and he comes out with the incredible 'I only love you, Mamma', the opposite of what he intended (XLI). In the face of

---

16   The original here is 'Beata! carola! papa-missas!' – whose brevity and sharpness are unfortunately impossible to imitate in English(-language) culture, where Catholicism does not have the same quasi-universal hold. A *beata*, in Portuguese and Spanish, is a woman excessively devoted to religion, who goes to mass every day and so on. [*Tr.*]

authority, his sense of purpose fails him. Another way out – in dreams, naturally – would be to ask the emperor to intercede with his mother, who would then in her turn give way to authority (XXIX).[17] In either case, Capitu's superiority is complete: she does not flee from reality into the imagination and is strong enough not to disintegrate when faced with the will of someone more important than she is.

This said, Capitu is not Capitu just because she thinks for herself. Inwardly emancipated as she may be from paternalist subjection, this is what constitutes her milieu and she must deal with it. The charm of the character lies in her natural way of moving in an environment she has outgrown, whose meanders and mechanisms she understands with a politician's instinct. It is as if the intimacy between intelligence and the retrograde context might allow a happy ending, a fortunate breach in the wall where class injustice and traditionalist paralysis could be made good, something like a local version of Napoleon's 'carrière ouverte aux talents'.

Speaking of his young friend's character, Casmurro observes that she was not short of daring ideas:

> But they were only daring in themselves: in practice they became clever, insinuating, stealthy, and reached the required end, not with a single bound, but with lots of little jumps. I don't know if I make myself plain. Imagine a grand conception carried out with small means. Thus, staying with the vague, hypothetical desire to send me to Europe [a hypothetical way out that occurs to the girl]: Capitu, if it were in her power, would not have me embark on the steamer and flee; she would stretch a line of canoes from here to there, by means of which I, seeming to go to the Laje fortress on a floating bridge, would actually go to Bordeaux, leaving my mother waiting for me on the beach. (XVIII)

---

17   Brazil, between independence in 1822 and the coup which brought about the republic in 1889, was an empire: *Dom Casmurro* is set in the so-called 'Second Reign' – that of Dom Pedro II (1831–1889). [*Tr.*]

This passage can and should be read in various keys because, as much as it expresses Bento's fascination with Capitu's femininity, it also is useful in the case brought against the wife by her husband, reminding us that from the beginning she was ambitious, calculating, sly and an enemy of her future mother-in-law. And yet another reading, attentive to the social content of the relations, has the advantage of articulating Capitu's conduct with that of the other characters, making the system that unites them visible. Indeed, the disproportion between means and ends, central in the story, reflects the practical constraints of the enlightened girl in local circumstances. The phrase 'daring ideas', with its suggestion of an oligarchic pout, indicates the possible outcomes of her independence of spirit, *individual* projects escaping the limitations of respectful conformity. The recourse to the 'little jumps', as opposed to the presumed openness of a big jump (would that be masculine, not feminine? Would it not be 'daring'?) registers the necessity incumbent on dependants of obtaining the favour of their protector at every stage, or risk falling into the abyss. It is part of the logic of paternalism that possible objectives are not defined as such and on behalf of the individual, but, with filial obedience, as something convenient for the protector, which makes them not only feasible but legitimate. That is the reason for the canoes to the Laje fortress, instead of the steamer to Bordeaux, since familiar aims are more easily commended to others. Capitu's 'clever' and 'insinuating' manners represent a policy of decorum, or, depending on point of view, of the hypocrisy required by this social arrangement. On the other hand, it is characteristic of Casmurro and his class ideology to present as a moral failing, as a lack of honesty, the policy of lowered eyes imposed by authority such as his own – though that will not prevent him from labelling the opposite behaviour 'daring'. It is part of its confusion, or its complexity, that a type of conduct with its foundations in the very structure of Brazilian society can appear to him at one moment as lack of honesty on his wife's part, at the next as an element of erotic interest, and finally as a general characteristic which does no credit to feminine psychology. This is clearly the common basis for Capitu's manoeuvres, José Dias's forced laugh, Bentinho's panic in front of his mother, and cousin Justina's shock on being asked for her opinion. The meaning of these variations on a situation of basic dependency remains incomplete, however, until we pass to the other pole, which determines them – the pole of the authority of the possessing class.

When she is widowed, Dona Glória sells the plantation and buys 'a dozen buildings and a quantity of government bonds', as well as slaves, whom she puts to work or hires out (VII). The Santiago family and the household on Matacavalos Street now live off rents and dividends. Not made to be the head of the family, the widow is a good soul, religious and attached to her son and devotes herself to looking after the house. Even so, her authority is unquestioned, as we find out by the care taken not to cross her, an obligation on everyone, without exception. Power derives from property, even if the proprietor does not take steps to assert herself. Something similar happens where virtue is concerned. Dona Glória, in the words her son has engraved on her tombstone, is *a saint* (CXLII). This in spite of the fact that she promised him to the Church without consulting him and sent him to a seminary against his will ('Stop playacting, Bentinho' [XLI]), and even though later she accepts a threadbare subterfuge to go back on her promise. In other words, a little superstition, authoritarianism and caprice do nothing to diminish the sanctity of the mothers of important families. In a patriarchal situation, the occasional slip-up here and there does not besmirch the transcendental virtue of fathers and heads of family, which forms a halo around property. The dignity of the narrator-husband, Bento, will enjoy the same unquestionable status – until it is turned into an object of satire. The respectable, civilized gestures of the possessing class make its actual conduct invisible, while Machado's critical spirit takes delight in detailing it.

In the second part of the book, Bento leaves the seminary, goes to study law in São Paulo and then marries, and becomes the property-owner in his turn. The education we observe in the first part of the book is now going to display its consequences. At first sight, this second part is a nostalgic memoir, full of maternal caresses and filial emotion, innocence and attachment to the scenes and places of childhood, all of it infused with shudders of lust and guilty feeling. Overall, it gives off a consistent, perverse suggestion, reminiscent of the family-oriented romanticism of Casimiro de Abreu, the pattern of feeling that Mário de Andrade identified in his essay 'Amor e medo'.[18] On the second reading, just as well-founded as the first, this nostalgic memoir turns into the documentation for a grim and unmistakably modern diagnosis of the paternalist world: here we have the irresponsible and capricious exercise of authority, which produces parasitism and sycophantic or terrified subjection; a higher education lacking seriousness or vocation, a mere ornament; an enfeebled, shallow religion giving cover for all kinds of rather less catholic interests. As Brás Cubas says of himself in relation to his education, at the end of a similar chapter in another of Machado's novels: 'From this land and this manure this flower was born'.[19]

This negative diagnostic derives from the *other* norm, now in fact the norm par excellence: the ideal of a society composed of free, responsible individuals; that is, not of slaves or dependants, an ideal in which European bourgeois civilization is steeped, and with regard to which Brazilian society – which had no way to avoid measuring itself against it, except by removing itself entirely from the historical present – appears as mistaken. Thus, methodically equivocal, the narrative gives voice simultaneously to the charm and the rejection of the paternalist order, imposing everywhere a preference, half-guilty, half-admitted, for outdated forms of existence.[20]

18　In 'Amor e medo', Mário examines the stuffy, repressed, even perverse way the Romantic poets of the so-called 'first generation', above all Casimiro de Abreu (b. 1839–d. 1860) and Manuel Antônio Álvares de Azevedo (b. 1831–d. 1852) treat the themes of love and sex.

19　Machado de Assis, *Memórias póstumas de Brás Cubas*, Ch. IX.

20　A suggestive illustration of these incongruities can be found in the irony with

Bento is now the head of a rich family, a well-established lawyer, a pillar of society. The internal disturbance that authority caused in him as a child has lost its rationale, or rather, it has changed its relative position, since he himself now *is* that authority. In the new circumstances, the old disturbances in his judgement, the inability to trace a boundary between the will of the person doing the ordering and his own change their nature. The most dramatic instance is his jealousy, which had been one of young Bentinho's several imaginative disorders, and now, linked to the authority of the lord and master, and husband, turns into a force for devastation. Although the subject matter lies within the private sphere, and the novel in its second part does in fact narrow into the difficult relation between two people, the theme is still what it was: the prerogative whereby the master Brazilian-style may confuse his own desires, even when they are hidden, with legal rights, dignity and so on, according to the convenience or the inclination of the moment and without the dependants being able to oppose him. Thus, there is a complementarity between these dependants' lack of guarantees and rights on the one hand, and, in the opposing camp, in spite of the appearances of civility, the lack of any clear limitation of desire, which in these

---

which the review *O Kaleidoscópio* (30 June 1860) deals with the social teaching of the liberal Tavares Bastos (b. 1839–d. 1875): 'His ideal in politics is *self-government* [in English in the original], as the English understand and practise the idea. However, to arrive at this point, you have to give the family a soul, so that the family can provide the local government that will provide the basis for the provincial government, and the union and prosperity of the provinces will be the source of the greatness and happiness of the nation. This is the yardstick for his governmental system. But oh, my dear Bastos! Do you think that ten or a dozen years will be enough to write the chapters of this work? Not in twenty, not in thirty. Look here: we need, at least, five centuries: one, to convince the paterfamilias that his wife is a woman, and his wife's children are in fact his; another, for that business about local government; a third, to persuade the Pernambucans that Bahians also descend from Adam and Eve; a fourth for the *self-governments* to discover where Brazil is; a fifth for everything to fall apart again and go back to its original state' (reprinted in Sérgio Adorno, *Os aprendizes do poder: O bacharelismo liberal na política brasileira*, Rio de Janeiro: Paz e Terra, 1988, 192–3).

circumstances has no way of perceiving itself from the outside. One of the original, profound themes of Machado's fiction is the mental indiscipline specific to the Brazilian conjunction of slavery, clientelism and contemporary ideals, and especially the madness of our 'right-thinking' men. From another angle, we can say that the misuse of narrative credibility, which in its own way is a breach of contract – this is the novel's crucial procedure – extends this one-sided power relationship to the level of form, where, when it is noticed, it appears as an intolerable abuse of trust.

Capitu's trajectory may serve as a commentary on the destructive meaning of this abuse of power. In making a good marriage, the girl escapes from the modest circumstances of her family and becomes – in Machado's beautiful comparison – 'like a bird out of its cage' (CV). However, the same clear and realistic social understanding that had allowed the girl's manoeuvring now means that, faced with her husband's jealousy, she tries to prevent confrontation by every possible means, renouncing the street and the window, ending up by living in self-imprisonment, all, naturally in vain. The cage of patriarchal authority shuts again, with no possible recourse to an appeal, as Capitu's final, lucid and moving resignation suggests. Another tacit commentary can be found in the episodes dealing with the theme of the confidence, or pact, between two people, with the element of equality that this implies. It occurs to Bento, very moved to be present at his son's breastfeeding, that this being exists thanks to the couple's love and constancy (CVIII). In the context, the passage naturally lends itself to a sardonic re-reading. Nevertheless, the emotion refers to something real, to creations of mutual agreement which, when the agreement is no longer there, collapse. The subject of mutual understanding had already appeared in the episode of 'the oath at the well', where the adolescents face their circumstances and promise to marry each other, a promise which is later fulfilled (XLVIII). Although the larger subject of the novel is ostensibly Capitu's infidelity, the supposed cause of her husband's universal mistrust, the real subject is Bento's own disinclination for any relation between equals, for a possible *modern* equality – if the measure of comparison is the patriarchal order, that is – which his mocking scepticism will defeat. Contrary to what the narrator's disillusioned melancholy would have us believe, in the absence of equals what is left is not the solitary individual but the master Brazilian-style, the big shot who need not justify his actions.

In the final chapters, we witness a strange succession of atmospheres, which figure, with precision, the sterilizing tendencies inherent in the narrator's social type – a Buñuelesque fusion of craziness, decorum and extreme nastiness. Thus, after preparing a theatrical suicide, inspired by the actions of Cato via Plutarch, Casmurro very nearly poisons his own child, who reminds him of his friend. Soon after, so as to separate from Capitu while keeping up appearances, he feigns a journey with his family to Europe, where he leaves his wife, the child and a governess, a journey he then regularly claims to repeat, making believe he lives with his family, whom, however, he avoids, and about whom he invents news to relay to relatives and friends. At a certain moment, very much in passing, he mentions the death of Capitu – the soul of his life and of the novel – in two short sentences, as if to rectify a momentary lapse. When his son visits him as a young man, the father wills him death by leprosy, but fate does not hear his pleas and kills the boy soon after of typhoid fever. The conception of the second-to-last chapter, 'The Retrospective Exhibition', is brilliant, so long as we see the real situation behind the euphemisms of the prose. Dom Casmurro is preening himself on his new circumstances: his soul 'didn't stay in a corner like a pale, solitary flower', nor was he short of 'female friends to console me'. If we look more closely, we see that these friends are poor girls, presumably prostitutes, that he brings to a distant mansion to listen to the reminiscences of a middle-aged gentleman, after which they leave on foot (*calcante pede*, he says, in Latin, with the same gentleman's modesty, but, also, to show his distinction from them); that is, except when it rains, in which case the owner of the house arranges a hansom cab.

How, then, are we to understand that the supreme elegance of the prose in the first chapters is the work and the pastime of the pathetic, noxious figure of the last pages? Whatever the answer, the question arises from the book's *composition*, which forces us to distance ourselves from what is said, or, better, incites us to give voice to corrections and addenda which the narrative situation imposes on the lyrical memoir in the foreground of the novel.

3

How are the first and second parts of *Dom Casmurro* articulated with each other? We have seen that in the first, the personal fulfilment of a young couple is set against the ancien régime, with its families of domineering and superstitious property owners, masters of their children's marriage prospects. At this point, Capitu is in charge of operations: she is more insightful and active than Bentinho, who is always emotional. However, quietly, the moral clarity of the fight is muddied by insinuations about the self-interested motives of the girl and her parents. So, the combat between the freedom of the individual and the order imposed by the clan, within which it is so easy to identify with the individual, also leaves space for a conservative evaluation, whose roots are aristocratic and Romantic, which deflects the focus onto a contrast between emotion, which is sincere, and intelligence, which is treacherous. From this point of view, the better person can only be Bentinho. However, the triumph of the young people is an easy one and does not sharpen the conflicts to the point where their limits are tested. This general absence of grave danger fits with the sepia-tint manner of the narration, with its circlet of delightful memories garlanding an idyllic, pseudo-innocent world that brings a smile, and where everything has a happy ending. And, in fact, though there is no lack of great moments in the first part, its strength does not come from the action but rather from the reflecting surface of the prose, whose complexity and ambiguity are governed by the events of the second part.

According to the narrator himself, the change in his character dates from the discovery of his deception, from the revelation that Ezequiel is Escobar's son. In the light of this certainty – which the novel disqualifies – Capitu's moral and intellectual independence, without which Bentinho would never have escaped the priest's cassock, changes its nature and confirms the insinuations of the beginning. The woman who had her own ideas had to end up by committing adultery and having a child by another man. Casmurro now identifies with the conservatism to which, to some degree at any rate, he had been opposed in the earlier period. Mental clarity, even in the face of authority, a taste for arithmetic, for grasping the meaning of situations and steadfastly maintaining one's aims or for being able to deal with money now become so many proofs of a false character, and, in the end, of a betrayal of the marriage. The rudimentary but effective obscurantism of these assimilations is directed against the element of calculation and reserve, of keeping a distance from oneself and from others, without which the individual cannot possibly hold on to rationality and cannot define herself as an individual. It is also directed against the use of intelligence on the part of dependants. The assault on reason is concluded in the refined forms of overbearing domination in the final chapters.

However, the most plausible way of periodizing the novel is not the one proposed by the narrator. The decisive turnaround happens earlier, when Bento stops being a son and becomes a husband and a property owner: at this point, his confused and 'burning' heart (LXXIII), which had put him in an inferior position, managed with great difficulty by Capitu, no longer has any opposition and is going to assert itself. The new Santiago is not born from his wife's betrayal but from the conjunction of his confused desires – some of them not to be confessed (his crazed jealousy, his varying sexual appetites) – with patriarchal authority; a conjunction that cancels, or betrays, the oath of mutual confidence and equality that the well-born young man had sworn to his poor neighbour. Thus, in spite of first appearances, Capitu's marriage does not represent a victory for the

Enlightenment but a reaffirmation of the traditional order, even if a delayed one. And Casmurro's universal scepticism, with its different intensities ranging from tolerance to ferocity, and equipped with all the paraphernalia of modern intellectual progress, serves him as a rational cover for his disobedience to the demands of bourgeois dignity; or, rather, it authorizes – without marring the civilized atmosphere – the brutality of the uncouth property owner. The critical reach of this self-exposure, as long as it is seen for what it is, is extraordinary.

Seen in terms of the novel's overall narrative movement, the dynamic element of the first and longer of its two parts is exhausted before the end, and thus is proved to be unreal, while a group of separate themes, with no obvious connection at first sight, at a certain stage coalesces and becomes the dynamic force in its own right, overtaking what promised to be the general tendency of the narrative and exposing its unreality. The love between the poor neighbour and the son of the rich family, with the corresponding desire for happiness, personal fulfilment and even a historic, progressive solution to a difficult class relationship, gives life to the book until it is well advanced, when the authoritarian dimension of property-owning comes centre-stage and galvanizes the late *nhonhô*,[21] who, seeing himself now as a victim, suspends and mocks his own previous tendencies towards understanding, equality, and lucidity, and affirms his readiness to issue orders without justifying himself – all this cast in a sophisticated, civilized language worthy of the belle époque. This is the curve the novel follows, one of its tacit elements of generalization, in which we can trace the line of a Brazilian road to modernity.

There is another historical specification embedded in the cast of characters itself. As the novel opens, Bento's father, a plantation owner and deputy in parliament, is already dead, and the family,

---

21   *Nhonhô* is a familiar version of 'Senhor', used by slaves to refer to their masters. The best English equivalent is 'massa', as used in the American South. [*Tr*]

having sold his lands, is living off rents. In this way, the political and economic activity of the owners is excluded from the novel, which devotes its space to the intra-familial sphere, where the relations of paternalist domination and subjection will be examined in a chemically pure state, so to speak; that is, left to their own momentum. The exclusion of external sources of life means that the system is fixed in its moment of decadence. This limitation lends a peculiar note to Bento's regressive tendency; his arbitrary acts, more or less self-pitying or furious, and confined to a narrow sphere, only signify his need to find himself. On the other hand, the rarefied atmosphere allows the confluence of Brazilian 'aristocratic' brutality and European decadentism, under the signs of psychological deliquescence; an ultra-nuanced prose; and the cult of uncertainty, all wrapped up in an aversion to 'the grunting of the pigs, a kind of concentrated, philosophical mockery' (CXLIV) – that is, the 'enlightened' point of view.

The rigorous continuity between the two parts of the book does not over-write its heterogeneous aspect and the romantic expectations of the plot, frustrated as they are. This eloquent, non-harmonious form illuminates the peculiar rhythm of the prose, in which we discover, sotto voce, the same tension throughout the book, in the form of enigmas, profound dissonances and resonances. As a whole, *Dom Casmurro* can be seen as an enormous, socially conditioned pun: an audacious narrative formula and one very difficult to carry off. The two faces of the narrator, so discrepant, have to be maintained by systematically ambiguous writing, which must be able to be read as the live expression of one and the other, of the naïve, betrayed husband as well as of the overbearing patriarch. A good example is the moment when Bento explains the aim of his book, which is 'to tie the two ends of life together, and bring back youth in old age' (II). Is there anything more estimable than the nostalgia of a widower who wants to reconstruct what time has scattered? But the poetry can also be an alibi, a way of affecting the impartiality necessary to accuse Capitu in public . . . The same goes for the quotation from *Faust*, presented soon after, which makes the memorialist's pen tremble with emotion: 'Ah, come ye back once more, ye restless shades?' (II). Is this the tremor produced by the return of youthful sensations? Or is it the shudder of a man blindly attacking a defenceless spirit, as the reader will come to see? Such is Machado's virtuosity in inventing subjects and sequences that highlight the duality of the narrator.

The first chapter, in which the title of the novel is explained, is a miracle of impalpable but functional organization. As an overture, we witness some slight skirmishes on the field of snobbery. In a railway carriage, returning at night to the suburbs, a distinguished gentleman nods off so as to escape from the approaches of a local bore, who speaks to him about the moon and ministerial comings and goings as well as reciting his verses. The bore, naturally, thinks of himself as ultra-civilized and is offended by the indifference of his fellow traveller – whom he goes on to call Dom Casmurro.[22] The neighbours approve of the nickname, for Santiago's reclusive ways irritate them too. In his turn, Bento tells the story to his refined friends in the city, who think it funny and adopt the new name, completing the circle. In a distanced, ambiguous transposition, the plot's themes are already here. The distant *gentleman* fits in with the model of European civilization, with his claim to *privacy* and habits of urban anonymity.[23] In contrast, the informality of the bore, who hadn't even been introduced, points to the provincial capital, the country where 'life is impossible', about which Casmurro complains to his elegant friends, who take tea, have a box at the theatre and a house in Petrópolis.[24] However, the figure of the unapproachable old grump also lets us glimpse the angry patriarch, who has fled to the 'lair' of the distant suburb to hide his 'secret wound', always taking

---

22   See commentary in n. 2 above. [*Tr.*]
23   The italicized words are in English in the original. [*Ed.*]
24   The routine of the Rio upper class included spending the hot summer months in Petrópolis, a mountain resort inland from the city. [*Tr.*]

care to look after appearances (CXXXII, I). There is no doubt that the refined memorialist, the frequenter of high society, is also the second of the two. The regular conjunction, articulated as it is at a deep level, between the iniquitous aspects of Brazilian society and its modern, refined sides is at the heart of Machado's writing.

It is worth considering the way in which Bento Santiago's nickname catches on. The new name is owing, in this order, to the accident of his nodding off, the resentment of a poet, the neighbours' dislike of his ways, a gentleman's joviality as he comments on his suburban misadventures to his elegant friends and to these same friends' sense of humour in finding the nickname apt. Bento himself does not dislike it; indeed it will become the title of his narrative, if a better one does not occur to him. Much of the sympathy the narrator achieves for himself at the beginning of the book is owing to this demonstration of tolerance, of openness to contingency and diversity, which suggests the enlightened superiority of someone who lives and lets live. In fact, this process of affixing the name according to the preferences of different people outlines a political and aesthetic ideology, with repercussions that go beyond itself – one of several episodes that themselves work like ideas, which, along with allegories and pocket-sized theories, make up the reflective atmosphere of the novel. The name is not actually necessary, since it could be another, but it satisfies the interested parties who have contributed to it in one way or another. All of which, along with habit and common use, gives it a certain legitimacy and stability, sufficient without being absolute. The name, like any other historical formation, is the consequence of life, time and adjustments, or, in other words, is not the product of a single, abstract aim against which it can be critically checked. There is an undeniable rightness in this mini-model of the social process, whose meaning varies a great deal depending on the context in which it is applied. Its antithesis, in the last instance, might be the French Revolution, to whose programme of radical and just reconstruction of humanity it stands opposed. Thus, as well as contributing to his civilized reputation, the narrator's show of amused tolerance in the face of contingency also functions in a conservative key, as a poeticization of the old Brazil, of the colonial inheritance, whose persistence confirms the unbreakable hold of the propertied class – and it is at this point that the charming memorialist shows his other side. In the closing sentences of the chapter, the narrator articulates these themes, which until now have appeared in the form of scraps of conversation, so that they suddenly and dizzyingly take on a new intensity, in zigzags that prefigure the rhythm and the reach of what is coming further on : 'Still, I couldn't find a better title for my narrative; if I can't find another before I finish the book, I'll keep this one. My poet on the train will find out that I bear him no ill-will'.

In other words, names and inventions are no worse or less useful because they're someone else's, a materialist truth, which should incline one to positive feelings: 'And with a little effort, since the title is his, he can think the whole work is'. Here, friendliness gives way to malice. Having adopted the other's find, cheerfully recognizing the non-individual aspect of his own writing and even glimpsing the rightness in not worrying too much about what is whose, the narrator changes, and insinuates that the poet on the train will not show the same detachment; in other words, he will not resist the whim of becoming an author himself, nor – is this the same thing? – of criminal theft. An appreciation of the social or collective foundations of life is followed by criticism of the individualist illusion of property, and that, in its turn, is followed by . . . *Stop thief!* The change of tone is completed in the final sentence: 'There are books that only owe that to their authors: some not as much' (II). After those unfortunates who, having contributed a name think the work is theirs, come the works not created by those who have given them their name (and therefore are fraudulent?), or worse, those that do not even carry their author's name. Nothing is left of the previous attraction of socialized operations, which take things from here, there and everywhere, and owe their beauty to this collaboration between many people, full of accidents and half unintended. In sum, these are daring speculations, contradictory and sceptical on the topic of the author's illusions, and they become much more drastic in their implications once we realize that authorship here is a first variation on the theme of *paternity*. In fact, if we substitute the word children for books – there are children who only owe that (the name) to their authors; others not even that – we have passed into the violent, crude universe in which the generic victim is the honour of wives who supposedly have children outside wedlock, a humanity made up, literally, of sons of bitches.

Dom Casmurro has taken its place in Brazilian literature as our *À la recherche du temps perdu* – understood as a piece of nostalgia, which would have made Proust's hair stand on end – or as the lyrical novel about the first kiss, the discovery of love, of naïve devotion, all destroyed by a woman's betrayal. We have found the reverse of this purity in the crudeness, the patriarchal and class authoritarianism that the narrator's performance brings into play. Machado's perception of the fundamental coherence and the ease of reversibility between the elite's beloved images of itself and the crassest manifestations of its barbarity is a critical insight of the first order. The greatest point of tension between the two is perhaps the quasi-impossibility, in terms of verisimilitude, of arguing that the monster of the novel's final pages and the sensitive, reserved memorialist of its early chapters are one and the same person. However, as we accompany the meanders of the latter's prose, we become aware of a sharp sting, disguised as elegance. On the level of the plot, the shipwreck of enlightened aspirations is part of its overall movement. The reign of Casmurro's mental confusion – in which there is even a place for unlucky Friday (CXXXIII) – expresses itself and finds its order in a refinement of language without precedent in Brazilian literature, a language with access to all the resources and opportunities that the literature, psychology and sociology of that fin de siècle, in its least naïve forms, could provide. What does this strange combination mean? On the one hand, it suggests that there is no reason to suppose that just because he is uncivilized within his family, the Brazilian oligarch cannot, or does not want to, enjoy the advances of contemporary civilization, when everyone knows that the opposite is the truth. On the other hand, by showing that his enjoyment is real, it offers an unflattering picture of progress – of the historical present in a strong sense in which there is plenty of room for every kind of regression. It is a sham version of enlightened tolerance, signifying above all an indulgent attitude towards those recurring moments of obscurantism. Both of Santiago's linguistic registers – the ignoble just as much as the idealizing one – operate, one might almost say, as *picturesque* indices of a second-class world, where individuality is limited and in which modern impulses stay half-baked. The very names of the principal characters, Capitu and Bentinho, discourage the thought that the novel might really be serious.[25] There can be no doubt about the Brazilian connotation of this diminished scale, backward in relation to contemporary levels of civilization, a size also suggested by the format of the chapters, similar to vignettes as they are. This gives the objectivity of literary form to the distance between Brazilian society and the other 'advanced' ones that provided us with the models. The surprise, however, is in the power that this universe, now past its time, has in relation to the very same categories that lower its prestige. The promiscuous picture of property, authority and caprice, with its long suite of attacks on reason and objectivity, in this case does not just describe a backward society. This subtle study of the intimate associations between these terms casts doubt on the very desire to separate them cleanly, and on the possibility of a society composed of rational, hermetically sealed individuals (the first-class world). In a characteristic movement, Machado's fiction first disqualifies local existence, which cannot even reach the point where it can be judged

---

25 Both protagonists' names are diminutives, of Capitolina and Bento respectively. [*Tr.*]

by the present-day norm, and then disqualifies the norm itself as
failing the test. The country's inferiority is undeniable, but the
superiority of our models does not carry conviction. The deceiving
narrator, who flouts the rules and subjects literary convention to his
class prerogatives, answers to both these movements. On the one
hand, he expresses arbitrary force, the madness of the oligarch faced
with his dependants, and strips it bare; on the other, he shakes the
belief in the universal model which not only prevents nothing but
actually helps the property-owning patriarch to conceal his shameful interests.

5

Another Capitu? Helena Morley's Diary

I'm almost fourteen years old and already I think more than all the rest of the family. I think I began to draw conclusions from the age of ten years, or less. And I swear I never saw anybody from mama's family think about things. They hear something and believe it; and that's that for the rest of their lives.

They're all happy like that!

— Helena Morley, *The Diary of 'Helena Morley'*[1]

In his remarkable preface to *The Diary of 'Helena Morley'*, Alexandre Eulálio observes at one point that there is nothing to prevent the reader imagining that the girl's writing, spontaneous as it appears to be, is in fact the work of an adult and thus a hoax. But he also reports João Guimarães Rosa as commenting that in that case the diary would be even more extraordinary, 'since, as far as he knew, in no other literature was there a more powerful example of such a literal

---

1   All references to the translation of *Minha vida de menina* are from Helena Morley, *The Diary of 'Helena Morley'*, trans. Elizabeth Bishop, London, 1997, except in the few cases where the relevant passage is omitted by Bishop. In such cases, the reference, given in italics, is to the original, Helena Morley, *Minha vida de menina: Diário de Helena Morley*, Rio de Janeiro, 1971. The epigraph is from the entry for Thursday, 26 July, 1894, 143. [*Tr.*]

reconstruction of childhood'.[2] In a later essay, in which he returns to his preface and extends it, Eulálio argues that the idea of a 'pastiche of genius' must be rejected and concludes, as if now in possession of further knowledge, and creating a new mystery, that 'we can but praise the lightness of touch of the experienced hand that prepared the girl's old notebooks [first published in 1942] for publication without disfiguring their genuine character in the least degree'.[3] In this version, the real author is the girl, but there must have been a final touch from a skilled and discreet writer, committed to preserving the diary's peculiar nature. Today, mutually contradictory versions of the story still circulate. The original manuscripts were burnt; and what is more, they never existed – the work is really a rejigging of family anecdotes – but they are quite safe, kept in an old trunk. The American poet Elizabeth Bishop, who felt the charm of the book and translated it into English in the 1950s, when Helena was still alive, says in her correspondence that she never managed to set eyes on the papers themselves, which were kept hidden by the family, who were supposedly ashamed of the girl's untidy handwriting and shaky spelling. Whatever the truth of the matter, Bishop's letters disclose the painstaking attention with which Helena's husband, the writer Mario Brant, followed the progress of the translation, and she herself guesses that the adult Helena's short preface addressed to her granddaughters, explaining why the book is being published so many years later, is his work.[4] Brant was clearly proud of his wife, Bishop recalls elsewhere, and of the initiative to make her old papers public.[5]

---

2   Alexandre Eulálio, 'Livro que nasceu clássico', in Morley, *Minha vida de menina*, xi. João Guimarães Rosa (b. 1908–d. 1967) was one of the greatest Brazilian novelists of the twentieth century, sometimes compared to Joyce in his experimentalism: his central work is *Grande sertão: Veredas* (1956). [*Tr.*]
3   Eulálio, *Livro involuntário*, Rio de Janeiro, 1993, 43.
4   Elizabeth Bishop, *One Art*, New York, 1994, 317, 318, 355, 376.
5   Bishop, '*The Diary of "Helena Morley"*: The Book and Its Author', in *The Collected Prose*, ed. Robert Giroux, New York, 1984, 84.

If and when the manuscripts are made available, these uncertainties may be resolved. But even then, we will not have explained the power of these pages, which is surprising, and should be the critical question to be addressed. It can be said without a hint of condescension that *The Diary of 'Helena Morley'* is one of the most distinguished books in Brazilian literature; Machado de Assis aside, there is almost nothing on a level with it in nineteenth-century Brazil. However, in spite of the many editions and the great praise that prove its success, its position has remained secondary: just the right present for curious foreigners and promising schoolgirls, perhaps, but beyond that? What is admired is the girl's liveliness, her unadorned prose and of course the collection of memorable anecdotes about family life in the provinces. I will try to show the possibilities of a reading that digs deeper. In fact, it is hard to avoid perplexity when faced with the infinity of correspondences – unplanned? tacitly understood? – between the diary entries. Once we have developed an ear for them, we enter a densely textured and at times revelatory world, which this girl's prose, free of any pretension of manner, serves with absolute propriety. As always, the perfectly achieved naturalness is linked to complex, unrepeatable circumstances. This case seems all the more notable when we think of the unfortunate but unmistakable link, so common in the writing of the time, between the crisis of the old Brazil, the stylistic contortions of *écriture artiste*, then fashionable, and the humiliating obfuscations produced by exaggerated respect for contemporary 'science'.[6]

The doubts about the diary's authorship and writing process raise questions of properly critical interest. Depending on the nature of the corrections – if there were any – the book and above all its writing style would belong *grosso modo* to the 1890s or the 1930s, or both, indeed. Think, for instance, of the rightness of Helena's

---

6　The best-known examples of this are *Os sertões* (1902) by Euclides da Cunha and the fiction of Henrique Coelho Neto. [*Tr.*]

Brazilian speech, which is innocent of literary flourishes and does not defer to the Portuguese of Portugal; or, again, of her very independent and unceremonious intelligence. At first sight, they seem to be instances of a reality, documents from the original and – when it comes down to it – harmonious depths of the ex-colony. Here is our true, unofficial civilization, averse to formalities, with no reverence for the State or for Europe, the same civilization that later dazzled Brazilian modernism,[7] which would try to make use of it, crying up its difference from the bourgeois model. But the reverse process is also thinkable: the girl's notebooks may have been revised and improved according to the prose ideal of the *mineiro* modernists,[8] to which the diaries would then owe what, according to the other version, they had brought with them – that is, a strategic fusion of Brazilianness, modest decorum and up-to-date intelligence.[9]

Thus, it is not impossible that there is a great difference between the original diaries and the book; that the prose has been normalized at a high level of literary sophistication; that sections of the book may have been taken apart and put back together again, by topic, so as to form more consistent, contrasting blocks; and even that the

---

7 Brazilian poetic modernism dates from the 1920s and was close to the European avant-garde of the time. It was also (especially in the writings of Mário de Andrade) a movement intending to return to the 'real' Brazil, as opposed to the official one. [*Tr.*]

8 *Mineiro* comes from Minas Gerais (general mines), the large, landlocked state inland from Rio, named for the gold and diamond workings discovered in the eighteenth century, which first brought Europeans and African slaves to the area. Diamantina, the setting of *The Diary*, is the centre of the main diamond-mining area. There was a strong modernist movement in the 1920s, of which the poet Carlos Drummond de Andrade (b. 1902–d. 1987) was the most distinguished representative. (For further discussion, see ch. 6.) [*Tr.*]

9 Qualifying these hypotheses, we might remember that a *mineiro* linguist, probably aware of the complications involved in this case, used Helena's prose as his principal document for a chapter on 'colloquial language'. Is this a testimony in favour of the book's authenticity? Since the study has no historical pretensions, it can perfectly well accept as colloquial a prose that has been corrected later. See Aires da Mata Machado Filho, *Linguística e humanismo*, Petrópolis, 1974.

dates which head the entries do not completely correspond to reality
and function sometimes as conventional indications that this is a
diary. This would be disappointing only if we read the book as a
document in the strong sense, from which even a small adjustment
would remove all credit. However, if the originals were to show
that the invention was total, even affecting the narrative situation of
the girl writing the diary, something would be upset and the nature
of our reading would change. Much of what seemed like curious,
lively detail when thought of as being jotted down in a diary would
appear as clumsy, pseudo-naïve and artistically inadequate if
thought of as composed in a strict sense, as a work of the imagination. The interest and the beauty of the work are tied to the feeling
that it was composed randomly, as the days went by, and 'with no
artistic intentions'.[10]

In aesthetic matters, nothing is more suspect than a preference for
an author who is not an artist. It is usually part of a regressive urge, an
aversion to calculated processes, technical discipline and engagement
with the complexities of contemporary life. It is quite possible that the
enthusiasm for Helena's writings does have something of this anti-
modern bias – but only by mistake, since they take pride in not being
naïve, and their beauty is of the present, advanced in every way, even
if involuntary to an extent. We will look closely at this prose that
values intelligence, free of the reek of literature or ideology, its attention fixed on the topics it deals with, which it commands with no
hesitation, and with the accuracy and economy that come with
complete familiarity. More than a simple knack or flair, this is true
mastery, with real artistic potential, but in a state we can call 'everyday' (as opposed to 'aesthetic'), and to which these qualities owe their
special poetry: for they exist in ordinary life, as well as in the book – a
kind of robust proof that beauty is of this world.

Indeed the diary as a whole has a poetry of this kind, exceeding
the reach of artistic *workmanship*. The diary entries form short units,

---

10   Eulálio, 'Livro que nasceu clássico', x.

centred on actual events and quite distinct from one another; they have no continuity among themselves and do not follow an overall narrative order. But of course their contiguity little by little brings the figure of the young girl into relief, and around her appears a whole social world, loosely assembled and teeming with interest. That said, there is a surprise in store. Beneath the surface context, and for all their picturesque diversity, the anecdotes and reflections have a pertinence that is, so to speak, systemic. Although they are always tinged with Helena's sharp sense of fun, they disclose a reality that is not easily grasped, of another order and greater weight, and which it is the critic's job to understand. We will see 'inadmissible' structural complementarities where common sense would not expect or appreciate them and rotations in the meanings of crucial categories such as work, property, kinship, favours, exchange, poverty and God. There are improbable dislocations in continuity, unorthodox functional parallels and discussions unintentionally given greater depth by the unexpected appearance of a different topic: all of this with a clear shape and awaiting a name. The intuitive, easy unity of a provincial diary, homespun and focused on daily life in its social context, holds within itself an unsuspected universe, full of abstract relations, as visible as they are unconscious, whose author, so to speak, does not exist.

If we set aside the unlikely hypothesis of a complete literary hoax, these nexuses integrate the very matter of the book, the ensemble of its numerous, recurrent entries, but only indirectly and to an indeterminable extent, as an effect of deliberate composition. They are unidentified sources of organization, whose formative power can only be brought into proper focus by active meditation on the contents themselves. The beauty of the book, much more compelling than the girlish subject matter, however amusing that may be, is owed to the unreflecting but ordering efficacy of a working, functioning society, cohesive in its own way. Like her talents, which shine out in her writing but are not created by it, Helena's memoirs, in their deep consistency, manifest in the most unexpected topics and manners (which in an imaginative work would be brilliant inventions), transpose *external* practical demands – also unconscious – which give the whole an *internal* form. In experiencing its tone, its achievements and its impasses, and above all by reflecting on its results and implications, we come into contact with the movement and the logic of a social formation. This has been the objective of modern realist literature, and it is achieved in this case – as in few novels in Brazilian literature – by a work that is not fiction.

I

The opening words of the diary, in which poverty and work are conspicuous, have something utopian about them. This paradox will serve as our starting point. As Helena explains, Thursday is the best day in the week: the family get up early, under mother's orders, tidy up the house and go into the countryside to work in what is 'the best spot in Diamantina', and, moreover, is 'always deserted'. In spite of the routine, the days and the places that life consists of are by no means indistinguishable from one another, and the best things, far from obvious, may in fact be the ones that are least expected. The boys take a basin of laundry, and the pots and pans go in the little cart. Later they will go to look for firewood, catch birds with bird-lime, and fish. The girls wash clothes under the bridge with their mother, who also looks after the lunch. In the second part of the day, they bathe and wash their hair in the river, while the mother keeps a lookout to see if anyone is coming. Then, they spread the clothes out to dry, and all the children run into the countryside after berries, birds' nests, butterfly cocoons and 'little round stones to play jack-stones with'. On the way back, along with the folded clothes and the pans, the boys bring the firewood and whatever else they have picked up, which they sell in the town the same day (3–4).

As we can see, this is a happy combination of simple, necessary, innocent activities, bordering on the idyllic. As well as being minimal in their own right, differentiation and division of work group people together more than they separate them. Besides, they are not irreversible: labour is almost unspecialized and demands little sense of hierarchy. It is obvious too that, even when in the foreground, work does not define everything. Looking closer, we will also see, already here, the signs of a social organization with a different spirit. Emídio, one of the boys, is a *crioulo*, an *agregado* in the grandmother's *chácara*.[11] He is the one who carries the basin of laundry on his head, while Helena's brothers carry the pots and pans in a little cart, just as it is him who goes in search of wood, while the others go hunting and fishing. A few more scenes, and the outlines of the large patriarchal family will emerge, with its rich influential property owners in the centre and relatives, dependants, godchildren, ex-slaves and down-and-outs scratching a living round them.

Taking both aspects into account, we can say that work, as we see it here, attenuates the crudeness implicit in the way society is organized. Or to put it another way, the typical Brazilian differentiation, originating in the rigours of colonial exploitation, is directed in this case towards much simpler activities, like collecting wood, which make it regress (or progress, according to taste) in the direction of universal cooperation.[12] Female confinement and the

---

11 For *agregado*, see ch. 4 n.11. Of *chácara* Elizabeth Bishop says: 'It means a house with extensive gardens, or even a small farm, but not necessarily in the country' ('Introduction', *The Diary of 'Helena Morley'*, XLIII). *Crioulo*, which means 'black', is omitted from Bishop's translation. [*Tr.*]

12 Here is the generalized version of this pattern as described by Gilberto Freyre, who writes the following about monoculture: 'Sugar not only stifled the democratic industries represented by the trade in brazilwood and hides; it sterilized the land for the forces of diversified farming and herding for a broad expanse around the plantations. It called for an enormous number of slaves. Cattle-raising, meanwhile, with the possibilities it offered for a democratic way of life, was relegated to the backlands. In the agrarian zone, along with a monoculture that absorbed other forms of production, there developed a semi-feudal society, with a minority of whites and light-skinned mulattoes dominating, patriarchally and polygamously, from their Big Houses of stone and mortar, not

stigmatization of physical labour, for example – both characteristic of slave-owning patriarchalism – are put in abeyance. Likewise, on the way back Helena's brothers carry wood in their turn, just as they never shirk carrying packages of all sorts – for this reason, the 'idiotic' relatives, who think themselves a cut above, like to take advantage of them like 'niggers' (67–68). In her turn, the girl struggles to escape classification, to the extent that her mother thinks it a good thing that she has hurt her knee, 'so she won't want to turn into a boy' (92).

The materialism of Helena's reactions is still impressive today because of the lively and surprising direction it takes. It cannot be properly understood without the background of slave-owning civilization. At some moments, though not always, the girl refuses to discriminate on grounds of skin colour: 'I don't make any distinction, I like them all' (98). More than the injustice done to the blacks, however, what she cannot stand are the blockages, the limitations that slavery, recently abolished, imposes even on free people, in particular when it leads to the devaluation of work and manual labour. We will see that the 'little English girl's' point of view may express something of the economic decline of Minas Gerais at the time. It is also linked to the Protestant, English half of her family, who find contempt for work unacceptable, though not when it is undertaken by blacks; and it owes a lot to the restless temperament of the girl herself, who hankers after physical outlets and shared work almost as if they were medicines.

Whatever her reasons, the fact is that Helena develops a very personal aversion to 'priggishness' (*enjoamento*) – by which she means a paralysing conformity with current social prohibitions.

---

only the slaves that were bred so prolifically in the senzalas, but the sharecroppers as well, the tenants and retainers, those who dwelt in the huts of mud and straw, vassals of the Big House in the strictest meaning of the word'. For our purposes, the differences are as important as the similarities. Preface to the second English-language edition, *The Masters and the Slaves*, trans. Samuel Putnam, Berkeley, 1986, xxix.

Her rebellion runs the gamut from an amusing, sometimes pointed lack of reverence to unsettling desires that are still challenging a hundred years later. Her impatience with her 'insipid' life (*a vida chocha*) opens her eyes to the hypocrisies of religious devotion, even those of people who are owed general respect. The same impatience informs the girl's desire to get her hands dirty, her sympathy with hard work and heavy-duty cleaning. Her humorous, intimate dealings with 'disgusting' things are part of a refusal to respect inviolable boundaries; and her preference for the open, no-nonsense atmosphere of the kitchen and the celebrations of the blacks is another aspect of the same thing.

But where her fearless disposition takes her further is in the *envy* that the needy sometimes awaken in her. It is always possible that the girl is showing off, being rebellious for the sake of it and trying to be edifying and self-denying or charmingly bucolic. But that is not the impression it gives. After all, she is just as energetically envious of her rich cousins. So, affectation or not, there is the desire to live like her impoverished little schoolfellow, in a bare hut at the edge of the woods, doing her lessons outdoors, sitting on a box (249); or to join the grape pickers' line in hard but enjoyable work, where 'we could eat a load of them' (*84*). Or, again, envious feeling appears in the surprising statement that the slaves do not incite pity because working all day long would not make her unhappy: 'To have nothing to do would be torture to me' (117). It seems clear that the envy has nothing to do with poverty or the inferior position of the family, much less with forced labour, but with the activity and the sociability that operates in these despised conditions, and is something like their real substance. Going right against the grain, Helena pays no attention to the 'external' frames, be they ideological or simply imposed by force, and concentrates on the life that, for good or ill, flows beneath them. It is true that this abstraction is arbitrary – unless history itself was operating an analogous dissociation, as in fact it was: with the coming of Abolition, the society engendered by colonial slavery was separated from its original institutional framework

and began to exist and persist under a different sky, with consequences that are, still today, difficult to gauge. Helena, when she
feels the pull of material activity considered in the fullness of its
content and stripped of conventional labels, points towards unexpected, quite unconventional perspectives, the more so in such an
unequal country. Once she has neutralized the stigma of class, which
complements oppression, the labourer's hut and work take their
place – like everything else – in a different, genuinely materialist
field of calculations and evaluations. In the case of the hut, instead of
signifying contemptible poverty, for her a reduced amount of housework and nearness to nature begin to count on the positive side; in
the case of the women carrying grapes, there is the pleasure of physical effort and of shared excesses. In other words, once removed from
the system of domination that created and polarized its values, the
differentiation of kinds of work and their associated situations
appears in a changed light, this time as a society's wide diversity of
experience, as an ample, loose cooperative order involving the possibility of self-realization for all its members. This is a breach through
which Helena's imagination enters with great energy. Suddenly, the
classic segregation of manual and intellectual labour, utility and
beauty, work and amusement, cleanliness and dirt, becomes fluid
and subject to new combinations, on which Helena's fantasy lingers,
unpretentiously exploring the heady, dis-alienating possibilities of a
materialist evaluation of things. For all the girl's cheek and her urge
to be original, it is good to think that the exuberance of her observations remaining infectious today may be an indicator of interests that
are not extinct.

The utopia of the opening pages also involves the alternation of
tiring tasks, exercises that require skill and games pure and simple.
This favours a notion of work that is sui generis, far distant from
God's curse on Adam and Eve. Are we dealing with a childish
idealization, or a reality in which a disillusioned onlooker no longer
believes, though it might raise a smile? The irony reaches its high
point at the end of this entry, when Helena, very much the

economist, expresses her regret that because of school the family
doesn't go out into the country every day. Her father's struggles at
the mine aren't producing 'diamonds any bigger than a mosquito's
eye' – less than the money-value of the wood and the birds the children bring back to the town. 'What a big saving it would make for
mama . . . [who] wouldn't have to work so hard' (4). The enjoyable
gathering of what nature readily provides fetches more than the
laborious excavations of the head of the family. Indeed mining itself
is not taken very seriously by the clear-sighted girl, who sees its
hopeless lack of realism and proneness to superstition.

'Today is the best day of the week': the book opens with these
words, which prompt the thought that the other days are *less good*.
A strong rhythm is then set up here, in two tempos, of effort and
immediate recompense: The family *gets up early* for Thursday,
which will be full and really enjoyable. They go down a narrow
lane and come out at the bridge, the best place in Diamantina.
Helena *carries* and *works*, and later has lunch and enjoys herself. The
children *set the bait* and fish for *lambaris* (minnows), *spread birdlime*
on twigs and catch *curiós* (seed finches), *look for firewood* and sell it
when they get back (3–4). This rhythm proceeds from the non-
specific to the good, from duty to leisure, from work to fantasy or,
looking at the scene as a whole, from the active morning to the
dreaming afternoon. Since the sequences are brief, the pleasure of
the second moment reflects back on the first, filling with happiness
the activities which, in keeping with the same rhythm, should
belong to the effortful, necessary part of the day. In this way, clas-
sifications are soon confused, and it becomes doubtful whether
rising early, getting down to hard work, washing clothes and
putting the bait on the hook or the birdlime on the twig are really
worse occupations than eating lunch, bathing in the stream, playing
in the countryside or catching the *lambaris* or the *curiós*. The liveliness of the episode also comes from its several simultaneous actions,
which are like voices. Some of the group do the washing, some
carry, some look for wood, some cook, others fish. These are simple

occupations, needing no explanation; each one fits in its own sentence, each with its own subject, creating a scene of general activity, in which nature itself seems to take part, the fish biting the bait, the birds landing on the birdlime, the wood and the pebbles offering themselves on the ground. Even so, we are not in the presence of pure anarchical high spirits, since everything takes place under mama's friendly coordination and in keeping with the objectives of a day's work, which are never lost sight of. The result has something of the happy, energetic movement of a musical divertimento, in which the note of Edenic inversion sounds throughout: note that the object of the trip was to do the laundry, and that the birds and the wood, which later provide some money, come as a bonus, as if to say that the superfluous is what allows one to live.

However, the real beauty of the scene, which transfigures everything else, comes in the final paragraph. Just as reward comes after effort, or afternoon after morning, or the return home after the trip to the countryside, here the recapitulation ends the day, transforming it into an internal movement, like a reprise in which we meditate on destiny. If we didn't have to go to school, thinks Helena, sisters and brothers could go out to the bridge every day and earn the money their mother needs. Or they could all stay at the mine with their father, so that mother would have to work less – 'it kills me to think of it', she says. But then, has the morning's fun been a hardship? The perfect happiness of the day is now replayed in a melancholy key, where even the idyll has an air of self-sacrifice about it. Of course the pity her mother inspires might in its turn be covering up the illicit desire not to go to school, but even this is, indirectly, another example of self-sacrifice. Sad or not, the final prize and the achievement of human freedom lie in these recapitulations of the imagination. Once noticed, the irony, the subtlety and the beauty of this movement are remarkable in the simplicity of their terms.

2

The first four entries in the diary can be taken as forming a single block. We have seen the Morleys' Thursday, in which the dominant tone of frugality and shared work dissolves social distinctions. Next, we see the same family at home, in their role as a respected, that is, a *distinguished*, family who offer protection, and from whom the poor ask a blessing. In the third scene, the positions are inverted, and this time it is the Morleys who will be on a visit, half out of courtesy, half on the lookout for favours, to the *chácara* of wealthy neighbours. The fourth entry, finally, brings all these themes together and puts the emphasis on the cruder relationship with private property and payment in money. The contrasts between the entries are sharp, displayed matter-of-factly and without comment, which makes them suitable for reflective contemplation.[13] Here are the Morleys, seen in four contexts, in potential contradiction with one another. Linked to them are others, equally suggestive. Thus, for example, the episodes are organized around different, precarious ways of getting a living, each one with its own truths to tell and its own differences from the others: going out looking for things that nature gives for free, trusting in God and his agents on earth, receiving favours from relatives and neighbours, working for others for pay, searching for the big prize in the mine. The surest way, of course, is to have property and augment it by business deals. There is a correlative variation in the ways nature is thought of. She can either be a wicked stepmother or be abundant and suddenly generous, just as she can either act for everybody or just for the rich and powerful. These variations interact with the first set, combining with them in different ways, each producing its own conflicts.

---

13   In another context, referring to the peculiar poetry of pre-modern stories, Walter Benjamin observes that compact narratives, which avoid the support of explanations, are the ones that speak most powerfully to the imagination because they leave room for it to operate. 'The Story-Teller' in *Illuminations*, New York, 1969, 91.

Criss-crossed by the random nature of the anecdotes, but also constrained by the limited number of the social relations that sustain them (kinship, neighbourliness, protection, enmity, waged employment, callous indifference), this multiplication of profiles and conflicts soon resolves itself into a rotation, which is repetitive to some extent and gives the density of literature to the disciplined and infinitely interesting movement of a real, existing order.

Between the first and second entries, there is an abrupt change of scene. Accompanied by her sister, Benvinda comes to inform Dona Carolina and Seu Alexandre, Helena's parents, of her coming marriage.[14] After beating about the bush, the girl reveals that her fiancé has a defect, a defect in his foot, or rather, he's missing a leg. Dona Carolina's reply would delight Machado de Assis: 'Oh, the poor boy! But then he can't walk, can he?' Straight away, Helena's mother asks if they know how they're going to live. Benvinda's response is: 'No, I hadn't thought of that, but we'll live the way people always live, somehow or other. God will help us' (5).[15] The comedy does not disguise the class viewpoint, with its focus on the drawbacks and surprises – if we can call them that – of the lives of the poor. The comic quality arises from the exaggerated worries of the unfortunate bride-to-be, who proceeds by stages as she struggles to confess the defect, as if caught in a breach of decorum. There is an amusing inversion of roles in this, for Benvinda, who after all is the one who has decided that the lack of a leg is not so important, makes more of a drama out of it than does Helena's family. Up to this point, then, we have had a comedy without surprises, or rather, one that conforms to the social order: on the one side, reason, naturalness, foresight, sound limbs, a superior position of sorts; on the other, poverty, pointless shame, mutilation, bad grammar, and a life

---

14 *Seu* literally means 'his' or 'your', but in fact this familiar shortening of *senhor* is (like Dona) a polite way for lower-class people or dependants to talk to or about their 'betters'. [*Tr.*]

15 Benvinda says 'a gente veve' for 'we'll live', where the correct Portuguese would be 'a gente vive'. [*Tr.*]

of 'God help us'. Of course, the superiority can be looked at in reverse shot, less sympathetically. Dona Carolina's ejaculation, 'The poor boy!' (*coitado*) – the first in a long series of them – assists the shift of perspective. On the explicit level is the compassion, half-generous, half-Christian, for everything that suffers. But the expression is also perfectly conventional, and moreover it is in this that it exhibits the unfathomable human quality, so familiar from Machado, that balances fellow feeling and basic indifference in the face of suffering and poverty. Brazilian local colour makes its presence felt here, in random fashion, in periodic encounters with a kind of deprivation inherited from the colonial period, wholly without social protection. Little by little, behind the mixture of familiarity and distance, there emerges the fatalism, the curiosity, guilt, fear and heedlessness with which enlightened Brazilians, even today, contemplate the destiny of the mass of the country's poor. The enlightened smile dominates the scene until the second-last line, where an amusing solecism points up Benvinda's ignorance. The change of register comes at the end, with her 'God will help us'. Even these words could be part of a scene illustrating local customs, as a characterization of improvidence. However, they refer to the *dissociation of the whole*: they are there, uncommented on, expressing a confidence that nothing justifies, an appropriate complement to the uncommitted pity felt by the educated class.

The poetry of this episode becomes more intense and complex if we relate it to the previous one. We have seen that the Morleys are disposed to look at social pretensions with some irony. And it is true that the repressed laughter that hovers over the scene with Benvinda has to do with the feeling of the ridiculous that polite pretences inspire in Helena, who does not believe in the role her parents take in the ceremony of respect – as indeed they have little belief in it themselves. This scepticism makes the penniless girl's trusting attitude the more pitiful, for, after all, divine protection will only come through the help of protectors aware of their own obligations. The all-purpose helpfulness of the Morleys, their immunity to disgust – their healthy attitude, in fact – is unexpectedly reflected in their way of looking at the physical defect. From the viewpoint of people who are well settled in life, the missing leg is one trait among others, you could almost say a picturesque one, in the life of down-and-outs. Not so for Helena, who looks at the defect as something between equals, with an amused, unpitying frankness and a touch of sadism. She almost envies the man his crutch, as, not much later, she will envy her sister's swollen cheek – a toothache gives her the right to go around the streets with her face tied up in a kerchief. Thus, overcoming prejudice puts everyone's fragility on display, against the absurdity of pretensions of caste, but without necessarily creating solidarity: it is a causal chain that forces one to think.[16] This said, the book is also full of movement in the opposite direction, as we will see later on, where Helena's universal sympathy and her mother's Christian charity are translated into dedication to the needy and an understanding of the situations of others. In fact, superior moral discernment is one of the eccentricities the Morleys cultivate.

Let us go back to the line 'God will help us'. This expression confirms the enlightened view of the calamitous fecklessness of poor people's lives. It brings it into play but at the same time checks it: the enlightened viewpoint itself, whose contented superiority dominates the rhythm of the scene, nevertheless soon reveals itself as useless when faced by Benvinda's helpless state and the undeniable nobility of her resolution. It is as if the humour had to bite its tongue. Furthermore, it is true that the Morleys, well educated and strong though they are, get by as best they can and need protection, without which they would have nothing. Thus, the context of incurable

---

16   The consideration of a physical defect via a class perspective was studied with a terrible acuteness by Machado de Assis in *Memórias póstumas de Brás Cubas*. Cf. Roberto Schwarz, 'Eugênia', in *A Master on the Periphery of Capitalism*, Durham, NC and London, 56–68.

precariousness that surrounds poor people is not unfamiliar to the family and sets an upper limit to respect for intelligence, forethought and other civilized virtues without discounting them altogether. This sense of the limited reach and the merely relative usefulness of the values of the Enlightenment, which the family cultivate partly as a sign of personal advancement and amour propre (even though it may be that those same values do not offer much in the way of advantage when it comes to circumstances), is one of the book's profoundly poetic conclusions, with a bearing on the slave-owning, clientelistic configuration of Brazilian society.

In the following scene (*6–8*) the Morleys are visiting the *chácara* of a neighbouring family, who usually favour them 'with fruit, eggs, chickens and vegetables'. These favours are linked to a move-ment, very Brazilian, of taking relations of patronage to imaginary lengths, in accordance with all kinds of needs and wishes. These neighbours say that Luisinha (Helena's sister) looks like their niece Quitinha, who is away from home. Quitinha's uncle and aunt, who are childless, are very fond of their niece. To compensate for her absence, they like to look at their neighbour's daughter, and comment on the likenesses between the two girls, as well as loading the family with presents. The Morleys are happy to play along: 'We carried on taking advantage of the likeness and eating the fruit'. The comedy – cheeky as it is – lies in the contrasting motives of those involved, well summed up in the dissonance between 'favour-ing' and 'taking advantage of', where the first term belongs to the decorous, so-called superior realm of personal favour, full of assumptions of something done for nothing and in freedom from commercial considerations, and the other belongs to the so-called inferior realm, and the overt calculation of interest. There is also the enlightened insolence with which Helena espouses ingratitude. Sustaining this feeling is the half-materialist, half-sarcastic convic-tion that similarities belong to the realm of fancy, while fruit and chickens are real. Nothing could be more beneficial than to concede the likeness, which costs nothing, in exchange for the food, which has a price. The irony goes up a notch and turns into a paradox if we remember, with Helena, the role that these same fantasies – similarities, intuitions, signs, which all make the world conform to an image conjured up by personal desire – have in the search for gold and diamonds. In these pursuits, however, lie the fortunes of the region, including, as one upshot, the Morleys' poverty, for at the vital moment they stupidly lent credence to a message from Saint Anthony, missing out on the chance of a lifetime (91). So, it seems, although chimeras do not exist, they have material consequences. Inversely, prosaic material goods are only partly separable from their owners' caprice and sense of their own importance – that is, chickens and fruit are not exchanged according to an impersonal economic law. In these circumstances, governed partly by custom and partly by calculation, what is an intelligent mode of conduct?

The episode reaches its denouement in a burst of laughter, which upsets the apple cart, and after which, sadly or not so sadly, there will be no more favours. When the opportunity finally comes to compare the girls and appreciate their similarities, the Morleys begin to laugh in an uncontrollable and unbecoming fashion – 'Just look, Zinha, there's the girl that looks like you' – and Quitinha's aunt scowls and takes her niece indoors. At first sight, the ones affected by the mockery are the girls themselves. In the scene's latent economy, however, the laughter has another function: it deactivates and puts on show a classic kind of unease in Brazilian society – the moral trap habitually set by the exchange of family kowtowing for material goods. After all, might it not be wrong, even in fun, to take advantage of their good neighbours' longing for their niece? In fact, might not agreeing that this same freckled girl looks like Luisinha be taking things too far? The laughter returns the Morleys to a state of equilibrium, not because it provides answers to these difficult questions, in which money and traditional respect create complications for each other, but because it marks them as insoluble and waves them away, even though the family loses out in the process. In other words, the current has changed direction. After the first phase, in which freedom takes on an enlightened air (the fruit is worth the kowtowing, which is unimportant), comes the criticism of the criticism: this same freedom reacts against the limitations imposed on it by cynicism (it's not true that hypocrisy doesn't lower one; it does have a cost, and family obligations do have a rationale).[17] These attacks of 'helpless laughter' are among the more attractive peculiarities of the Morley family, who for good or ill resign themselves and live with them, just as Benvinda 'veve'[18] with her fiancé and his missing leg. The defect in both cases has a cost for the interested parties, but that does not stop them dead. Of course, Benvinda's deprivation when she entrusts her survival to God, not knowing how her lame husband will be able to work, is the more radical, because determined by her helpless situation. The Morleys, when they give themselves over to laughter, at worst give up the neighbours' fruit and chickens, not the protection they enjoy as poor (and valued) relatives of an influential family. Nevertheless, the structural parallel exists, and its refraction in the difference between the class situations – because of the very disproportion between them – illuminates the internal organization of a system of inequalities. When they laugh at the people doing them favours, the Morleys conjure up in a more attractive form the same fatalism, exemplary so to speak, be it drastic or obtuse, with which Benvinda goes out into the night. Trust in God, the protector who would make all the others unnecessary, allows the penniless girl an integrity free of utilitarian calculation that,

---

17   En passant, the reader interested in the social core of the artistic form will clearly recognize the conflict that gives shape to the novels of Machado's first phase, where the moral dilemmas of the characters derive from the struggle between individual reason and paternalism. It is undeniable, I think, that the question appears with greater variety, depth and humour, here, in Helena Morley's book. See Roberto Schwarz, 'O paternalismo e a sua racionalização nos primeiros romances de Machado de Assis', in *Ao vencedor as batatas*, São Paulo, 1977.

18   See n. 15 above.

with numerous variants, will be one of Helena's references, a constant object of envy for her, humiliated as she is by the computation of social goods and favours.

There is here a noteworthy reflection of the opening scene by the river, where the free, happy life existed thanks to the abundance of nature. In Quitinha's aunt's *chácara*, where all you have to do is pick the fruit and eat it, something similar happens, with the difference that there is an owner. Here too the plenty is natural and unshadowed: the accidental resemblance between two girls opens up the richly laden trees to some half-famished neighbours. We could say that the resemblance is a gift from heaven, which needs no thanks, just as is the profusion of *lambaris* when the children were fishing in the previous scene. It happens, though, that the consent necessary for it to take shape carries a certain cost in social recognition, which can be used for bargaining and so reintroduces the element of exchange, of 'you scratch my back, I'll scratch yours'. In this sense, the comparison between the two girls has 'computational' implications, involving property and neighbourliness, which transform this piece of luck into a problem: the memorable but inconclusive laughter is a commentary on this.

We see, then, how the amusing and picturesque externalities of situations have internal repercussions, opening up a space for questioning. This is in fact one of the miracles of Helena Morley's diary, which never leaves the day-to-day life of the provincial town, yet never falls into mere blandness. The movement will be repeated in the next episode, triggered this time by a diamond the children find in an escarpment. The stone causes a series of moral tensions. The general framework of relationships does not change, but the dominant tone does. The generosity of nature, with its aspect of sheer chance, the ignorance and the enigmatic good nature of the very poor, who need the protection of the educated, who in their turn, however, have interests of their own – all this reappears in a different light, and a harsher one (5–6).

At the end of the afternoon, when the workers have been dismissed, it is the children's turn to play, barefoot, in the muddy waste of the mine. Suddenly Helena's friend Arinda, who is out with the gang that day, bends down and with a scream 'pick[s] up a really big diamond'. The gang run to Helena's uncle's house, since he is in charge of operations. He examines the 'beautiful' stone and gives the girl five hundred-*milreis* notes for it. The gang run off again, this time to her parents' miserable little hut. They are 'crazy with joy', and 'her father folded up the bills and put them in his pocket, took them out again and looked at them, and put them back again'. More beauty? Their happiness is such that Helena is sorry for them and agrees that 'it was best that Arinda had found the diamond'. The poetry of the gang of children rushing hither and thither, still united by the new toy, and already threatened by the resentments of property owning, is striking. Sour grapes apart, Helena resigns herself to the other girl's luck, seeing in her penury a justification for her own bad luck. Hidden beneath this is the conviction of the educated, according to which very poor people do not need the money, which they do not know how to use. There is also the paradoxical tone of their 'pity', which in this case has to do more with the degree of happiness brought by the hundred-*milreis* notes than with the poverty of the family, in whose house 'there is nothing but a cowhide for them all to sleep on, *coitados*'. Put another way, for Helena it is less a matter of charity than of contempt for their undisguised desire to better their lives, which she sees as more humiliating than the poverty itself. Is this lordly contempt for a poor relation? Or the enlightened contempt of someone who thinks that money and expensive things will never change a no-hoper? The same desire to better oneself is very strong in Helena, and that is why she despises Arinda's father for his indiscreet enthusiasm. Straight away, he says that he's going to use the money to dig 'in a place he knows is going to produce diamonds'. Back home, when Helena recounts these plans or dreams, she hears the following commentary: 'That poor fool! I know where he's going to bury that

money; it's in that hill at Bom Sucesso where we've mined already'.
Now, Helena's pity is prompted by her father's lack of it, since he is
normally so good, and by the ignorance of Arinda's father, who is
going to work over worked-out excavations, and waste the money.
In the end, the earlier hidden thought is bound to return: would it
not have been better ('more methodical and reasonable', Machado
would add) if Helena and not Arinda had found the stone?[19]
Separated from the rest of the text, with a paragraph of its own, so
as to leave the various sides of this on show, is the final sentence:
'Arinda didn't even get a penny but she didn't care'. Plainly, luck
does not improve the lives of the poor, for they squander it; they
rarely try to fight for it, and only look wretched when they do. That
said, they are incomprehensible, as well as admirable and saintly,
especially if we consider the sequence of moral revelations, the
apprenticeship in property-related bourgeois iniquities, that Helena
has just gone through.

At the beginning of this episode, as an introduction, there is a
brief humorous comment: 'When I am envious of other people's
good fortune, mama and grandma say, "God knows who's fortunate". Here in Boa Vista I've learned to believe it. I've already told
grandma that she's almost always right about everything she says'
(5). The scene is so homely that its ironies might pass by unnoticed.
We need to rub our eyes and read again. At first sight, when they
say that God knows who is fortunate, the mother and grandmother
are teaching a rather unlucky child resignation in the face of
Providence. But they might also be having a joke at the expense of

---

19   The quotation is from the beginning of ch. 3 of Machado's 'O alienista'
(translated as 'The Psychiatrist' and 'The Alienist'), a long short story published
in 1881. In the piece, the alienist's wife wants to go on a trip to Rio de Janeiro but
dare not suggest it because of the cost (and because she is terrified of him); it is
thus (ironically) 'better, *more methodical and practical*, that the suggestion should
come from him.' In the only translation I have been able to consult, that of Helen
Caldwell and William L. Goldman, *The Psychiatrist: and Other Stories* (Berkeley,
1973), the quoted words are unfortunately omitted. [*Tr.*]

a girl who is a fearful nuisance. In this case, God changes roles and
becomes a hidden ally in the family's guerrilla warfare. Helena's
commentary underlines this duel between two ironies: in Boa Vista,
when God gave the diamond to Arinda, she finally believed in His
wisdom – for the family in question was truly needy. But is it wise
to give money to someone who doesn't know how to use it and isn't
even bothered by receiving it? If that's the case, why not give something to Helena too? And what if God's wisdom is nothing more
than a grudge against the girl, known as she is to be unlucky time
and time again? In this case, would God be evil, and is the girl
saying that she has just learned to disbelieve in Him, when she
really has believed in the past? The sarcasm also turns against the
grandmother, who is 'always right' and wants to teach her granddaughter patience. What the girl is saying is that she does, in fact,
need patience, but she needs it to put up with the bad luck that dogs
her, and which readers, the further they go into the book, have no
difficulty in seeing as the weight of poverty and family duties, rather
than of divine purpose. In sum, God can be provident, unwise and
unjust; He can be of use to adults when they want to plague children, and it may be that He does not exist.

We may say – mistakenly perhaps – that Helena is training
herself in an established, settled form of prose. I am thinking of the
ruminations of an egoist in the face of fickle fortune, a *mineiro* form
of humour, unblinkingly analytical and with a touch of indignation,
possibly associated with the ups and downs of mining, but with a
structure as universal as private property itself. This para-literary
model, in which the enlightened and antisocial dimensions of individualism are sharply stylized, evolves through the medium of
anecdotes from a still-colonial world, whose make-up and possibilities are of a different order. The conjunction of clear, objective
prose, reasoned in manner and guided by personal interest, with
traditional religiosity, large extended families, social classes
excluded from owning property and a mass of goods that only occa-
sionally have market value is a real cultural and aesthetic event.

Along with the individuality of each situation, which naturally adds a great deal, this combination creates a complex unity with its own perspectives and dilemmas; this is material charged with great historical energy.

Just a few diary entries, which could hardly be more unpretentious, are enough to put a surprisingly extensive system of variations and echoes into movement. The social topography, the graduated differences in the values of things, the different modalities of work, the kinds of appropriation, the explanations given for these things: everything is linked, in relationships which in general are mutually confirmed by each component. This is where the feeling of natural, harmonious functioning has its roots. The revelations, for their part, come at those moments, also structural, when the usual hierarchy no longer convinces and is turned upside down. Parallel to the order of social inequality, for example, there is an ascending scale that goes from the wild berries to the orchard fruit and the diamond. The first belong to those who pick them in the fields; the second, grown in the orchard, have an owner but hardly circulate as commodities since they form part of the domestic economy and the politics of favour among neighbours; only the diamond circulates strictly as property with monetary value. In the same spirit, picking fruit allows one to live 'at God's mercy'; favours, half way between dependence and the market, go together with services and personal obligations; while the mining gives life to property, business, political influence, contracts, paid work – the whole mass of important economic activity, oriented towards the international market. Even here, however, one ingredient is still pure chance, and this fact turns everything on its head, making the search for diamonds and gold the most irrational of all activities. Thus, adhering to a commonplace of enlightenment, Helena thinks it more intelligent to plant crops than to work in the mines. But what she really likes is the freedom to pick berries 'out in the country' (7), which demands no social qualifications, where she need not suffer the embarrassment intrinsic to relations of favour or observe the discipline imposed by property, which the girl both despises and admires in her business-oriented uncles. So, contrary to appearances, the life that gives the greatest satisfaction is not lived at the top, even though Helena makes a great effort to get there. In another perspective, it is clear that the rich see themselves reflected in the diamond rather than in the wild berries since it is precious and perfect. But if the mirror were turned around, the figures who, for the same reasons, could be likened to the diamond would be others, like Arinda and Benvinda, ignorant perhaps, but innocent and unstained by bourgeois calculation, which is something whose human cost Helena has a crystal-clear notion of.

These are not arbitrary speculations: the reflection of the social order and its ambiguities, in the system it imposes on nature, sustains the hidden architecture of the book, and in this sense validates that order . . . However, there is no lack of inversions in the established hierarchy of good and bad. They range from the innocent to the truly important: those valued least may be the best; the blacks' festivals are more fun than those of the whites; there is more dignity in persons abandoned to their own devices than in those who depend precariously on favour; religion, which is civilized, may be no different from superstition, which is backward; and imagination may be better than either, and is in fact quite like them – and so on. These anti-ideological discoveries are not the result of a simple inversion of the conventional point of view and cannot be reduced to a rhetorical artifice. They presuppose an active and unprejudiced curiosity about the less-esteemed areas of life, and go further, reaching an enlightened, genuinely rare understanding of the reciprocal character of social relations and the positions they define. They are nourished also by a taste for dismantling the pretensions of the rich relatives, and, movingly, by the pride Helena takes in exercising an exceptional intelligence, which from early on is recognized by the family and then by the town. We have the pleasure of witnessing her successive youthful jibes aimed at clan and class obscurantism. Instead of closing herself off from the condition of the poor, she understands it as part of her own, identical or complementary, and much of her ambivalence and perspicacity spring from this. Thus, she applauds the insight in the reply of a shabby cousin, an incorrigible drinker, whose relatives offer protection so long as he stays polite and sober: 'If I had enough will-power not to drink, and some good clothes, I wouldn't need Seu Antônio Eulálio's help! I'd look after you and him and everyone else' (215). The argument applies equally to Helena's family, who are more amusing and less organized than their relatives in business, and also need support. At another moment, a lad tells a poor woman to work instead of begging for alms. 'She answered, "Me work? I'm so poor!" We all laughed. Then I thought and said, "No. She answered very well. Could she find a job as a cook? Nobody has cooks here. Could she gather wood? Nobody would buy it here. What work could she find to do? Poor thing!" The woman was pleased at my taking her part and said "Yes, that's it, she understands"' (273).

3

What are we to make of *The Diary of 'Helena Morley'*? Does its appeal lie only in the writing or also in the world it records? Against a Brazilian background marked by slave labour, uncontested patriarchal authority and all the other consequences of colonization, its humanity and charm pose a problem. How did these inversions of perspective, the constant reference to the unseen side of things, the sympathy with despised points of view, the distance taken with respect to esteemed opinions, and above all the sense of mutual, back-and-forth conditioning become possible? What is the meaning of the ubiquitous hidden reciprocities? There is no doubt that overcoming one-sided points of view is one of Helena's passions, and we will return to this. But it is also obvious that wishing is not enough. In a simple diary of day-to-day events, generalized inter-connections depend on suitable material, things that actually happen and confirm their existence; otherwise they are just pious wishes. They presuppose the normality of contact between opposites, recip-rocal knowledge and interest, without which they have no real content. We have seen that such relations do in fact occur in the book, where sometimes they seem to be consciously noted and at others to take shape unintentionally. But did they exist in Brazil itself? Today's readers concede, with some surprise, that they did not know the country could be so civilized, at least potentially. The same enigma is at the heart of several of the best moments in Brazilian culture.

In other words, there is a constant circulation between the differ-ent social poles, the various forms of work, the types of goods people own, the forms religion can assume and so on, which little by little form into repertoires. This movement to and fro is owing to Helena's restless intelligence, and to the routine of her world, which is always picturesque because of the family-focused, unstable adjustment between social spheres that normally would not mix. Like the girl, her little brothers sometimes do work normally done by blacks, or become poor cousins, exploited for domestic work by wealthy relatives, or take their place as members of an important family. This alternation between more or less incompatible roles, far distant from one another in the social spectrum, is lived as an everyday experience, so that the system of social differences is transformed into an interior reality marked by a surprising objec-tivity and irony of manner. Mutatis mutandis, something similar holds true for the chickens, which may go into the pot because they are homebred or as a favour from a neighbour, as an occasional theft or as merchandise bought and paid for. Belonging to the everyday world, these functional variations nevertheless have major historico-structural import, which gives the prose a substan-tive rhythm as well as laying out the complex of relevant questions and determining its own peculiar humorous atmosphere. There is an extraordinarily lively relationship between the writing, the contradictory way things happen, the social framework and the way it is interiorized by the inhabitants of Diamantina, which, if this were a work of imaginative literature, would itself be a great prize. What are we to think of it when it is found in a diary from a backward place out in the sticks?

Helena's writing, we may say, is driven by a convivial impulse whose counterpart obstacles are the segregations and the forms of stupidity peculiar to Brazilian society with its colonial matrix. It may be that the moment and the place of origin of the diary tell us something about this. Slavery had just been abolished, and free labour was not yet set in the alienation of a wage system. While the brutality of the slave-owning economy was coming into question, the degradations specific to abstract labour were as yet remote, and this created an interregnum, promising or chaotic according to the circumstances, an ill-bounded space in which the sociable, human idea of collaborative effort, which Helena invests in and which today sounds utopian, could more easily make its way. Commenting on the diversity of labour relations in Rio de Janeiro after the end of the international slave trade in 1850, when this transitional phase began, Luiz Felipe de Alencastro says that the city was one of the world's great social laboratories, which gives us some idea of the far-reaching relevance of what was happening.[20] In a similar spirit, Antonio Candido analyses the energy of a novel by Aluísio Azevedo, *O cortiço* (*The Slum*), and reveals its affinity with the new rhythms of money making, based on a newly extended gamut of primitive ways of exploiting and robbing others.[21]

For all the differences between the big cities and a certain kind of place in the interior, the same breath of innovation enlivens Helena's

20   'Machado de Assis: um debate', in *Novos Estudos Cebrap*, 29, São Paulo, March 1991, 60.
21   Antonio Candido, 'De cortiço a cortiço', in *O discurso e a cidade*, São Paulo, 1993; *The Slum* (1890), trans. David H. Rosenthal, eds. David H. Rosenthal and Affonso Romano de Sant'Anna, Oxford and New York, 2000.

notebooks. But here the changes move in another direction. In the area where the diary is set, the wound of slavery seems to be healing over: the ex-slaves would be absorbed by the owner's families and integrated into their domestic and economic activities. The gamut of assimilation is varied, with leeway for many very personal ways of adjustment, which in their way are forms of freedom too, made possible by the weakening of social domination. Thus, when he needs workers, Helena's father has recourse to some old maids in the neighbourhood, who 'have two Negroes, [whom they previously owned as slaves] and rent them out to work and divide the money with them, because that's the only way they can support them' (28).[22] Another moment brings an unexpected inversion: Helena's brother, who can't find anyone to buy his *curiós* and his brushes, is contracted at ten *milreis* a month to give lessons to the children of a couple of blacks who are very clean and well-educated (277). There are also blacks who mistreat one another with a domineering brutality imitated from their former owners (30). There is the *agregado* who gets hit a few times because he thinks he can treat one of his boss's relatives without due deference, because 'Aren't I as good and as free as he is?' (80). Like some of their aunts, Helena and Luisinha love looking after black babies and are grateful to their mothers (23, 54, 147). Júlia, a former slave who has the bad luck to be chosen as Queen of the Rosary, spends the savings she has put by for a hut on the festival instead: is she crazy or admirable (35)? The same *agregado* who gets hit sends the whites crazy when he cures himself of toothache by applying a red-hot iron to his gums; here again Helena doesn't know whether to admire this or to think it weird (80). But she is openly admiring of the black woman who, the day after giving birth, starts the housework again, so as to 'feel lighter' – quite different from the whites, who are swaddled in excessive precautions (278). Thus, in the universe of hard work, or of African traditions, forms of wisdom and even of lunacy have

---

22   Bracketed phrase omitted from Bishop's translation. [*Tr.*]

been developed, with enough strength to survive and prosper. Seen as a whole, these are examples of a far-from-uniform process of redefinition of previous social relations, always involving some overcoming of the barriers created by slavery. Without idealizing it, we may note its evolutionary openness and the outline of a more integrated existence.

However, in the economically dynamic regions, Brazil's course was quite different. Once the euphoria of Abolition had passed, what actually happened was that the former slaves were abandoned and forced labour was replaced by semi-forced labour, preferably done by immigrants. The oligarchy renounced its rights of property in human beings (and shrugged off the attendant inconveniences, to say nothing of obligations) but not the prerogatives of social irresponsibility formed under the regime of slavery and intrinsic to its barbarity. Emancipation did not fulfil its historical promise of incorporating the blacks and the poor into contemporary society, nor can it be said that it civilized their social relationships, which changed without improving. The new urban chaos, as well as being modern in its way, was anything but integrated and renewed the terms of the old social divide. Within this picture, where are we to place Helena's world, whose humanity we have highlighted? This is and is not the same country. To what, then, can we attribute the easier social relations, with their element of reversibility, of lively mutual interest, the propensity to question, the moral concern in the face of indifference, which in the context really constituted progress, in the strong sense of the word? Is this just a peculiar case; or even, perhaps, just one more family-oriented idealization of Brazilian conditions?[23]

---

23   Readers of Monteiro Lobato's children's books will feel the affinity between Helena's Diamantina and Lobato's Sítio do Picapau Amarelo (Yellow Woodpecker Farm), our favourite idyllic place. Here, with hardly any changes, are the warm-hearted grandparents, the world of the cousins, the cult of pranks and practical jokes, the girls who have an answer for everything, the saintly black cook, and, above all, informality, the remedy no evils can resist.

Combined with Abolition, without which the rest would not be possible, the other reason for this progress must have been the economic decline of the area. This is an interesting paradox, one that illuminates the narrowness of the usual biases in favour of 'progress', which have no way of sensing real improvement in society. A social advance possibly encouraged by a decline in the economy is a thought-provoking combination. The improvements that arise in the space opened by the de-activation of the dominant enterprises – linked to world capitalist accumulation – are a living critique of those same enterprises and the order they consolidate, above all in ex-colonies, where the profit-making potential of a few export products helps to stabilize centuries-old kinds of barbarity. Elsewhere, that same order of things is still in place, demonstrating its primacy in other parts of the country – precisely the most prosperous ones – as well as in the international sphere. None of this, however, invalidates the problem: it simply relativizes the relativization itself, creating still greater complexity. However tangible they may be, the advances made by backward Diamantina, which make Helena's diary such a remarkable work, may have no future.

The decline of Minas Gerais, caused by the exhaustion of its gold and diamonds, is an academic specialism in its own right.[24] For our limited purposes, all we need to note is that in the professional literature its movement is described either as an involution or as a peculiar form of growth. In the first case, the emphasis is on the loss of the links to the world market of metals and precious stones, this accounting for the impoverishment and regression of a society that

---

24　Amilcar Martins Filho and Roberto B. Martins, 'Slavery in a Nonexport Economy: Nineteenth-Century Minas Gerais Revisited', *Hispanic American Historical Review* 63:3, 1983, 537–68. In the same issue, there are critical commentaries by Robert W. Slenes, Warren Dean, Stanley L. Engerman and Eugene Genovese. For the authors' reply, see 'Slavery in a Nonexport Economy: A Reply', *Hispanic American Historical Review* 64:1 (1984), 135–46. My thanks to Luiz Felipe de Alencastro and Fernando A. Novais for their help in this connection.

has lost almost all contact with civilization. In the second, the focus is on the reorganization and the particular kind of expansion of this same society, now focused inwards, towards local and regional markets, and growing with less inequality and greater responsiveness to the elementary necessities of the population. What for some is a step backward is for others an advance in civilization, though opinions on the subject are not necessarily the same in different sectors of society. Indirectly, this disagreement is a commentary on Brazil's alternatives and on the nature of the ideal society itself.

Much of the poetry of Helena's book belongs to this historical constellation. When the link to the world diamond market slackened, the economic collapse was immediate; however, the old order based on the overly simple aims of colonial exploitation persisted without its mainstay. In compensation, there arose in the political sphere a new and enlightened awareness of necessities at a regional level; that is, within and between its constituent parts.[25] Meanwhile, in the context of everyday life, the family framework of property ownership and economic enterprise came into the foreground, in experiments with a truly paternalist way of overcoming the anti-social character of the previous society. The separation between classes was qualified, and patriarchal authority itself, without the spur of infinite riches, became less distant. A certain level of de-specialization – or of family cooperation – allowed the social division of labour to function also as an enrichment of individual experience, and not just as a force for segregation and subjection. In the same way, the intricate connections between 'serious' production (for larger world markets), local business, the subsistence economy, the gathering of free materials in the countryside and housework began to favour a sense of the relativity of values, and a wider sense of reality, of which Helena gives numerous examples. Contact between these different spheres of life promoted realistic

---

25   José Moreira de Souza, *Cidade, momentos e processos: Serro e Diamantina na formação do Norte mineiro no século XIX*, São Paulo, 1993.

self-regulation of work done in common. The fetish of wealth lost its absolute value and opened up, for the imagination and for rational thought, the little piece of paradise that was actually available. These are obvious improvements in a human sense, and it is no exaggeration to call them disalienating. They fail to conform to the commonplace notion of progress only because this notion itself is open to criticism. The curious process of 'ruralization' of the town, to which Helena's intelligent love of the countryside is linked, can be seen in this perspective. We are, in fact, looking at a structural variant of Brazil's evolution, which here seems to be on the road to something better. This must be one of the reasons for the charm and interest of the book – and its potential use for idealizing arguments about the country's social structure. On the other hand, it remains true that the plenitude we are describing does not offset the relative backwardness, or the corresponding awareness of provinciality and lack of contact with the progress of the world, even of Rio de Janeiro, which is always very acute. The general appetite for novelty and money is great, and it is quite clear that the balance that has been achieved between the two is a half-accidental intermission, which will be ended at the first opportunity. Even here, the girl's diary yields nothing to kitsch or sentimentality.

Helena's situation, seen within the ensemble of social relations that compose it, has little exceptional about it: she is the poor cousin, the adored granddaughter, the restless, lively daughter, the dominant sister, the lazy schoolgirl. What is unusual is the girl's very open, complex response to these relations, whose degree of inner articulation is highlighted far beyond what we might expect. Her more critical, truthful presentation of everyday life answers to a high literary ideal, which requires nothing less than a superior viewpoint, tested in the context of *shared* forms and subjects, and with no recourse to the authority of artistic *specialization*. At one moment, the girl says that she is writing her diary at her father's suggestion, to preserve her memories for the future (*47*). But this

is not the tone of the diaries, in which she is always trying to identify something beyond the details of daily life that clarifies existence
and shows how to avoid the traps it lays; this is when, in her own
eyes, Helena has achieved something. She has no interest in noting
things just for the sake of it, recalling the past simply to recall it. It
is the activity of a young mind eager to observe and understand the
daily life of the family and the town that gives the diary's episodes
the tension of rationality, far superior to a simple chronicle of
provincial life.

In fact, the habitual topics of the Enlightenment are to the fore:
superstition and sanctimonious religiosity, the fanatical Italian
priest, airs of grandeur, the misdeeds and absurdities of absolute
power, the mania for sacrifice, lack of hygiene, misgovernment in
the town, education unsuited to local conditions, hypocrisy in the
nuns' school and so on. This identification of obscurantism, in a
provincial setting and coming from a child in the process of discovering the critical faculty inside herself, naturally has its own poetry.
The best writing, however, is in a less orthodox vein. From time to
time, Helena surpasses herself, extending the force of criticism to its
own findings, preferring the spirit to the letter, or better, recognizing the part frequently played by obscurantism in overcoming
obscurantism, observing how class repression and oppression are
part of the conduct of enlightened people. This marvellous twist
reveals that her attachment to progress is not automatic and shows
up the breach between reason and the advances of civilization.

Perhaps because she is a child, female and from a needy family,
and because she will not give up the fun she gets from the street,
Helena objects to the adult, masculine, wealthy and white notion of
progress. Like a social scientist, the girl explains that Uncle Conrado's
children get on better than her at school because a shopkeeper's
family has a more regular and organized life than a miner's. However,
she wouldn't swap one for the other because she also has an exact
notion of the cost in happiness of a sedentary life full of rules: 'I can't
stand Uncle Conrado's being so orderly and methodical, with a set

time for doing everything. It may work all right for my cousins' study-ing, but for everything else it makes me sick!' (49). What's more, the simple duty of sitting still, though indispensable to study, is a sacrifice for someone who likes to be out in the fresh air. Even the novelties of civilization, to which money gives access – ice cream, the telegraph or the little machine that generates electricity – interesting though they are, provide material for the iniquities of the rich relations, who use them to flabbergast and humiliate others. The social distancing and oppression that accompany the manifestations of progress do not escape her. Of course, she reacts above all against the paralysing forces of backwardness, like superstition, credulity, resignation and apathy; and sometimes this even includes the Church and the exist-ence of God. But it is not, then, that she loses her enthusiasm for religious festivals; their principal attraction is the way they bring classes together, and exclude no one, which for her is obviously a good thing. See, for example, the parlous state of the Ash Wednesday procession, which goes out into the streets with its ramshackle saints, the head of one attached to the body of another, since there aren't enough whole figures: 'I liked the procession very much but my father said it looked like a carnival, and my mother thought it was a bad sin of my father to say that' (17). With its three points of view and its echo of the several variants that *The Diary* happily includes, this sentence is a world in itself. As in other moments of a similar kind, with cloth dolls made any old how, extremely primitive theatrical shows, a pretty chamber pot used as a soup tureen or another featur-ing polite ways of hiding chicken droppings on the table, Helena finds a special charm in the resourceful imagination that can make do with poor or unsuitable material and yet so hold on to its integrity. There is a hint of provincial pride here, which has no reason to feel inferior, and of the life of the common people, with its superior kind of happiness.

In this case, the questioning, reasoning disposition associated with the Enlightenment participates in an atypical set of alliances, from which dependants and those without property are not excluded. The immediate cause must be Helena's *precocity*, which develops her critical sense and capacity for self-expression at an age when children still prefer the kitchen to the drawing room, servants to parents, the poor and the workers to the 'best' people and the social and racial mixture of games in the street to property and class distinction. There is nothing unique in these 'childish' preferences; but what is certainly unusual is her ability to express them in a polemical vein, without belittling them, exposing the injustice and sacrifice imposed by propertied reason, which also happens to be the order of the adults. It makes a difference that this critical sense emerges early, lending her intelligence its peculiar social drive. The result, at the level of literary prose, is a particular kind of enlightened attitude, free of automatic class alignments, opposed to old seigniorial absolutisms, critical of the social divisions brought about by civilized property and, above all, sympathetic to those who need protection, whose interests she recognizes and interprets, partly because she shares them – though this does not prevent her seeing the elements of the absurd, which in any case are also far from absent in the world of the rich.[26]

Helena's willingness to see things from the other side, and think about socially interlocking points of view, does not exhaust her rebelliousness. At times, this is also fed by a kind of self-questioning, which gives her inner strength to oppose the others as a group. In this context, the formative episode is the funeral of her paternal grandfather, an English doctor and distinguished citizen of the

---

26   To appreciate the effects of this distribution of emphasis, in which ideas based on the Enlightenment do not operate as class prejudice, we need only note that they do not allow the formation of the ideological opposition between civilization and barbarism, which in this period imposed a kind of stupidity on the acts, the thoughts and the prose of many of our illustrious compatriots. (The two most famous examples of it are the Argentine Domingo Faustino Sarmiento's *Facundo*, subtitled *Civilización y Barbarie* [1845; Mádrid, 9th ed., 2011], and, more relevant to the present turn-of-the-century context, the Brazilian Euclides da Cunha's *Os Sertões* [1902; New York, 2009].) [*Tr.*]

town, who cannot be buried in hallowed ground because he was a Protestant: 'They speak of it in Diamantina until today. When he was about to die the priests, the Sisters of Charity and even Senhor Bishop, who was very fond of him, argued with him to be baptized and confess so he could be buried in holy ground. He answered: "Any ground God made is holy"' (79). The question divided the family, as we see when Helena says 'Papa, if I hear you say one thing, and the girls and mama and everybody say another thing, it drives me crazy' (79). The inner certainty she reaches with great difficulty is that God will be just and that a good person can't be in hell, an enlightened – and foreign – idea which leads Helena to oppose the Catholicism of family, town and school, where, whenever there is a fight, her schoolfellows tell her that her grandfather is in 'the heaven for the English' (79). In His turn, the reformed God was not pure goodness either, judging by her father's advice: 'Tell them that it's where you're going, too, child, and that it's the heaven of the whites and not of the Africans' (79). This is the other side of strongly held principles that help one resist adversity as well as discredit one's adversaries.

The free examination of controversial matters and, above all, of established traditions and institutions defines Helena's intellectual personality, developing in her a clear feeling of superiority and distance in relation to her milieu but also the openness of mind that allows her to understand it. Even here, the surprise is in the nuance, for the girl thinks that people who are innocent of doubt are happier than her, and that it would be better to be like them. In spite of this toss of the head, the realistic notion that thinking for oneself, as well as indicating superiority, is a painful effort is plain enough. The subtleties of these pros and cons are great, especially in the moving case of the mother, with her impulsiveness and great capacity for devotion, which Helena at bottom admires but which she believes cannot be separated from her unlimited religiosity. The comings and goings of Helena's self-examination often lead to barefaced rationalization, lending petty thefts and other dishonesties the approval of her conscience. Thus, the confrontation of Protestantism and Catholicism has unforeseen consequences. One nice case of balance, which also gives pause for thought, because of the mental reservations it implies, concerns the religious festivals, which fill the girl with happiness – which is not to say that she overlooks the element of superstition and the dubious economics of almsgiving.[27] This tendency is fulfilled in the moments when Helena's impartial thinking and pleasure in telling stories make her forget family decorum and her own interests, when the diarist does not exempt those dearest to her, or even herself, from the negative conclusions that apply to others and so reaches a kind of youthful probity, or the high-mindedness of criticism without acrimony.

The conscientious, good-natured father, who does nothing wrong, naturally does not fit in with the town. The same goes for the English aunts, who earn their own livings, cultivate personal discipline in everything they do and keep a strict watch over their expenditure, as well as recommending readings to strengthen character. Even here, Helena learns judiciously, without losing sight of circumstances. After listening to a lecture on the wastefulness of the hired servants, and the right manners when being served at table, the girl observes that, since she hasn't a maid to serve her and it's her that clears the table, this advice is pointless (14). Even her own conscience, which provides the necessary distance for independent

---

27 'Without wishing to overestimate a conflict which, to tell the truth, is only there in outline, we can attribute part of the protagonist's great psychological versatility to the echoes of a British, Protestant, liberal education, resounding in a Catholic, Iberian atmosphere, which has only just emerged from a slave regime. Colouring the emotional independence of youth, this case of the girl with auburn hair who, although she is completely identified with the milieu of people darker-skinned than herself, and is the only one who knows it and loves it, doesn't hesitate to criticize it with notable precision and wit, has a strong sociological flavour to it. This lucidity transposes the intimate coexistence of two divergent cultural worlds, who look at and judge one another inside a self whose harmony is itself the product of the balance between its contradictions.' Eulálio, 'Livro que nasceu clássico', xiii.

moral discussion, serves above all as a space in which she tries to find herself and so understand the proportions of diplomacy and confrontation necessary when affirming her own tastes and satisfying her own will, in opposition to Catholic mortification. Maybe it is an adaptation of Protestantism, changed into a very active but not-too-repressive conscience, more focused on questions of desire than morality. Always guided by a questioning instinct – or a habit of intelligence – the girl rejects what she hears or sees and immediately moves to look at the reverse side of things, the unnoticed, the relational, even the taboo, thereby widening the horizon and escaping from the prison of individual and class interests. The victory over social compartmentalization also happens inside her, through her apprehension of the conflictual nature, social in the last analysis, of the very difficulty of understanding itself.

Although commented on in the family, Helena's intelligence is not obvious to the girl herself, and it makes her uneasy. After three days at the Normal School,[28] this worry produces a passage notable for its rapid fluctuations of self-belief. A paraphrase, making some things more explicit, might go something like this: the others – her grandmother, father, aunt and Joaquininha, her primary school teacher – think Helena is intelligent. She herself, in humility or distress, and anyway, with a certain humorous detachment, thinks they may be deluded – which however puts the adults' judgement in question, and in a flash turns her inferiority into superiority. What she really is quite sure of, however (superiority), in opposition to her own and other people's notions (inferiority), is that she doesn't like to sit and study (inferiority? superiority? – it depends on your point of view). As a consequence, she'll be a bad pupil, even if she's intelligent. Or will she be a good pupil without studying? In either case, someone will be wrong, and in any event, she prefers them to

---

28   Bishop: 'The "Normal School", for training grade-school teachers. Equivalent to high school in the United States', 8. [*Tr.*]

think she's intelligent, even if she isn't, rather than to think she's stupid, 'which is what I'm afraid they're going to say when they see I'm not going to be what they hope for, in Normal School' (9). Here is her deepest worry. However, the reaction is not long in coming, and soon the girl is boasting of how easy it is for her to remember things by heart (superiority), and so, even if she doesn't understand a thing (inferiority), she'll know how to hoodwink everyone (superiority? inferiority?). But what's to be done about subjects that can't be learned by heart? After all this toing and froing, her childish conclusion is touching: 'I'm going to go to bed and ask Our Lady to help me study and make me more intelligent, so I won't disappoint my father, grandma and Aunt Madge' (9).

These twists and turns bring Helena's insecurity to the surface, but they also disclose the disputed and uncertain nature of definitions of intelligence, subjected as they are to a kind of tug of war between different interests, which more or less reveal the shape of the social conflict governing these matters. Thus, each one creates the perspective that suits them best: the enlightened adults' opinions, the family members' vanity and the new authority of the Normal School; the child's resistance to discipline and study and her anxious desire to live up to what they expect of her; the distinction between understanding and memorizing, in which the former is superior from a progressive point of view; the prospect of appearing in a good light while hoodwinking everyone; and the final recourse to Our Lady – all this, not to mention the abyss between those who think about these things and those who do not. And yet in spite of the bumpy terrain, this passage does not go beyond conventional limits: the focus is more on the girl's fear of failure than on questioning the value of study or the importance that relatives and hangers-on accord it.

Already in the next entry, thanks to one of those near-parallelisms that give the book its density and resonance, the same topic appears in a less decorous and more hidden form – but hidden by whom?

This time the controversy surrounds porridge and cucumbers.[29] To start off, Helena protests: 'There are so many things you can make with *fubá*: couscous, corn bread, doughnuts, cakes, and no one wants to make anything but porridge' (*12*). 'No one' is the adults, who want everything to stay the same, and are in opposition to the girl's varied, experimental appetites, which they try to repress. In their own sphere, these desires are a form of mobility and mental openness. Is it going too far to compare this to the dislike of immobility (the seated, studying girl) in the previous entry, of which it might be a less inhibited form? And might the adults' praise for Helena's intelligence itself have something to do with their fixed preference for porridge? If this is so, then there is no point in pushing oneself to deserve the praise, and real intelligence may have nothing to do with studying. What is more, Helena at another moment observes that her grandmother is intelligent even though until a short while ago she didn't know how to read (89). She also notes that Seu Pitanga,[30] though very ignorant, is 'clever, and funny when he's clever', and 'has an eagle's eye' for life (*255*). These are rather unconventional conclusions, which take the side of the real substance of things, against official, prestigious definitions. There is nothing more instructive than the difference between a thing and its name, when the former is understood in its content and social development, as we see in the same passage about porridge and cucumbers, when a neighbour, Siá Ritinha[31] – another 'eagle' – spends an evening telling stories of people who got ill from eating cucumbers: '"Dona Carolina, you mark my words. The cucumber

---

29 'Porridge' is Bishop's translation. The Portuguese word is *fubá*, which literally means 'cornflour', which is mixed with water to make *angu*, a kind of porridge. [*Tr.*]
30 Here, the *seu*, in contrast to the use commented on above (n. 14), is a familiar, semi-respectful way of referring to a local character. A *pitanga* is literally a small red fruit, also known as a 'Brazil cherry'. [*Tr.*]
31 *Siá*, though less common, is similar in meaning and connotation to the *seu* in *Seu Pitanga*. [*Tr.*]

is so poisonous that if it so much as touches the hem of your skirt, it's dangerous'" (9). The object of this intervention, soon worked out, is to curry favour with Helena's mother and support her in her struggle to make her daughter lose her taste for eating cucumbers with salt in the morning and go back to porridge. An alliance has been sealed by the right-thinking, spoilsport adults against the fancy and enjoyment of others. If Helena likes cucumbers, why this objection to them? But the neighbour is poor, owes the Morleys favours and needs their protection, so that her teachings about cucumbers not only are not disinterested, they're a shameless service rendered to Dona Carolina, to the detriment of the happiness of the more vulnerable member of the family, with the added advantage of compensating for the humiliations of vassalage by stirring it a bit. Besides, Siá Rita has the reputation of being a chicken thief, something which Dona Carolina, at the moment she gets her support, conveniently forgets – unlike her daughter, who understands all the clientelistic jockeying on which the imposition of a certain diet and, by extension, maternal authority itself, depend.

Simplicity does not exclude subtlety, and these episodes teach us a great deal, if we see their latent similarity, which allows us to use one anecdote to see deeper into another. Thus, in the defence of her taste for cucumbers in the morning, or for less common uses of *fubá*, Helena uncovers the obtuse, blinkered side of those responsible for order, who like to prohibit, even when the prohibition seems to make no sense. In its way, it produces the didactic effect of Brechtian estrangement, revealing in detail the authoritarian substratum of the very Brazilian alliances between the cultured classes and *agregados* and their many hidden dimensions, with which aspirations to freedom are bound to conflict, even when the subject is only cucumbers. And what if the approval surrounding school, study and intelligence were no different, in substance, to that which imposes porridge?

4

At a certain point it becomes clear that the family cannot manage Helena any more. She decides, on her own, in consultation with her friends and against the will of her elders, that she's not going to the nuns' boarding school. It is a good example of her character, at once individualistic, sociable and rebellious. The extent of the disagreements cannot be easily divined, and the reader suspects that the girl's independence of mind, with its practical effects, has not just excited admiration. Over the course of the book, we witness the transformation of the observing, critical child into the bright, astute young girl, who resolves everything in her own head, where she decides what to do, for good or ill. The atmosphere of simple family life hides the exceptional nature of this second character, who constitutes a historical novelty. One sign of this strangeness is perhaps Helena's own surprise at the unorthodox suggestions of her own mind. 'In my imagination, I'm an only child',[32] she notes, to explain the profitable use she has made of her sister's money (54). At another moment, ashamed at her 'uniform all faded, and mended at the elbows' (171), Helena prays to Our Lady, who inspires in her the idea of stealing a brooch from her mother to raise money to buy a new uniform: 'Sometimes I'm amazed to see how intelligent I am about certain things. But it was all Our Lady. She saw I needed a dress and a uniform at the same time, and inspired it directly. The dress was made up entirely out of my head, without seeing the fashion plate. How could I have such a good idea!' (174). In a less scandalous vein, Helena distances herself from her mother's self-sacrifice: 'Mama's sorry for me because she says I'm never going to be happy in life as long as I keep wanting to enjoy everything; life is made up of suffering. But I'm not going to be so foolish as to make

---

32 'In my imagination, I'm an only child': ibid., 54: Bishop's translation is possible; but the sentence – in the original, 'Na imaginação sou sozinha na família' – can also mean 'As far as imagination goes, I'm unique in the family'. [*Tr.*]

such a wonderful life a life of suffering' (32). A little earlier, a propos of fasting on Good Friday, she says with remarkable honesty: 'I'm very unhappy about making sacrifices. I don't like to make sacrifices' (22). And again, near the end, comes this argument: '"Daughter, do you think the world is coming to an end? That's what I think when I see you so anxious to amuse yourself. You're just beginning life, daughter. Don't be so greedy about it . . . Anything that isn't natural is scandalous, my child" . . . I let mama speak until the end. Then I said, "Do you know why it is you're so nervous for no reason at all, mama? It's because instead of staying there watching us play and dance, you came home and shut yourself up in this dreary house, and worked all day long, and you should get the idea out of your head that life is made up of suffering . . . Think about it and tell me" ' (268).

As the episodes succeed one another, Helena's deliberate and forceful disposition to enjoy life enters into conflict not only with Christian abstinence, the precedence of family interests, provincial limitations and the resignation of the poor but also with the new, utilitarian civilization of the bourgeoisie. The aura of the book is conditioned by the unexpected character of this conflict zone, partly to do with adolescence and partly with the uncertainty of the historical moment and the perspectives it opened up. But Helena is far from being a Romantic heroine radically opposed to her world, and there is no one more family-oriented, impregnated with religion, savvy about social differences and aware of the advantages of an ordered household than she is. In this sense, her case is not one of clashes in which a new rationale aims to suppress others, and it would be better to speak of a conquest of space or of an enlightened adjustment within the family. Her unexpected angles and acute formulations owe a great deal to this intimacy with the opposing camp, toned by full awareness of the prevailing conditions and the desire not to pass up anything good or sacrifice oneself to principles for nothing. In order to rebel against obstacles in one area, Helena invokes the values of another, which in turn become obstacles themselves, and so on until the circle is complete. So, at the end of a certain number of episodes, we know not only what meanings the social order takes on for a young girl who has no desire to be silly; we have also witnessed the clash of several important views within society, which in this process become more specifically defined. It is no exaggeration to say that we are in the presence of the rich and differentiated many-sidedness that distinguishes the realist novel.

The diary's procession of anecdotes takes apart and shows off, in all its aspects, Helena's appetite for the good things of life, from the brilliant and liberating to the conformist and questionable. And rendered in the same youthful tone, her materialist good sense and the aptness of her formulations gradually win recognition, and even give her a kind of authority within the family. So much so that at a certain moment the grandmother says – though it is hard to understand exactly what she is thinking of – that Helena will manage to free her parents from the economic difficulty they live in. The fact is that the girl gives guidance to her mother, observes that the family would not suffer hardship if her grandmother looked after her money better, explains that the nuns' school will put an end to Luisinha's happiness, has proposals for the reorganization of work in the household and opinions about street lighting and the postal system, points out how useless it is to drill La Fontaine into the heads of *mineiro* schoolgirls and so on. She is brash, no doubt, but her talent for administration and her superior realism, which, moreover, accord with the town's aspirations to progress, are obvious. When the mother criticizes her daughter and reminds her that in the olden days modesty brought girls a reputation and attracted offers of marriage, Helena replies in terms that could not be bettered: "'You were homebodies because you lived in Lomba [i.e., in a mining settlement, far from civilization]. And besides, the reputation was the pot of diamonds that grandpa found. Homebody – doesn't the Senhora see that nobody could have that reputation? How? If nobody saw you?" (197). Here, we are a long way from the child at the beginning, who when she was low thought of herself as 'the most miserable, the skinniest, the stupidest of them all . . . inferior in everything' (156), to which her grandmother, to console her, would reply that she was 'the best girl in Diamantina' (*115*). Now Helena has discovered that she is pretty and special, and in fact 'everyone loves her'; she is the teacher's pet. Her schoolmates complain that 'everything's different' for her (267), while the teachers comment on her exams and find them amusing, whether because of her impudence when she cheats, the cheek of her answers, her exceptional memory or just because of the figure she cuts overall, which takes on a triumphant aspect; all of this at the expense of the nonconformism that impelled her to find meaning and taste, where order – that is to say, money and the 'best families' – failed to see them. In another register, there is a good illustration of the seduction exercised by Helena's rough-and-ready ways, when, arriving home one rainy day she 'came in the door shaking [her] legs and throwing the boots off in the hall'. The boy who accidentally witnesses this scene says to his sister that 'he knows he's going to be a bachelor, because he'll only marry a girl who'll do things like that and he knows he won't find one' (168). Who would think of this exact erotic image in the poor, supposedly naïve atmosphere of a provincial town?

The relationship between Helena and her grandmother is delightful but also complicated, and tests both of them. On one side is the rich family matriarch, worshipped by all; on the other, the poor child, exceptional and with a difficult temperament, whose cousins' wealth sticks in her throat. At the beginning, the focus is on Dona Teodora's worries, concerned as she is about a girl from a home that does not always have food on the table or money for necessities. Well-defined personal preferences are antipathetic in this setting, seen as caprice and injustice or as a restraint placed on the normal course of things. For her part, the granddaughter defends this partiality by all kinds of means, facing down the jealousy of cousins, aunts and uncles. Her weapons go from enlightened personal understanding – which is mutual – to bursts of tears and ingeniously conducted manoeuvrings. The economic basis of the dispute, in which the matriarch's fortune is at stake, is no secret to anyone. It revolves round the controversial possibility of the old lady making discriminations among her heirs, some of whom are rich and some poor. Suspicious vigilance is in the natural order of things, to the point where the grandmother says: '"Carolina, I'll really have to die to make things better for you, daughter." She used to talk like that because she couldn't give us money while she was alive because Uncle Geraldo took care of her fortune and he wouldn't let her' (280). As a humane response – understanding, acknowledging and at the same time rising above a social order – this would be hard to outdo . . . The commentary, inevitably brought on by life itself, comes in the fight that the grandmother's death causes among her children. As for her manoeuvres, we may instance how Helena manipulates her stomach ache, her dislike of the purgative castor oil and Dona Teodora's alarm, so she can get a dress in exchange. 'Pretty clever!' say the aunts, turning their backs.[33] But even here, where we might expect some kind of sentimentality, her jottings resist idealization. The close, diligently cultivated ties with her grandmother, whom she holds so dear, weigh on her like a real sacrifice, which, as she explicitly says, she would like to escape. The girl has a notion, too, of the scandalous favouritism of which she is the object (according to her schoolmates, 'Your grandmother looks more like your boyfriend'[*209*]) to the point where she takes steps to avoid it. Towards the end, when the preference is well established, Helena diplomatically tries not to go to the *chácara* with her cousins to avoid occasions for envy and complaint. Thus, her individual inclination at one moment coincides with self-interested calculation, to the detriment of her loyalties; while at another it does not; and at yet another it exists alone in its own right. Something similar is true of other elements in play. Each

---

33   Bishop here adds a note: 'Literally: "She's an eagle!"' (a genius).' [*Tr.*]

alliance and each conflict constitutes a substantive problem, welcome or troublesome according to whether it is overcome easily or not.

5

Readers of *Dom Casmurro* will – I hope – have recognized the outlines of Capitu's situation. Here is the poor and intelligent girl, with advanced ideas, who is manoeuvring to make herself the favourite of the clan's matriarch amid the rivalry of relatives and dependants, some of whom have nothing of their own, in an atmosphere composed of the inheritance of slavery, Catholic decorum and aspirations to progress. There are similarities in the basic social coordinates of the two books: in the practical and moral content of the constraints within which a nascent individualism pays tribute to the old order, in the brilliant intellectual character of the young girls and even sometimes in the tone. For instance, when Helena 'gets so mad and hates [Chininha] so much' for 'roll[ing] up her eyes at Our Lady', 'pretending to be a saint all the time just to please grandma', we are not far from the 'furious words' – 'The sanctimonious so-and-so! Always at the altar rail! Never away from mass!'[34] – which Capitu's future mother-in-law provokes in her. The suggestive parallels between the books can be multiplied at will, and there are amusing things to discover in the haughty, meddling subservience that Siá Ritinha shares with José Dias, the *agregado*. At the level of the literary whole, there is also the effect of *constant variation* in both, produced by the many anecdotes that have repeated elements. Marked by Romantic *costumbrismo*,[35] both bring into play a simple but also multidimensional view of relations, which is an achievement in itself, involving as it does kinship and

---

34   See ch. 4, n. 16, p. 74 [*Tr.*]
35   The vogue in literature in Spanish and Portuguese during the Romantic period for the description of local customs, usually seen as picturesque. [*Tr.*]

protection, poverty, money and work, along with the parallel circulation of hangers-on and tittle-tattle; the routines of housework; the
barbs inspired by social hierarchy; the lax, oppressive atmosphere
of Catholicism and religious festivals in town and city; and so on.

But what is the point of juxtaposing the loose jottings of the girl
from Diamantina with what is possibly the most refined and
composed novel in Brazilian literature? Why compare one style of
writing 'with no artistic intention' and another in which artistic
calculation and faith in the efficacy of the form reach an exceptional
intensity? There can be no question of equating the two works, of
transforming *The Diary of 'Helena Morley'* into a novel or viewing
Dom Casmurro as a collection of historical vignettes. With this
proviso, however, the common universe, which does exist, allows
for sensible reflection on the relation between the two kinds of
prose, which is more interesting and complex than critics may think.
We can say that the two books disclose, in differing but comparable
keys, the peculiar universe of social positions and relations that
could be called the matter of Brazil and which has developed in
ways that still have relevance for us today.

Having insisted on the difference between the two books, we can
begin to relativize it. We have already suggested that the novels of
Machado's first phase are no match for Helena Morley's diary in
respect of literary quality. The problematic substance of the social
matrix they share exists with more variety and spirit in the schoolgirl's compositions. In other words, literary quality can exist – for
us, a hundred years later – where it was not planned and can be
missing when even it has been pursued with deliberation and determination. We are not imagining, on the other hand, that Helena has
not cultivated an ingenious way with narrative, a sense of humour,
of the mot juste, as well as an understanding of conflicting interests.
However, these – undeniable – formal refinements were developed
in a non-artistic context, such as an enjoyable conversation, a
school composition or a diary to be read *en famille*, close to the
demands of daily experience and far from (but not entirely outside)

the literary system and its rules. In sum, the book is an example of aesthetic accomplishment detached from artistic specialization. This is something very different from what happened with Machado de Assis in his first novels, when he deliberately broke with fashionable liberal-Romantic illusions and their corresponding European narrative models. In opposition to these prestigious templates, which he saw as not fitting the country, and with the clear purpose of putting Brazilian fiction on a more realistic path, Machado tried out non-canonical plots driven by the practical moral dilemmas of a modern individual entangled in clientelistic relationships or even in direct personal subjugation. The change, which later on would be decisively fruitful, at this stage approached – with a struggle and without much artistic success – the same mix of subjects that was Helena Morley's point of departure. These are normal paradoxes of the history of art, which in this case show that the elaboration of a form happens as much outside the literary field as within it, converging with it or not. And in this dialectic of literature and society, everything depends on the total context: proximity to daily life can favour conformism, but it can also have a critical effect, just as ruptures can open up new perspectives or create other orders of conformity. This is what happened in the case of Machado's early novels, whose turn towards the Brazilian social context – a very considerable achievement – was accompanied by an edifying tone that today excludes them from the list of books that are still alive; Machado would have to free himself of this tone to become a great writer.

But let us return to the comparison with *Dom Casmurro*. Both the fictional character Capitu and the real-life girl Helena are figures who stand out; they are the sort who will make good marriages, with the attendant rewards, though Helena hardly touches on the theme. The Morleys achieve economic security at the end of the book, when the father starts work for an English company; this puts an end to the uncertainties of mining on his own account, and releases him from the position of poor relation.

Without further explanation, Helena attributes the change to the protection of her grandmother, who by that time is already in heaven. In any case, they are on the way up: 'We shan't suffer for the lack of necessities any longer, thank God' (281). Capitu's early initial trajectory, from poor neighbour to Dr. Santiago's wife, also leads upwards. In both cases, the poetic force of the climb is linked to the correction of a 'mistake of nature' that allowed talented girls to be born with few means at their disposal.[36] Since the correction of the 'injustice' is owing in great part to the intelligence and initiative of the interested parties themselves, who have succeeded in finding the right protection, we are left with the impression of a society that is unequal but flexible, open to the demands of merit. Confirming the impression of fluidity, Helena and Capitu make no bones about the realities of poverty but do not lose their sympathy for the poor; what is more, this provides them with their insight into the falsity of the airs of class superiority. Thus, their upward passage seems to be representative of a change for the better, a general tendency towards civilization, in which for good or ill – and sometimes as a matter of sheer luck – the propertied classes show themselves capable of recognizing and raising up the gifted poor, who in their turn, having a less inhuman view of social inequality, will hopefully widen the process, which will thus benefit from the paternal enlightenment of the rich and the gratitude of the poor. Helena's diary and the first part of Machado's novel share this optimistic notion of the workings of co-optation and chance.

The first part but not the second, for the greater achievement of *Dom Casmurro* has to do with the opposite conviction, with the certainty of the arbitrary and destructive vocation of paternalist

---

36   The expression 'mistake of nature', slippery in its own right, lies at the heart of the novels of Machado's first phase, and it can be read in that context in a cynical or a providentialist key. See Machado de Assis, *A mão e a luva*, Rio de Janeiro, ch. 9.

protection, which is far from being providential or enlightened and to whose polemical demolition the novel, without ever speaking directly, dedicates the best part of its *formal* ingenuity. To conceive of the similarities and differences between the books, and the intricate design of Machado's experiment, it is enough to imagine Helena's life being recounted, like for like, by an obscurantist cousin with money and superior airs. Half-shocked and half-attracted by the boldness of his poor relation, and anxious to hide the confusion of his own feelings, this second Bentinho would lend an incriminating – as well as emotionally involved – air to his unforgettable memories. Though centred on the disturbing girl, his writing would convey the unsettling of the patriarchal presumptions and prejudices of a rich cousin both by her and by his own reaction. Likewise, there is no great difficulty in speaking about Capitu in Helena's terms: the former could well arise out of the latter's situation, and this indicates their interchangeable nature and the universe they have in common. On the other hand, the change brought about by our Casmurro-esque change of focus affects the whole, since in *The Diary of 'Helena Morley'*, the sympathy, the initiative and, above all, the analytic thrust are on the side of the disadvantaged, against oppression and inequality and the 'idiotic' uncles, aunts and cousins, as indeed also happens in the first part of the novel, with its truly Morleyesque charm. We can say then that the disconcerting strategy of the author of *Dom Casmurro* consisted in inverting, with an obliquely realist aim, the so-called modernizing strategy of social representation. Instead of making Brazilian property owners, with their aura of privilege, impunity and ideological rationalization, look at themselves through their dependants' aspirations for progress, rights and equality – for civilization, that is – Machado, as it were, handed them the mirror. And in fact, seen from the self-justificatory angle of an oligarchy jealous of its own authority and confident that its dependants are laden with favours, the claims made by such people, however timid, can only look like so much ingratitude and meanness.

In other words, Machado chose the cunning option of claiming the sincere first-person singular for a singularly retrograde personage, who meditates, gravely and poetically, on the lifelong exile he has imposed on his forward-looking wife with her humble origins, whom he accuses of adultery. As is natural, or almost natural, we hurriedly assent to the thoughts of an important person, still more since he is the narrator, whose impartiality and understanding of situations flatter the reader and act as an a priori in the novel's artifice. Thus, shielded by the reputation of the refined classes and by the credit owing to belles-lettres, the narrative function comes down into the arena and gives scandalously illegitimate cover, using the most effective means a cultivated man could dispose of, to the 'wrong' side of the conflict. To complete the confusion, the upper-class and, so to speak, anti-romantic polarization of the perspective turns the book's horizons, and their vanishing points, upside down, destroying with them any hope of a way forward; instead of setbacks and advances on the road to freedom, we witness the *effrontery* of this same freedom, followed by its just punishment.

As everyone knows, jealousy clouds Dr Bento Santiago's judgement from time to time. His memories of Capitu express, as well as his troubled feelings, the fantasies of the patriarch, the old-fashioned property owner, the father who thinks his son looks like someone else, of the husband who is less intelligent than his wife and prefers his mother, who really is a saint – all this dressed up in a backward-looking kind of poetry. The transformation of these regressive emotions into a model of literary elegance widely accepted in Brazil was one of Machado's greatest acts of sarcasm. That said, what is the purpose of this subtle malice? Why give the last word – or the appearance of the last word – to an authoritarian, disturbed point of view? Why make its confused pulsation the organizing principle of the story? There is a chess player's ingenuity in this set-up, which delegates the initiative, the angle of observation, the prestige of a refined sensibility and an axiomatic

moral creditworthiness to the very character whose inner movements and intellectual procedures are the ones to be investigated,
with the indirect intention of exposing the ignominy and the disastrous dynamics of his class.

This masterly solution, which set up a new endgame involving
the best-known figures of Brazilian society, is admirable for its
novelty and its difficulty. This is clearest when looked at from
inside the pattern of power and culture that allows it to exist, and
whose unacceptable face it reveals. The example helps us to understand what the invention of the plot and of the narrative situation
consists in, in a great novel of realist inspiration. Let us suppose that
the writer, his eyes fixed on the small world shared by *Dom Casmurro*
and *The Diary of 'Helena Morley'*, was also reflecting on the direction of Brazilian history. Did integration and reconciliation under
the aegis of property-owning families or the healing of the wounds
left by the colonial order and by slavery really happen? What was
the artist's duty, once he had perhaps concluded that the property-
owning class would not be forced to opt for civilization, much less
opt for it of their own accord, even though they might be family-
oriented and adepts of progress? Putting it another way, when the
novelist understood that Brazil's 'reputable' classes would not
loosen their grip on their unfair prerogatives, the corollaries of
slavery, which, when slavery was abolished, were left intact, it was
his role to imagine narrative situations equal to this, and able to
develop the logic of this new state of affairs, difficult to face as it
would be, and quite thankless. By giving Dom Casmurro the 'final'
word, specious and cultivated at the same time, when he had already
given him the power of unilateral decision, Machado was setting up
a deliberately unbalanced plot pattern, opposed to justice in general,
and in particular to poetic justice, with an intolerable class bias –
and imitating the course of history. After the opening situation, in
which the relationship between dependants and owners had seemed
unequal but remediable, warm-hearted and open to change comes
the second and final one, in which property disclaims all

responsibility and brands the opening situation as itself an illusion. The qualities developed by the poor in the effort to educate themselves and civilize their protectors, who should have civilized them – a process whose many implications are evidenced in the figure of Capitu, in Helena's world and in Machado's own career – are in vain, according to this view. There is no need to comment on the implications, at a national level, of this dramaturgic invention. And we may add that this fusion of archaic patriarchal traits with aspects of fin de siècle decadentism make Dr Santiago a representative not only of Brazilian backwardness but also of the progress of the West; it reminds us of how, in the contemporary world, modern appearances are quite compatible with the persistence of the substrate of barbarism.

6

What do the careers of Capitu and Helena have to say about one another? Helena's, which is made up of triumphs in which her intelligence plays a part, reminds us of what happens in the idyllic part of *Dom Casmurro*, in which Bento's clear-sighted sweetheart has the initiative and achieves her aims, managing to work her way round the obstacles of the old Brazil. The other half of the novel, twisted and sui generis, does not follow the parallel. Now, the active role passes to the 'casmurro', that is, to Bento the husband and proprietor, inflamed with jealousy as he is. Capitu, who had directed her friend in his resistance to the obscurantism of the family, social prejudice and his own confusions will now be forced to renounce the liberties and equalities she thought she had won. Just when it seemed to be a dead letter, the universe of patriarchal dominance, reeking of incense, is back, dressed up in the new clothes of the belle époque but with the same authoritarianism. The second half of the novel, gloomily destructive, corrects the optimism of the first, and in the light of this, the looser version of the similar relationships which we have seen in Helena Morley's Diamantina comes to look, to a certain extent, simplistic or unreal. Thus, it is as if the biographical curve traced out by Capitu includes and calls into question that of Helena, which it repeats for a limited stretch; her prospects are denied, however, by the later development. In analogous fashion, the Brazilian relationships and the subtleties and solutions that correspond to them are very similar in the two books but with a difference of tone. In *Dom Casmurro*, the accent falls on the precedence of property and its ghosts, which are first questioned and then reaffirmed with arbitrary fury. They block and stifle the dependants' desire for autonomy, producing the uniquely crazed atmosphere of a 'restoration'. Even here, the comparatively open world of *The Diary of 'Helena Morley'* has its equivalent within *Dom Casmurro*, and one with a decisive structural role, what is more, for it functions as the illusion to be destroyed.

The raw material the two books have in common is made up of observations and anecdotes about Brazilian life seen in a 'picturesque' light, caught between patriarchalism and urbanity, to which the girls' critical, undefeated point of view gives its special charm. These are materials of limited scope but with a mutual attunement that gives evidence of a powerful, objective subterranean organization, independent of authorial intentions, particularly in Helena Morley's diary.

Of course, in Machado's work the observations are sewn together by the thread of the contingent, logical and properly fictional plot, which invents incidents and develops their implications, always in line with the narrative situation and the class relations embedded in it, which is the secret structure underlying the novel's complexities. The plot, in this case, functions as a true instrument of exploration, made to measure for the material it reveals, and with which it has a structural relationship, in which the agent of revelation is in its turn revealed. Reflected in the mirror of Bento's intense suspicions (and reflecting them), everyday Brazilian informality, so engaging and full of promise and in which from time to time the hopes for the patriarchal regime's self-reformation are founded, simply ensures that in the moment of truth, the weaker side is defenceless. One example of the treacherous but functional operation of the story is its profusion of coincidences and likenesses, so indispensable to Dr Santiago's jealousies. This would be worthy of the best sub-Romanticism were it not that these coincidences are rigorously balanced to cancel each other out, allowing the reader to glimpse the novelist's scepticism and along with it, behind the emotional tumult, the persistence of the same social blockage and the same correlation of forces that were there at the beginning. On the other hand, it allows full and self-compromising expression of the discomfort the paterfamilias feels at the thought of the rights of others. The fictional necessity of the outcome is proportionate with the general class features that compose the negative figure of the narrator, constructed with scientific care by Machado, who understandably wanted to outdo his naturalist rivals in this field. Here, ironically disguised as a nostalgic memoir, was *a modern explanation* of Brazilian backwardness.

In its way, the unhealthy atmosphere in which *Dom Casmurro* ends allows us see something in the nature of a historical conclusion. Though the explicit context is that of private life, the traces of a more general meaning within it extend the reach of the anecdotes and the denouement, and of our way of thinking about them. We have seen that the narrative situation dramatizes a Pyrrhic victory, which has a class character, a Brazilian resonance and a contemporary twist. The combination of forces it transposes to the level of the form is confirmed in the internal logic of the plot, which develops it or reveals its authoritarian secret, discarding as less substantial, artistically speaking, the more democratic and equitable outcome. In this way, the novelistic imagination concentrates and foregrounds an aspect of things that remains diffuse in *The Diary of 'Helena Morley'*, where the writing looks for justification to the precision and intelligence of its observations. No one will be surprised if we say that in *Dom Casmurro* the material common to the two works is composed in a superior way, one that allows us to see more and goes further.

However, anyone reading the young girl's exercises with the novel in mind may have the opposite surprise, realizing that much of what *Dom Casmurro* elaborates in a more subtle, profound way is also to be found in Helena's book, in an occasional form but still rich and complex. An example might be the incessant denigration of the girl by her uncles, aunts and cousins, who want to supplant her in the grandmother's preferences. These religious zealots insist that Helena's dedication is self-interested and insincere, and make her independence look like disrespect for religion and a moral defect. All very like the murmurings destined to prejudice Capitu's standing with regard to Dona Glória, or the methodical insinuations with which Casmurro tries to bring his sweetheart down in the eyes of his public, describing the best features of modern intelligence in pejorative terms, inspired by patriarchal suspicion. On the opposite side, Helena is at her best when she demands her right to be herself and reproves her detractors' hypocrisy in the same combative, enlightened spirit that gives Capitu her dignity – and perhaps gives her readers their dignity too, for it is only by striking out in a critical spirit that we can free ourselves from the tendentious conversation Dr Santiago wishes to engage us in. Thus, the struggle between positive or negative characterizations of one's own conduct and that of others, responding to defined social interests, is in the order of things; and Helena too practises the form of sarcasm that consists in adopting the adversaries' words and point of view to reveal their faults, in the manner Machado de Assis took to its furthest limit in the construction of *Dom Casmurro*.

Capitu's story, which has an unhappy ending, is no more likely than Helena's, which ends well. On the contrary, in fact, because it is hard to believe in the drastic turn in Capitu's fortunes. Yet the difference points up the rigorous, non-trivial element in the story-telling of the great novelist. When Helena (like Capitu in favourable times) uses her intelligence to fight against stupidity, we are the delighted witnesses to the victory of the Enlightenment, and of the defeat of forces that no longer have a raison d'être, in particular those characteristic of the backwardness of the ex-colony. However, though her constant reflections highlight the wider relevance of the girl's manoeuvres, the obstacles that are overcome do not go away: they remain, waiting for their next victim. From the collective point of view, there is more reality in them than in the triumph of the occasional lucky individual. Thus, when at a certain point the novelist becomes convinced that Brazilian society will not take the much-awaited step forward, his opinion of movement between classes also changes. This upward movement is not the harbinger of a general progress and must be understood in the light of its cost in unsatisfactory compromises, or, as in Capitu's case, in complete disaster. The demand for social truth – as opposed to the Romantic impulse of an isolated adventure – made the novelist conceive of the destiny of a poor person with merits and potential who is defeated by the common enemy, that is, by the arbitrary conduct of her 'betters', as *representative*. In contrast with Helena, Capitu refers us to a Brazil where all things do not come out right in the end. But even in this respect, *The Diary of 'Helena Morley'* has its surprises. It may be that, within the change from the critical child into the clever girl who can look after herself, there is a variant of this process of reconfirmation of a social divide. In either case, the system of Brazilian class relationships reveals its impasse.

It is certain that the affinities between these books cannot be due to influence, and in this lies their interest, since the shared mould that these affinities imply must be looked for on another level outside literature, and can only be Brazil's social formation at this time. This formation is given shape more or less unintentionally in Helena's diary, which portrays it from its own particular angle. Behind this transposition – which, even when the writer is as young as Helena and as lacking in literary self-awareness, cannot start from square one – there are, naturally, literary and cultural patterns. There are, for example, the European fashion for keeping diaries as part of a girl's education or the templates for school composition as well as the diffuse presence of Romantic values, which draw attention to the relational side of social life, especially to its more curious aspects. These are real forces existing in daily life, and to call them artistic would be excessive. The powerful organization of the observations comes from material shaped by ordinary daily existence and captured with an admirable acuity. In this sense, nothing could be more distant from the mature, independent historical reflection, calculated composition and impeccable construction of *Dom Casmurro*. Nevertheless, the work of fiction, with its highly wrought formal arrangement, studies that same area of interests and social contradictions. This internal relationship is confirmed by the presence in *The Diary* of embryonic forms that are developed further in the novel. The daring composition of a masterpiece opens our eyes to random forms, operating at a lower level of stylization, but which are also interesting and aesthetically forceful, and active in works that represent daily experience but are not fictional. In this heterogeneous diptych, which nothing forces us to put together, what can be discerned and apprehended are the forms through which reality itself functions, in the variants of a novel and a diary. Thus, form is not the exclusive attribute of art; its logic and even its aesthetic possibilities are also present in practical reality, though naturally without the refinements of artistic technique. Conversely, the ultra-sophisticated invention of *Dom Casmurro*, far from exhausting itself in pure art, if such a thing exists, brings out the logical shape of real-life connections and develops them. This work of making explicit a real order that is itself well structured gives another kind of weight to the discussion of the novel's artistic properties, for they now exist as a function of questions raised inside *and* outside literature.

7

More than a century on, Helena Morley's diary entries show no sign of ageing. The course of Brazil's experience as a nation has favoured them, deepening their resonance, and educating our minds in her unerring spontaneous judgement, which is never simplistic. The decision to collect the old diary in 1942 must have obeyed some similar kind of feeling as well, perhaps, as reflecting the new interest in Brazil's social make-up. The surprising integrity of her observations, in which time has discovered no weaknesses, is a challenge to critics and all the more so if we think of famous contemporaries who almost without exception have aged badly, figures who, in comparison with the girl, look as if they come out of a museum of mistakes. The homespun, schoolgirl genre of the diary, far removed from the pseudo-superiorities in which the country's cultured production was alienating itself, might explain something. *The Diary of 'Helena Morley'* does not pay homage to the patriotic mission of the arts, to rhetorical liberalism, to linguistic purity, to ornamental language, to the invention of great achievements in the past, to the whiff of Catholicism or to the temporary triumph of pseudo-science (with its 'difficult' terminology and its erudite clichés about race and the tropics), which, separately or together, invested the intellectuals and the literature of the period with authority. Of course, to write truthfully, it is not enough to escape from contemporary defects, and these defects themselves can empower great literature, so long as they are integrated in a critical spirit, as in the case of Machado de Assis. Yet it remains the case that, seen in the light of Helena's complex simplicity, much of the scholarly and artistic exertion of these contemporaries sounds hollow, and lamentably ideological.

In a suggestive episode, a pretty, well-dressed relative comes to Diamantina. She 'speaks very clearly and very correctly . . . without swallowing a single *r*', and when offered a tray of grapes, replies: 'I would appreciate a bunch of grapes exceedingly, Dona Agostinha'. The cousins are open-mouthed and afraid to talk near her. Later, 'eulogizing her and comparing her with us', an aunt observes that in the old days girls paid attention 'in order to learn the really refined words'. For example, they used *chamber pot* instead of 'the other word'. 'These days, you don't pay attention to anything, and you speak like riff-raff!' At dinner, the girls take revenge on their aunt:

'I would appreciate a drumstick exceedingly'; 'I would appreciate the fried potatoes exceedingly' (258–9). Amongst many other things, this scene shows the bellicose, youthful irreverence that feeds Helena's aesthetic, with her aversion to all social pretension. Seen from this point of view, affected language is of a piece with other harmful forms of upbringing – 'idiotic' in Helena's word – that a healthy mind should not submit to. It goes along with false religious devotion, looking down your nose in general, annoying prohibitions that plague the girls' daily lives, prejudice against manual labour and against blacks, the presumption of the important families – in short, the whole system of segregation and prerogatives typical of old Brazil, felt by Helena to be just so many obstacles. It is within this lively picture that the un-literary style, in its enlightened impatience with the ostentations of caste and class, shows its polemical edge.

Fifty years later after their composition, when the notebooks were turned into a book, the scenario had changed. According to the author's introductory note, her childhood jottings might now have an educational function, making 'a book that might show the girls of today the differences between present-day life and the simple existence we led at that time' (xxxvi). The volume presents the past to modern youth, a modest life to those with a comfortable one and a – very charming – provincial world to the capital and the whole country, which at the time was living through the dictatorship of the Estado Novo.[37] The idea of national cultural integration was in the air, and could find at least the appearances of confirmation in the democratic habits and civility of an influential family from Minas Gerais, the land of politics itself.[38] A further ten years

---

37 The Estado Novo was the authoritarian state set up by Getúlio Vargas in 1937. It lasted until 1945. [*Tr.*]
38 *Mineiros* are regarded in Brazil as politicians par excellence. The saying goes: 'Mineiro faz política, paulista faz dinheiro, gaúcho manda'. Interpreting slightly: 'Mineiros engage in politics, paulistas make money, gaúchos push everyone around'. Some of Brazil's most dictatorial rulers – Getúlio Vargas,

on, when Elizabeth Bishop arrived in Brazil, two or three people recommended *The Diary of 'Helena Morley'* as the country's best book since Machado de Assis.[39] We do not know who these enthusiasts were, nor what their arguments were, but it is easy to imagine that they would have combined the daring, irreverent quality of the modernists – the brilliant girl, so superior to the 'masters of the past' – with the familistic traditionalism (now, in a cosmopolitan vein, installed in the capital of the Republic) for which the delight of the real Brazil was to be found in the life and prose of Diamantina, and with a universal appeal, besides, notwithstanding later (or even contemporary) distortions. The combination is paradoxical but has its logic within the framework of a conservative modernization. Modernism itself had found in the country's colonial heritage – antediluvian, familiar and still present – the *objets trouvés* that its writers would use as trademarks of a new Brazil with an up-to-date look.[40] Indeed, Helena's remarkable book might function as an *objet trouvé* in its own right.

However, *aesthetic* judgement was concerned with the work itself, according little importance to intentions, and overturning the conventional rankings of literary importance, which generally reflect the doctrinal conflicts and the conscious aims of writers and their works. For all their unpretentious origins, the girl's jottings rose to an unexpectedly high position. The comparison with the greater part of Brazilian literature spoke in their favour – or, more polemically, they reflected badly on the literature itself. The new framework of attention posed a peculiar critical problem: how to identify and explain the formal qualities that give life to Helena's prose, qualities which endow the work with beauty, distant though

---

Emílio Garrastazú Médici, Ernesto Geisel – came from the southern state of Rio Grande do Sul, whose inhabitants are known as *gaúchos*. [*Tr.*]

39　'Introduction', *The Diary*, ix.

40　For the implications of this aesthetic-ideological operation, cf. Vinícius Dantas, 'Entre "A negra" e "a mata virgem"', *Novos Estudos Cebrap*, 45, 1996, especially 110–112.

they are from literary procedures as, in their specialized sense, we normally understand them.

Even the avant-garde reader, used to seeing conventions overthrown, or finding them acceptable only when parodied, is surprised by their absence, pure and simple. There is nothing more 'ordinary', to use the aunt's word, than the niece's writing, averse as it is to external marks of distinction, whether social or linguistic. This is poetry without prior warning – that is to say, with no support from figures of speech, syntactic refinement, learned references, unusual words or concern for euphony; without links to literary movements and free of all esotericism. In positive terms, the poetic quality has to do with its strictly prosaic character; the common diction, objects and situations; and the greatest possible clarity, in deliberate contrast to the whims of the world, where colonial inequalities with their accompanying pretentiousness make themselves felt. The form, which is almost completely de-conventionalized, matches the wealth of internal relations in the material. The anecdotes and sayings, and the brief reflections on this material, echo one another and multiply the perspectives; they make up a whole in which everything is seen in relative terms, and in an ironic light, according to its own characteristics. This web of relations that sustains the book is inherent in its materials, making for a literary economy that is rare, and realizing one of the most influential *idées-forces* of modern culture. Instead of erudite ornamentation, we have the resonance of objective complexity.

On the other hand, there is no shortage of entries where the composition retains something of the school exercise: the episodes end on an almost sentential or at least detached note, as in a fable, where the ending sums up the lesson or meaning. But the relation between the anecdote and the moral is not always clear, and sometimes they do not fit one another. In general, the anecdote carries more meaning than the moral (which seems comic in its almost childish awkwardness, fitting into the setting as if it were just another feature, unintended but meaningful). Thus, after recounting how her mother's forebodings had stopped her father when he was two steps away from finding an unworked deposit of diamonds, which would have enriched the family, Helena says: 'I don't believe that money brings bad luck to anyone' (91). Rather than an abstract truth, of superior usefulness, what we have here is the girl who has decided to reach her own conclusions. At the same time, even when it does not work, and is no more than an echo, the model of the fable-with-its-moral makes explicit the enlightened tone of the whole, in which there is a continual effort to observe and understand, to learn and communicate. The best thing, however, over and above the didactic form and the urge to reach conclusions, comes in the discrepancy with the next entry, where the account of a day full of happiness in the countryside, which money can't buy, relativizes the utilitarian lesson of the preceding episode.

That said, we cannot appreciate the tone of the book without taking into account that everything in it is steeped in family life – even what in principle might seem to escape it, like the analytic distance, the laconic humour, the refusal to indulge in fooling around, the coolness of good sense; the instruments, that is, of individualist reason. Even in the episodes in which outsiders come to the fore, there are always relatives present, setting up, so to speak, an inner, intra-familial space, and causing the observation and the reasoning to be impregnated with these relationships, which the episodes respond to and which in the last resort set the tone. Since the author is a child, there is nothing unusual in this – and not much promise. Although natural, the constant appeals to mamma, daddy, granny and aunty are grating, and the sober reader has trouble conceding that a literature with authorities like these can be of value. In fact, because of what they mean in terms of deference and dependence, these words seem to give the girl's formulations an infantile bent, in which the limitations of child-hood and the homely atmosphere, along with maudlin sentiment, all seem to play a part.

*   *   *

How can these conditions, regressive in principle, sustain strong prose with a clearly critical aspect? Later, we will return to the historical circumstances in which the paternalist model could unexpectedly change aspect and look *modern*, an inversion which would happen again, moreover, in the modernism of the 1920s.[41] Meanwhile, we may note that in the Morley family, the patriarchal order has lost its authoritarian aspect. Helena listens with amused curiosity to the stories of the olden times, when her grandfather married his daughters without consulting them or when the simple presence of the patriarch made an aunt's stomach give way (252, 53). For the younger generation, the extreme manifestations of family pride have become anecdotes. In the school, the girls are amused by a schoolmate with 'tangled' hair who shouts at another: 'Do you think you're my equal? I, with my hair, am worth all of you here, you cats! I'm Dinis Varejão's daughter!'[42]

It was natural that in remote parts of the country, far from the official sphere, public matters should be dealt with in everyday language, as it is spoken in the family. The picturesque aspects of the mixture have become famous, together with their quota of semi-utopian sympathy, associated with the – anachronistic – suggestion of government without formality. The drawbacks are obvious too, since nothing suits the despotism of the propertied class better than informality. Helena's prose, which is distinguished by special qualities tried and tested within the family, can be seen as an evolved version of this model. Around the father, with his mania for even-handedness, who likes to explain everything, and of whom his wife and children are unafraid, a different microclimate is created, one that is far from obscurantist. In a paradoxical way (for they are pressured by backwardness), their relative poverty also pushes in

---

41   Roberto Schwarz, 'The Cart, the Tram and the Modernist Poet', in *Misplaced Ideas*, London, 1992.
42   'Tangled' is a euphemism for African. The insult-word which Bishop translates as 'you cats!', is in fact *sua cachorra*, which would be more accurately translated as 'you bitch!' [*Tr.*]

an enlightened direction. In forcing them all to do something of everything, it attenuates the colonial element embedded in economic specialization as well as favouring improvisation, so that social conditions are looked at from the point of view of a spontaneous, innovative calculation of what is best to be done, unaffected by fixed formulae. Moreover, in the Morleys' house, study and intelligence are valued, so that the precariousness of everyday life, instead of being greeted with fatalism, works as a stimulus to humour and a sharply critical attitude. At one point, the father counts the proceeds of the moneymaking efforts by which his wife is trying to make up for his own ineptitude. 'When he saw the loss he turned to her in his quiet way and said, "Carolina, my child, you're killing yourself for nothing. These businesses of yours are getting us into debt. It's better for you to go visiting your mother and sisters and not try to be a business woman" ' (169). The salience of economic interests, constantly relativized as they are, however, by considerations of family happiness, makes for a scene of rare balance and open-mindedness.

Returning to our starting point, and without disavowing personal preferences, we can say that Helena's familiar, non-literary diction is alive, while the stylistic and scientifico-philosophical displays that marked the turn of the century impress us, above all, with their very characteristic failure to grasp reality. For an anti-modern reader, this contrast will reveal the victory of eternal truth over mere fashion, the provinces over the capital, authenticity over foreign imports, the natural over the artificial and so on. This essay moves in another direction, aiming to identify the historical energy in Helena's spontaneous disposition, which gives expression to a defined group of social, personal and stylistic achievements with obvious value in themselves. These achievements have artistic power, even though they came into being at the margins of literary history, which, however, threatened to appropriate them from the moment the book was published. Helena Morley's writings, which are the product of a coherent advance in a direction peculiar to her, cannot serve as a recommendation of intellectual innocence or be taken as gesturing to a sphere of beauty indifferent to classes and above history. Rather, the contrast with the partisans of prestigious verbalism, of modish scientifico-philosophical pyrotechnics, makes one think, for it throws into relief the false positions and the malformations created in peripheral countries by the desire to keep up to date; it points up the regressive, disastrous character of Brazilian modernization, which from time to time turns our necessary and inevitable aspirations to progress into their opposite, in the arts as elsewhere.

8

We have already commented on the relational density, rich in subversive acts of integration (as opposed to the primitivism of dissociation), which the familiar, advanced prose allows one to glimpse in everyday life. This life is reflected here to its real advantage: it takes on a slightly out-of-phase air, with a ubiquitous irony born of the movement of real and possible relativizations, which are a kind of progress – a victory over unrelatedness – with a *local* referent. A touchstone can be found in the ways of looking at the dominated classes, the Other par excellence. Transformed into a cognitive relationship, *the characteristic familiarity seems to presuppose a generalized form of kinship*, one expressed, in a modernist vein, in Drummond's line: 'At least we know everyone's rubbish around here'.[43] This removes the basis for the distancing and the absolute objectifications, which even when practised in a scientific fashion, are ways of mystifying the radical class estrangement inherited from the slave-owning past and renewed now in the beginnings of a wage economy. Thus, for example, it is by basing herself on the informality of her home existence that Helena tries to understand

---

43   Carlos Drummond de Andrade, 'Explicação', in *Poesia e prosa*, Rio de Janeiro, 1979, 98.

the 'incomprehensible' behaviour of the blacks, whether this behaviour has African origins, has grown in the slave quarters or been learnt from the whites. Magna the cook is in the habit of thrashing her husband Mainarte and ends up in prison for trying to strangle him. Her explanation repeats the lesson of some upper-class lady: 'I can't stand laziness'. Trying to kill him, however, was a mistake. Helena's grandmother asks: 'Why did you want to kill that poor man who wouldn't hurt a flea?' And Magna replies, 'No, Senhora! He's just the kind that dies easy! I only squeezed his throat and he stuck out his tongue in order not to answer me. I didn't mean to kill him, no, Senhora' (30–31). In another episode, which is in two parts, Emídio, the black lad, is thrown down the stairs for treating a respectable person as an equal. Helena thinks this is a good thing, because she thinks the *agregado* is 'far too nosy'. Then she observes that he is strange: 'he puts his finger in the lamp oil and licks it as if it were molasses'. What are we to make of this piece of lunacy? Can it be that the lamp oil is tasty or good for your health, and Helena didn't know about this? Is there a link between this and his earlier misbehaviour, which earned him his punishment? On another occasion, the same Emídio cures his toothache with a red-hot spit: 'I heard the flesh hiss and I was horrified. He didn't complain about his toothache any more after that' (80). In this case, as in Magna's, there is an element of uncouth stupidity which fits easily into the daily life of the families, and is a profound comment on it. Even the part we would call barbarous, or foreign to civilized people, is not so extraordinary, and in the case of the red-hot spit is not even seen as absurd. Helena is horrified by the hiss but still records that the *agregado* stops complaining, unlike many white people, who in the same situation go around complaining for days – not to mention the case of Dona Augusta's daughter, who dies as a result of a tooth extraction (15). It's not impossible that if necessary Helena might try Emídio's method. Magna's truculence, too, though linked to the slaves' world, could easily appear among the whites. Finally, even extreme forms of ignorance and superstition, which cost lives, or, in one case, a child's sight (211), are not attributed simply to poor folks, who do not constitute a separate species.

How would these same episodes appear in the lens of the scientistic writing then fashionable in Brazil? Their aspect would change, for in the last resort they would have to be linked to some racial defect, to the African climate, to a succession of geological periods, to religious atavism or whatever. Little would be said about who owned the land, about kinship, labour relations, authority or slavery, so recently abolished. In other words, the explanations would appeal to remote natural laws, light years away from everyday social conflicts. In converting to a scientific view of things, and above all to the terminology that went with it, the conforming 'modernized' writer gave up on the understanding of things present in everyday language and logic, political practice and the rules governing his own place in society. Or, better, he pushed into the background what he knew through his own experience and that of others about the way the country worked, in exchange for a dubious superiority, nourished in part by the cult of science and progress but also by traditional credulity and a primitive admiration for unpronounceable verbiage. The mental discontinuity introduced by this reform in ways of thinking, which was not the last of its kind, is worth consideration. In part at least, it reconstituted, with a theoretical façade, the social rupture that Abolition was supposed in theory to overcome. As a contrast, we may recall Joaquim Nabuco's *Abolitionism* (1883),[44] a contemporary and far superior work that accorded the highest value to terms *in current use* to express the struggle over slavery in Brazil, in the world, in the author himself and in his opponents, as it attempted to increase and deepen critical awareness of the subject. Where evolutionist philosophy measured the archaic nature of slavery in centuries-long anthropological

---

44   Joaquim Nabuco, *Abolitionism: The Brazilian Antislavery Struggle*, trans. and ed. Robert Conrad, Urbana: University of Illinois Press, 1977, originally published 1883; regarding Joaquim Nabuco, see further ch. 4, n. 13. [*Tr.*]

epochs and underplayed its continuing effects in the present, Nabuco looked for contemporary expressions of the conflict in order to analyse them and understand their historical strength, to elucidate the workings of the social order that sustained these forces, and try to transform it. Even today, the integrity and profundity of his book are disconcerting.

Meanwhile, our 'scientific' critics, faced with the self-examination that the dissolution of the slave-owning order invited them to undertake, went to look for authority and intellectual resources in the mirage of European science, which was assimilated in a degraded, almost superstitious version. There is no doubt about the polemical value of evolutionary convictions, with their attack on Catholic providentialism and the idealization of the traditional order. But their legitimating possibilities in a country that, once Abolition had happened, had no intention of admitting its poor to citizenship, are also evident. The fanciful but always extra-political arguments about the foundations of our social backwardness were perfectly adapted to the new inequalities of oligarchic Brazil. The ironies of this affinity did not escape Machado de Assis, who summed them up and immortalized them in his character Quincas Borba's philosophy of Humanitism.[45]

The disastrous aspect of scientific prose in Brazil was this *regressive* core, in which the ultra-critical urge includes an element of bedazzlement, authoritarian and complex-ridden, and fatalistic, too, in its own fashion. Although not everyone sees it that way, we cannot fail to recognize the obscurantist workings of

---

45   Humanitism is a satirical mixture of Positivist and Darwinist doctrines, by which its (mad) exponent, Quincas Borba, explains that all is for the best in the best of all worlds, because he himself is well off (from an unexpected inheritance). The suffering, and the great disasters of history – slavery included – can all be explained in this fashion. Humanitism is expounded in ch. 117 of *Memórias póstumas de Brás Cubas* and, with slight changes of emphasis, in Machado's *Quincas Borba*, where it is summed up in the famous phrase 'The winner gets the potatoes!' [*Tr.*]

techno-complicated terminology. The use of esoteric vocabulary, impregnated with pseudo-science, contemporary prejudice and ancient dogma, and sounding its own Parnassian note, gave the writer his credentials as a member of the worldwide elite of savants, and included him too in the stratum of men who should be running Brazil were it not for the usual injustices. The unfortunate objects of naturalist conceptualizations, meanwhile, were placed at a distance that left no hope of reply: 'A bubble has no opinion', Quincas Borba explains to his 'ignoramus' of a disciple.[46] Nabuco and Machado de Assis are writers who tried to educate themselves by the analysis of the *social* (as opposed to *natural*) relations they formed part of and which they forced the incoming tide of naturalism to pass through. Mutatis mutandis, something of the same kind is true of Helena Morley and her colloquial, irreverent writings. 'The other day, when I told him a cousin had told me that man is descended from the monkey, Father Neves said it's a great sin to listen to such things. Hadn't I read the story of Adam and Eve in Sacred History? I didn't say anything. But if Father Neves knew the monkey we have in our neighbourhood, even he could believe it. This monkey's more intelligent than lots of the boys I know. He belongs to Siá Ritinha, the woman who steals her neighbour's hens' (114).

The clarity and concreteness in which Helena specializes satisfy modern taste, which discovers in them the opposite of our prolix, opaque sameness. By an easily comprehensible paradox, they had to do with the relative impoverishment of the region, which did not wipe out the urban, enlightened point of view but combined it with a picturesquely compact assortment of goods, opinions and activities. Later, associated with the primitivist trend in the European

---

46   The quotation is from ch. 6 of Assis's *Quincas Borba*, where Quincas Borba explains to Rubião (the 'ignoramus' to whom he is expounding his doctrine) that 'individuals are just transitory bubbles' in the great process of history. When Rubião asks what the bubble's opinion might be, this is Quincas's reply. [*Tr.*]

artistic avant-garde, this picture of a reduced state of things would turn into an aesthetico-political proposal for the country, in Oswald de Andrade's modernist manifestos, which revolutionized Brazilian taste and brought it up to date, creating an image of ourselves 'for export', in which our relative lack of civilization took on a new connotation: 'Poetry is in the facts. The saffron and ochre shanties in the green of the Favela, under a blue Cabral sky, are aesthetic facts . . . Brazilwood Poetry is a dining room on a Sunday, with birds singing in the reduced jungle of a cage, a skinny individual composing a waltz for flute, and Maricota reading the paper'.[47] The surprise in Oswald's construction appears in the compatibility – half-patriotic, half-utopian and humorous as well – of these innocent figures with the daring of modern art and technological progress. In Helena's prose, where there are hardly any material advances, much less any of the inventions of the avant-garde, the affinity with modernity comes from the multiform existence – clear, however, and without shadows – given to people in the varied ensemble of their activities, *beyond which there is nothing*. This clear light, the enemy of reaction and superstition, favouring contentment for all, is *advanced* in the best sense of the word.

As in Oswald's writing, backwardness is not seen in an immobilizing perspective. It is noteworthy that in the book there are no descriptions properly so called, of the kind that, on the pretext of impressing us visually, in fact throw ideological dust in our eyes. In spite of the importance of fruit and vegetables, chickens and cats, neighbours and relatives, we know little about their physical aspect, which does not prevent them all figuring vividly in their different roles. In one episode, Helena's brother comes back from school and notices that the eggs the hen was about to lay are not there. In no time, the lad grabs the broom to kill the house cat, who is cleverer

---

47 Oswald de Andrade, 'Manifesto da poesia Pau-Brasil', in *Do Pau-Brasil à Antropofagia e às Utopias: Manifestos, teses de concursos e ensaios*, Rio de Janeiro, 1978, 5, 9.

than him and gets away. The mother, less impulsive, thinks the thief might have been a *teiú*, a kind of lizard, that has been sucking eggs in the area. Good sense then tells us that if that is so, the shells must still be around. Not finding them, the boy concludes that it really was the cat, which had already eaten his sister's chicks. Dona Carolina reminds him that chicks are not eggs and tells him to go and see if the door into the street is perhaps open, for the street kids might be the culprits. And in fact the door was not shut, to Renato's chagrin; according to his sister, he's crazier about eggs than the *teiú* itself, and was intending to fry them up that night (*113*).

The bald concatenation of these acts, all unmysterious in themselves, puts in motion a lively poetic system, quite sui generis, revealing an intimacy and a certain reversibility among categories that, according to the norm, should not mix. The richness of the scene comes from the set of combinations the anecdotes and their elements can enter into, or from the synchronic order, of whose possibilities this episode is one particular case, and which takes its interest from what suitable – and ironic – comparisons may suggest. Depending on the immediate opportunity, the hen's eggs are for the consumption of the owner, of wild animals, of domestic pets or of the local children – one of whom, at other moments, is the furious owner himself, for he is no saint. Once the common hunger, shared by man and beast, by owners and neighbours on the qui vive – a troupe of heterogeneous composition, and curious from the point of view of social history – has been established, the differences within it claim our interest, because each one of these appropriations satisfies individual, competing needs as well as prompting specific thoughts, which are amusing to think through. Who is the worse thief: the kids from the street, the sister's cat or the wild lizard? The question of property is present, but wrapped in an objective irony, shorn of any excess of morality or certainty, and without excluding animals. We can add that these opinions also work in the opposite direction: the sister thinks Renato is almost an animal, and the cat seems to have made up its own mind about him, while the mother, who thinks his conclusions precipitate, is determined to educate the turbulent boy. Note, too, the complete list of possible thieves, which points to a consummate knowledge of the situation, giving a peculiar authority and balance to the familiar tone as well as exemplifying in a simple way what we can think of as a life lived in full daylight. In this sense, Helena's passion for experience fully laid out in all its elements, as an ensemble, with its corresponding internal music of differences and similarities, is a decisive factor in the mastery of her prose, in which knowledge matters. There is, for example, the passage in which the peculiarities of the women in the family are listed and commented on; another in which the vices most common in Diamantina are evaluated; and a third one in which local superstitions are passed in review (187–8, 159–60, 142). These are the result of a kind of studious accumulation, in which an assiduous interest in stories about the family and the town takes on, as if spontaneously, the character of an abstract, analytic system in which the collectivity appears in a reduced form. Without their individual presence being at all diminished, things, acts and subjects are directly grasped in their social existence, as part of a transparent, bustling functional whole, with a cast of characters and a distribution of roles that do not correspond to their (normative) image of themselves.

As for the eggs, there's nothing more certain than their several uses – they are good to eat, raw or cooked, appreciated by humans and lizards (but not by cats), easy to steal, ideal for selling, necessary for raising chicks and so on. These uses form a contrastive list, or an abstract system, in which the family and the society appear in a summary. Those who make use of them make up another contrastive list of this kind, concrete, abstract and also offbeat: there are similarities and differences, for example, between the *teiú*, the cat, the owner of the hen and the children in the street; each one belonging to a single category (wild animal, domestic pet, breeder-owner, coveter of others' goods) or all united and lumped together in the same one (as possible thieves), depending on the angle and the moment. Even the eggs, to be what they are, are differentiated inside many other lists, which vary or coincide according to their user: for the *teiú*, they perhaps come before insects and larvae, which however make humans uncomfortable; their lists, which reflect society's divisions, are headed by gold and diamonds, which are of no use to the cat. These are clear divisions, founded on the diversity of living beings, things and interests, as natural as they are social. Consideration of their possible permutations can be taken too far, perhaps, losing contact with the anecdotes; but it is wholly in keeping with their spirit. Beyond the Morley humour, the ever-present reversibility among the terms of the series is in itself a historical index because of the fluidity it reveals within the social set-up, on which the new market economy had not yet imposed its hegemony. In fact, economic value appears as one more attribute of things, almost like one use among others. Alternating here with no break in routine are the contexts of whole civilizations, fostering the encounter, as relative equals, between the activity of gathering, a subsistence economy, the inheritance of slavery and patriarchalism, civic, urban values and the new post-Abolition horizon in an inex-haustibly interesting experiment. The terms on which these forms of life fit and interact raise their own questions, which despite the author's childhood perspective, sometimes close to mere cuteness, have the unavoidable seriousness of what is structural. The disin-terested movement from one point of view to another makes one ask, for example, more as a practical question than as a moral one, whether it is better, or more natural, to raise hens than to look for eggs in the countryside or take them from the garden opposite – unless, maybe, it is more appropriate not to bother with such choices. 'Sin? I was born knowing that it's a sin to steal and not get away with it', says the good, amenable Maria Quitéria, justifying the stewed chicken on the table (196). Isolated examples like this do not sufficiently convey the great liveliness of the whole, within which the promises, the horrors and the absurdities that life's sub-systems hold for each other are made tangible. Helena's artless, strictly referential sentences accompany and bring to life the diversity and the shifting oppositions of the anecdotes, with their – always amusing – reversals and exchanges and give her prose its lively rhythm, which leaves no room for the anodyne. Now that market values have almost totally swallowed up the natural substratum of life as well as making societies' process of self-reproduction a matter of guesswork, this series of differences that are not indifferent has taken on a kind of luminosity.

At one of the several festive blowouts the diary records, Helena sits near the Portuguese teacher, Seu Leivas, the biggest drinker in town. At one point, after Father Augusto has recited some verses in honour of the lady of the house, the teacher fills his cheeks and makes a funny face. Without understanding why, the girl fixes her eyes on him and starts laughing. The neighbour opposite, who is savvier, grabs the platter of roast pork and potatoes and hides it under the table. Straight away, Seu Leivas's cheeks fill up again, and this time 'two spouts of beer came out of his nose and sprayed all the dishes that were in front of him!' (46). At least the platter with the pork was safe. The clarity of the sequence and its elements is reminiscent of slapstick comedy. This gift and the taste for looking and distinguishing, which can be applied just as well to the stages of a disaster as to the phases of a perfect day, to the different sides of a question, to possible ways of survival, to the aunts' temperaments or to the squares and streets of Diamantina are perhaps the writer's basic impulse. Realized in a prose with no need of adjectives or of a web to join it all together, Helena's discrimination takes on a bright, brisk quality, as if it were saying that the elements, separated and underlined as they are and more defined by practical contexts than by literary tradition, have a right to consideration. The constant changes in their profile are part of this. Are eggs the result of a process of rearing? What if they were natural food, to which we have a right, as the *teiú* does, or like the air we breathe? And are they not also an incipient form of money? The language, which steers clear of poetic connotations, opens up a space for the objective poetry of actions, situations, things *and language itself*, all of this unstable and multifaceted within the general stability.

The precise visualization and the direct verbalization carry the mark of the skills characteristic of a provincial and in great part illiterate society. This, if not mistaken, is an interesting paradox, worth thinking about. The complete memory of what has happened and been said, of the order of things, and so on, which gives the notes their air of freedom from subjective deficiency – you could almost say their impeccable finish – has to do with an oral culture, where illiteracy is common. The same can be said of the flawless verbal appropriateness, founded on the authority or objectivity of common use, that reduces the personalized aspect of the choice of terms. However, the more-or-less unchanging, collective character of these skills, which inhibit individualized expression, does not stop Helena's prose from fusing them with a critical intelligence to which they lend an unexpected dynamism. We can say that enlightened – or individualist and self-interested – curiosity, once moulded by the language of the patriarchal family, and through it by stable forms of authority and of the popular life, *which informality makes reversible*, hits on a linguistic register full of possibilities, in which, time and again, reason changes sides, at one moment on the side of the masters, at the next on the opposite. The unforeseen affinities, and the obvious tension between the components, which tacitly reflect one another, do not break the naturalness of the combination, in which the simplicity and the tone, ambiguous and sometimes problematic in a strong sense, coexist. We have already seen the mischievous and profoundly witty rhythm that Helena achieves within this framework: individualistic, that is, opposed to the constraints of family and customs but family-oriented, against the break-up of the clan and its abundant life; modern, against the pretensions of birth; rebellious, against class and race prejudice; enlightened, against superstition and ignorance but all in favour of popular and religious festivals and allergic to utilitarian discipline; allergic, too, to all immobilism, be it humble or well-to-do, and aware of the mobility and the advantages conferred by money. The last Helena considers to be 'a piece of dirty paper, to which we attach more importance than to all the good things in life' (47). A clever child, a poor relation, she nevertheless specializes in showing conclusively that money, which you sometimes have to steal, doesn't buy what's best about life; she is an enthusiast for a life without humiliating calculations – for freedom, perhaps? – that belief in divine protection gives to the poor. The element of reasoning and lively preference – that is, the element of logic and fellow feeling in each of these incompatible positions along with the limited historical prospects of such combinations – needs no comment. The strange thing is that in context these positions have an atmosphere of relative realism and do not seem merely childish. It is as if the de-activation of their contradictions has found some kind of real guarantee, which stops them looking like fairy stories. Earlier, I suggested that the destruction of slavery took different paths and opened different perspectives depending on where it happened. Left to itself, the process separated out in the old order those elements of social cohesion that did not consist only of brute force, or in which necessity found minimal levels of consent or even identification, bringing into existence atypical, non-bourgeois tendencies of social reproduction, whose *advanced* character in relation to the previous situation, impracticable in relation to the march of history, may not reach viability on a large scale but does give them a lasting capacity to speak to our imagination.

9

The subtitle Helena Morley gave to this collection of her old papers, 'a provincial girl's notebooks from the end of the nineteenth century', is accurate but does not do it justice. It is as if the publication were excusing itself from any possible vanity through the laudable aim of documenting the Brazilian past. This classification, a little condescending towards young female writers, backward places and past times, scarcely conveys the acute vitality of the anecdotes. Moreover, it is not as if the girl had no notion of her age, her relative position in Diamantina or the picturesque nature of old Brazil, which for her, however, had to do with the present and were untinged by nostalgia. Indeed her sense of local colour, showing Romantic influences but dispensing with their sentimental and patriotic components, has something intriguing about it. By what right does the young girl see the familiar figures of her daily life as *curious?* The scattered but real presence of the model of enlightened values made normal relations look exotic as well as normal, even though they were more familiar than the model itself. One way or another, Helena thinks that the beggars, *agregados* and ex-slaves, the enormous extended families, the counting up of favours and giving of alms, the recourse to the free contributions of the surrounding countryside, the life in closed houses, the thick rind of superstition, the innumerable religious festivals, and the rest constitute something worthy of attention, a present time that is colourful but out of place in the present proper, so to speak, a deviation in relation to *normality*, which in its turn, however, for all practical purposes did not exist. For, of course, there would be nothing more anomalous than a small family, freedom of labour and unfettered individual self-interest – which are the substance of this normality – were such things really to appear on the scene. Even in Diamantina, at the same time the back of beyond and the centre of everything, the enlightened schoolgirl was experiencing within herself the clash of the discrepant phasing of the contemporary world. Immediate reality jars, if only at a secondary level, with the normative, progressive background of the present day, which, however, finds little corroboration in the things she lives among; and this backdrop itself looks barbarian if nearby reality provides the norm. As the result of historical alienation, or, as far as possible, as an overcoming of that alienation, this movement between two norms traces discontinuous horizons on the empirical facts, giving them a specific relief and reality in time, or, by the same token, giving an actual presence to the ideological instability of the young, ex-colonial country.

So, at a distance, the new bourgeois norm put pressure on and in a way condemned to limbo a system of relationships that, nonetheless, however, it would take time for it to replace. The intelligent, individualist little 'English' girl had a notion of this process, which, however, she very often did not accept, and to which she reacted with suitable answers, all of them having to do with intelligence and self-realization but pointing towards a different course of events. Put to the test in the circumstances, intelligence and self-realization revealed themselves to be less simple and above all less bourgeois than was suggested by the accepted model, whose absurdities cropped up here and there. The critical fruitfulness of this questioning is what ensures the modern and *universal* interest of the book – adjectives to be taken in a duly modest sense. We see the splendid balance of Helena's reactions: she never pretends that provincial life is anything but precarious and backward but never thinks this is a reason for belittling or condescension, and, furthermore, she has the strength to take from the experience available to her the terms that give her room for independent judgement in the face of the polarizations brought by progress. As well as shrewdness, she shows a certain courage in overcoming the one-sidednesses and regressive temptations her situation at times lead her into. Progressivism itself, cultivated in the abstract, might well be one of them, and perhaps it can be said that her rebellious instinct for seeing the relative side of things, or her opposition to formality, is her governing faculty (as it is Capitu's). An example is the case of the two lads from Rio who come to Diamantina to set up the lottery. The relatives who know the capital tell their cousins they should not trust them, since 'in Rio de Janeiro a man who runs a lottery is considered very low class'. Helena disagrees: "'What does it matter? They're considered low-class there but here they're considered to be quite all right and so we can't be rude to them, since they're such nice, agreeable boys"' (270–1). The lack of presentable young men in town makes her refrain from a judgement that in Rio might be apt. In another case, she decides that the mania for thinking everything that comes from outside is better is absurd, particularly as regards dentists: 'What we have is worthless; only things from other places are any good. Even I used to think that way. But from now on I'm not going to' (107). More significantly, there is the father's resolve 'not to let my brothers refrain from work, saying that work is only dishonourable here, because only slaves work and work is honourable where there are no slaves' (*260*). Here is an example in which foreign and indigenous rules coexist, but the former are the right ones. In other cases – for good or for ill, it is impossible to tell – distance cancels out Rio de Janeiro's importance: though she is amused by forced voting and the family's political passions, Helena doesn't believe that the presidential election will change anything in Diamantina.[48] As a whole, her exercises in relativizing and inverting common notions create a lively atmosphere, notable for its intellectual nonconformism, the wide reach of the questions involved and the impartiality she shows, all of this with obvious human benefits. Accepted truths are seen in different, even opposing perspectives and criticized in the light of the particular situation. More than this, she does not want to exclude any of the possibilities for fulfilment to be found in local existence, or, for that matter, to accept the emptiness to which the dynamics of the modern world condemn its so-called backward parts. The decisive potential of these latter tendencies does not cross the girl's mental horizon – she is young, after all – but they pervade her more daring sallies, even when they are innocent. Of course, irreverence has a right to be acute in ex-colonies, in proportion to the damage caused by the complexes and illusions of the colonized people themselves. But, even putting decolonization on one side, Helena's ironic eye for situations differing from the 'norm', which raise doubts about the

---

48 'Forced voting': *Voto de cabresto*, literally 'halter voting', by which a powerful landowner's dependants and neighbours were forced to vote for him (as if led by a halter). Secret voting was only instituted in Brazil in 1932, and even then these practices continued. [*Tr.*]

general value of accepted generalizations, is a triumph for critical independence, whether in Diamantina or in the most advanced European capital.

Although alert to peculiarities, Helena's writing is sparing with local colour, without treating it as taboo. Much of her literary distinction has to do with this wise parsimony, which avoids isolating particularities, while still highlighting them. Spontaneous as it may have been, it is a profoundly appropriate response to the Brazilian setting, which did not itself suggest it. Attentive to the country's distinctive features – which are really the effects of colonization and slavery – she does not turn them into absolutes by the common routes of patriotic or traditionalist exaltation, abstract indignation or 'scientific' labelling, nor, much less, does she hide them. Framing these features by means of an interesting anecdote, which aims to clarify, and in which actions, the relationships between them and witty commentaries on them stand out, she creates a kind of sober distancing, in which the immediately picturesque and the conventional evaluations do not disappear but act as backup to the main argument, with its additional element of critical acuity. It might be said that the idea of place with which the prose accords is made up of relationships, in contrast to a facile localism tied down to fixed signs. We need only recall the wonderful episode of Arinda's diamond, where God *grants* luck; the uncle *buys* whatever comes his way; the impoverished child *finds* the diamond but doesn't get any reward, while the ignorant father *deludes* himself about the future; and Helena, *resigned* to her own bad luck, *feels sorry* for her little friend's poverty. The secret is in the shaping force of this gamut of verbs, which among other things conveys the *active* feeling of life – a real novelty – that distinguishes the writing. If each expression is taken on its own, it tells us nothing about local things, but the whole sets up a universe with its own social logic and moral problems, and this without recourse to – say – descriptions of the mine, the physical types of the people, the sparkle of the Brazilian stone and so on. To illuminate the aptness of the solution, which does not spring from artistic concerns but still escapes from the usual disharmonies of Brazilian prose, all we have to do is imagine, with a little exaggeration, what Romantic, naturalist or regionalist writers would do with the scene. This is another aspect, in this case a stylistic one, of Helena Morley's exceptional poise. For immediate, fleeting reasons, and with no need to hide historical 'anomalies', the forms of local life seem to have a fluid and substantial relationship with contemporary life, neither despised nor over-praised but appreciated as they happen, with freedom, in the presence of a world that transcends them. This distribution of localism and generality will not be given its real value if we ignore its internal tension, or its triumph against the odds. When enlightened civility and the refined and passionate sense of a special form of life come together, conflict usually results. This passion for the local, especially when it is linked to the susceptibilities of the provincial backwater and of national backwardness, and its own forms of class resentment, is an open invitation to an easy indulgence in incivility by those involved, who are happy to reflect one another in a confined space – or in their own private means of expression, impermeable to all external evaluation. In their turn, the absurd pretensions to cosmopolitan urbanity in societies with a colonial formation are well known. However, in spite of the familiar tone, which in its way also represents a kind of collusion – you could almost say a commitment – Helena's writing always maintains the *decorum* proper to the struggle to understand and civilize, rejecting the obtuse, collusive aspects of local colour. Outside the confines of nationalism, reactionary tradition, or the scientific hierarchy of races or of regions, not to mention cocooning pure and simple, the sense of particularity shines with a different light.

In its way, *The Diary of 'Helena Morley'* is a confirmation of Machado de Assis's project, which prefers the 'intimate sense' of the country and the time, the famous interior Brazilianness, 'different and better than if it were merely superficial',[49] to explicit, emblematic Brazilian subjects. Helena's sense of the real context of relationships and of their precedence over the conventional definition of their terms never ceases to surprise. Along with Machado's, her writing seem to be immunized against the coarseness of the time; that is, against the mental confirmation of the separations, the stigmas associated with the persistence – or the modernization – of the colonial matrix. Her treatment of the humiliated sections of Brazilian society leaves today's reader open-mouthed in the humanity of its depiction. The absurd improvidence of these people, their abject social dependence, the darkness of their skin, their grammatical mistakes, the constant thieving, their superstition and the rest are not debited exclusively to the account of the class they belong to – better still, they are mentioned ironically within the context of the better-off, which leaves the reality of social disjunction with no ideological support. The anti-barbaric bent, in this case, is not anti-popular. There is no better indicator of the exceptional character of this attitude than the difficulty we have in admitting, in imagining, that it might really have existed in its own moment, functioning exactly like this from day to day, without interruption, in the immediate presence of the prerogatives it opposed.

In fact, the diary has something of a perfect finish, more appropriate to literary works than to actual conduct. This might be one reason for thinking that the book was fundamentally rewritten in the 1930s, when the artistic avant-garde, inspired by a new historical situation, had already decided that our inherited colonial relationships, anomalous from the point of view of bourgeois civilization, could become a trump card, at least aesthetically, in the country's ever-so-modern – post-bourgeois – play to join the near future. Along with elements of undoubted genius, the modernists' valorization of old or popular Brazil included a lot of rather

---

49 Machado de Assis, 'Notícia da atual literatura brasileira – Instinto de nacionalidade', in *Obra completa*, vol. 3, Rio de Janeiro, 1959, 817.

aggressive, shocking humour and went on its way with the insouci-
ance and the authority of artists who, in a country full of boors,
were up to date with international fashions. In Helena's diary,
however, whether it has been rearranged or not, there is in the clash
with backwardness the simple seriousness of everyday questions
brought into consideration in their common-or-garden practical
guise. The enlightened dimension of usefulness makes its mark,
even if it is out of phase with the features that progress showed to
the world at that time, and which in their turn were losing contact
with the idea of progress itself – all of which produces a paradoxical
combination of ideas.

From another angle, and since this is Minas Gerais, the reader
may find in the pastoralism of many of the episodes an echo of the
Arcadian conventions of the eighteenth century,[50] in which we have
the pleasant places, the rustic contentment, the dignity of work and
the ideally simple society in a reduced material setting, all of this
expressed with clarity and composure. The pastoral life, in which
Reason and Nature are in harmony, seems almost to be realized in
this impoverished little town, halfway to becoming rural, yet at the
same time very civilized. Helena's prose, too, fuses family informality with strong elements of an enlightened point of view, such as
her convivial, business-like outlook on things, her openness in the
consideration of individual interests and her confidence in the practical advantages of reason, elements which the town's traditions
must have conserved, and which already in the Golden Age of the
late eighteenth century contrasted with the general lack of culture
and with the bare countryside. Coloured by the stoicism and cheer-
fulness of a girl who never gives up, the constant search for fruit to
placate hunger, very often in other people's gardens, the careful

---

50   In the latter half of the eighteenth century, a group of poets centred on Ouro
Preto, the most important town in the gold- and diamond-mining areas of Brazil,
wrote in the pastoral mode then popular in Portugal and other European countries.
The most famous of them are Tomás Antônio Gonzaga (b. 1744–d. 1810), Cláudio
Manuel da Costa (b. 1729–d. 1789) and Basílio da Gama (b. 1741–d. 1795). [*Tr.*]

watch over the family's hens and eggs, so they are not stolen in their turn, the tiring housework that prevents her studying: all these things take on the tone of humorous pastoral. However, stylized or not, her needs have nothing to do with convention. The reflections they prompt are practical, with something of that seriousness in looking at daily existence that is one of the advanced conquests of literary realism, according to Auerbach.[51]

Modern literature has accustomed us to seeing its achievements as the result of effort, discipline, self-denial and so on. Flaubert's correspondence tells us of the hard work and sense of responsibility involved in the search for the mot juste. In an analogous fashion, unconventional prose depends on a struggle against the prestige and the automatic habits of rhetoric, just as clear outlines can only be achieved by an arduous process of purification. In all these cases, it is a question of rejecting a lie – a bourgeois lie above all – embedded in social relations, in ourselves, in language and in artistic tradition. Without forcing unwarranted comparisons, we can see the 'para-modern' quality of Helena's prose, which is more satisfying than many others in all the features mentioned but which is the result of a different historical conjuncture. Her precise expression is not a victory *over* anything; rather it is a victory *in favour of* common usage, which seems to contain more truth than lies, since its opposite is highfalutin language, and, in general, the occlusion of trivial, laborious daily life. The source it draws on is spoken language in its popular setting, in circumstances where belles-lettres are in the service of class distinction. The non-conventional rhythm of the prose is sustained also by the realism of childhood and family experience which, under the influence of enlightenment – and of the historical moment – escape from their intrinsic narrowness. It gives voice to a group of unrepresented interests: the unprotected, poor relations, ex-slaves, women, the hungry, animals, as well as the

---

51   Erich Auerbach, *Mimesis: The Representation of Reality in Western Literature*, Princeton, 1968, 480, 490.

children themselves, escape from silence and come face to face with
the rules of property and authority. In this prose, the mixed energies of rejection and adaptation join and take a spontaneous new
direction. Then, finally, there is the surprising complexion of the
prose, which unites attributes that our own times have made incompatible: it is clear, without being dry; resonant, but without diffuse,
vaguer connotations; beautiful, but without losing contact with
practical reality or adding perfume to the flower or poetry to the
poem – to recall João Cabral's famous instruction, which, in its own
inverse manner, is emphatic and poeticizing.[52] The diary entries
present themselves with all their clear, substantive ambiguities, the
result of loyalty to a contradictory experience, both individual and
collective. In many ways Helena Morley's writing realizes, quite
spontaneously, one of modern poetry's ideals. Far removed from
the over-abundance or the parsimony of literary schools and
sustained by the good luck of a particular historical situation, the
girl, without trying, hits the spot that others aim for in vain. There
is something utopian in such ease, which, though it cannot be
repeated at will, remains an achievement to ponder.

10

Trying to understand the charm of *Memoirs of a Militia Sergeant*,
Antonio Candido discovered its depth, and there, a hidden axis on
which Brazilian literature turns.[53] His starting point is the law that
governs the novel's fabulation: the characters merrily circulate

---

52   João Cabral de Melo Neto (b. 1920–d. 1999) was the leading poet of the
generation after the modernists. His poetry often deals with the poor of the
Northeast of Brazil, where he was born. His poetic is harsh, ascetic and dry and is
summed up in these words from 'Alguns toureiros' (in *Paisagens com figuras*,
1955): one should write poetry 'sem perfumar sua flor / sem poetizar seu poema'
(without perfuming your flower/without poeticizing your poem). [*Tr.*]
53   Manuel Antônio de Almeida, *Memórias de um sargento de milícias* (1853). See
ch. 2 above for further discussion.

between the hemispheres of order and disorder, moving innocently to and fro, in a 'dialectic of roguery'. Something similar happens with the writing, which in the style of the popular humour of the time clears a space for the two sides of things, with its balanced sentences and cheerful equanimity. Thus, the book's economy presents as equivalents and intimates the two hemispheres that the conventional ideology of the young nation kept separate, like good and evil. Given the rigidity of slavery, the charm of this feeling for life, full of fluidity and good humour, is surprising. Was it pure fantasy? Or did it approach history in some way, as the references to the Rio de Janeiro of Dom João VI might suggest? Candido's reply is nuanced. Manuel Antônio's book imagines the *dynamism* of society in depth, according to the way of life of one of its sectors, and so satisfies an essential, modern aspiration of realist literature, and its most valuable one at that; yet if the trademark of realism is the complete, positive reproduction of reality, *Memoirs* is excluded from its canon because of the many vestiges of 'gently fictitious' folklore it contains and because the social panorama it offers is incomplete. To put it simply, the ease of movement stylized in *Memoirs* is conditional on what it excludes. The novel omits the two decisive social realities of the time, slave labour and the propertied class, in order to concentrate on the zone between, where the poor, without work or property, get along as best they can, living off the leftovers of the other sector and developing the mechanisms and rhythms that the novel valorizes. Here, then, is a real, partial and extraordinarily attractive vision of the country, glimpsed thanks to the providential disappearance of its elite and its basic form of production. Deliberately or intuitively, this subject is the central structural problem of Brazilian culture, which is always occupied with the task of curing or disguising the wound opened by the colonial economy. For all the difference in genre, there is no lack of parallels with *The Diary of 'Helena Morley'* – and readers will already have noticed how much this essay has borrowed from Antonio Candido's.

In an aesthetic analysis of *Memoirs*, Candido first tries to capture the particularities of a mode of existence. He then identifies its historico-social foundations and finally contrasts it, in a discreetly meditative register, and as a suggestion, with the Puritan forms of life examined in the North American fiction of the period. The political horizon of the essay, published in 1970, was the military regime installed in Brazil in 1964, with its anti-popular proclivities, and the deepening capitalist integration of the country, which occurred in those years. Its theoretical context, which harmonized, however obliquely, with these tendencies, was defined by vulgar Marxism and anti-historical structuralism, both of which 'The Dialectic of Roguery' opposed as a more convincing alternative, though without labouring the point. Then, possibly less ephemerally, the composition of the essay, very carefully thought through, offered a critical and academic model for some of the long-term aspirations of Brazilian letters; in particular, the desire to win recognition for aspects of national life thought to be worth valuing. It is obvious that this ambition carries a risk of becoming ideological, but this is no reason to reject it, if, avoiding cliché, it makes sense and enlarges our idea of the present. Carried through with discernment, and, above all, without exaggerated patriotism, it is a difficult project, entailing a combined reflection on the country's historical experience, marked as it is by an incomplete decolonization, and on its contemporary situation, in a doubly critical movement back and forth. Now, if we look at the substance of Brazil's most salient cultural formations, those in which, for good or ill, we feel energy and universality, we will find – I believe – that they involve some kind of desegregation, of liberating mobilization – illusory, in general – within the deformed world produced by the modern-day recycling of the colonial matrix. It is as if they were pointing to the country's historical duty, the worldwide disaster to be made good, the real strength that confers universal significance on the provinciality of our internal problems. When any prospect of overcoming them seems possible, the lamp of interest is lit. When this fails to happen, it's back to the old routine.

I I

Modernist prose offers an exemplary instance, in the work of Mário de Andrade, with its unmistakable tone, especially his famous way of placing pronouns,[54] which is popular and Brazilian, grafted onto a style of dazzling flexibility, the product of a very sophisticated, erudite literary culture. The historical and social dovetailing of this style, very much composed yet aspiring to a higher kind of naturalness, takes us back to our problem. Mário's aim was to expose the colonized, anti-popular, unreal and truly *uncultured* character of Brazil's cultural model, and to clear the way for its substitution by another, more appropriate one. Taking the scandalous initiative of making 'mistakes' in his writing, with an attendant self-denying willingness to bear the insults of the 'well-spoken', postulated a kind of leadership by example. In placing pronouns in his own way, which was that of the majority of people, Mário took a complex position, whose libertarian aspect is worth defining. To avoid misunderstandings, the iconoclast himself explained that the mistakes were deliberate and their purpose was militant. Using the pronoun in the Brazilian fashion is the rule among the popular classes, whether or not they are illiterate, but also among the educated, so long as they are not writing or speaking in official contexts, where the rules of metropolitan Portuguese grammar support the identity of an elite – an 'occupying' elite, in Paulo Emílio Salles Gomes's terminology, having nothing to do with

---

54   For Mário (see ch. 2, n. 4), modernism was not a purely artistic endeavour. He intended to produce a more genuinely Brazilian art, one more in contact with and reflecting the life of the whole population. This includes reflecting normal Brazilian speech patterns, which differ considerably from those of the Portuguese ex-metropolis, notably, in this context, in the use and placement of pronouns, both subject and object: Portuguese as spoken in Portugal tends to put pronouns after the verb (*vejo-te*: I see you), whereas Brazilian speech usually places them before it (*te vejo*). [*Tr.*]

colonial riff-raff.[55] This is the context, coherent on the one hand, fractured on the other, within which Mário invented ways of giving everyday language its due recognition, freeing it from stigma and relative confinement. At first sight, this change meant promoting the popular milieu. However, it had more to do with the cultivated classes, who were being urged to transfer their linguistic loyalties. The crucial move was the rupture with the Portuguese model, seen by a few members of the cultured elite as an outdated obstacle to a new kind of development with a new internal impetus. The task of integrating the nation culturally had come into the foreground, enjoining modern people, au fait with new international aesthetic trends, to work to articulate these trends with the richness of Brazilian poverty, in an exciting synthesis incompatible with the current bourgeois norm, which was made to seem *backward*. The country's colonial base, with the addition of the masses of immigrants, who were also reduced to a state below citizenship, now became the repository of its strength. The disalienation of the elite through this alliance, overcoming the previous mental subjection, would open up a national space of originality, dynamism and regeneration. Developmentalism was knocking at the door, in a pre-1930, non-economic variant, which gave thought its own new direction. The reorientation of modernism, especially Mário's, had roots that today's progressive thought does not sufficiently appreciate.

The Brazilian positioning of pronouns crystallized a strategic complex of polarities, themselves differing internally from one another. Incorrect language caused a polemic of the imagination between Brazil and Portugal, the people and the 'frock-coated' minority,[56] the real country and the official country, the genuinely patriotic and the alienated sections of the elite, modern freedoms

---

55   Paulo Emílio Salles Gomes, *Cinema: Trajetória no subdesenvolvimento*, Rio de Janeiro, 1980, 77.
56   The word *casaca* (frock coat) has survived the garment itself, typical of nineteenth-century politicians, to signify male members of the traditional ruling classes. [*Tr.*]

and sclerotic conventionalism, and so forth. The second term in each of these pairs is the defeated one, or at least deserves defeat. The first, positive terms are not correspondingly identical in their libertarian meaning, however; and investigating these differences can lead us to a more discriminating view of modernism. For instance, the shallowness of the official, legal, grammatically conformist country made the real country no less authoritarian, even as it benefited from sincerity in the matter of pronouns. In the same order of ambiguities, there is a decisive connection between the Brazilian use of pronouns and the universe of informality, allergic to official situations and thus to the normative dimension of the public sphere. Informality, which is a near relative of naturalness, seemed to represent the extension of family relationships into the street and the whole social context. So, the family model, with its characteristic forms of authority and intimacy, seemed to take the place of politics, which was reduced, as a consequence, to a useless luxury. In the guise of promoting popular life, the personalism of rural relationships and the correlative powerlessness of the State took on a *modern* aesthetic gloss, even if this was qualified by a humorous proviso. In order to understand the dubious character of these comings and goings, it is enough to recall the formal, non-spontaneous – frock-coated? – aspect of the idea of citizenship itself, even that of the poor.[57]

This said, the aggressive didacticism of Mário's stylistic choices, acquiring added value and even a kind of nobility through his erudition, linguistic alertness and unlimited dedication to the immense virtual family of all Brazilians, and especially to the unvalued culture of the poor, certainly did symbolize a national project, which was at once mistrustful of politics and political in its own way. He was trying to unite and embrace, in the informal erudite manner of his prose, the drastically unequal complex of regions,

---

57   The classic exploration of these themes can be found in Sérgio Buarque de Holanda's *Raízes do Brazil* (1936).

cultures and classes in the country; the power of real inquiry and modern artistic freedom; and an enlarged sense of what was owed, as a matter of programmatic obligation, so to speak, to the Brazilian kind of extended family, which he widened to include the whole nation. The best feelings that paternalism was capable of when taken to its own limits, freed of its material interests but still mindful of the corresponding duties, grew on a truly Amazonian scale reaching as far as the country's borders and beyond. The modern individual – here is the avant-garde note – would be liberated and inspired by a certain ideal pattern of Brazilian family existence, flexible, extendable and open to adjustment within the wider collective whole, would take a revolutionary turn, overcoming egotistical isolation. Alien to the rigidities of the law, these family ties would be the inspiration for an order that, overcoming the estrangements of the old Brazil, would also be equal to the modernist critique of the new alienations of bourgeois civilization, to be avoided at all costs. The misplaced nature of this aspiration, on the eve of the Revolution of 1930 and of the industrial growth it brought with it, is nowadays very obvious.[58] But that does not mar its beauty. The paradox lies in the aesthetically advanced external features, which are owed to the adventurous or extravagant activism of our pre-bourgeois substratum in the field of advanced artistic experimentation; an unlikely combination making for an impractical political hypothesis but a powerful ideal image to set against a frustrating social inertia that persists today.

Everyone who reads Mário recognizes the rather cloying tone of his prose, in which the immense, writerly freedom of movement combines rebellious gestures and the aim of edification, arising from his vocation as a teacher. The transgressive dimension, very

---

58   The Brazilian revolution of 1930 ended the 'Old Republic', dominated by elites from the southern, particularly the coffee-growing states of Brazil, brought the *gaúcho* Getúlio Vargas to power, which he was to institutionalize in the Estado Novo. The thirties also saw the first steps towards industrialization. [*Tr.*]

varied in its motifs and gestures, deserves a separate study. For our purposes, its unexpected aim – in part Mário's alone, in part common to the modernists in general – is enough. The point was to take features of Brazilian life that might be thought embarrassing, for example its parochialism, its proneness to childish enthusiasms, its complicated family relationships, its malarial hallucinations or its adolescent rebelliousness, and show them off in the open, in the contemporary world, where they would operate as trump cards of advanced thought – not to say of subversion. It was as if a river were flowing uphill . . . Such inversions are partly just a *boutade*, but they owe their force to a certain endorsement provided by the local course of history, and above all to the crisis of bourgeois reason, which causes supra-individual mechanisms, even if they are soaked in backwardness and localism, to bear promises of future harmonies. Readers will have noticed the parallel with Helena Morley's critical spirit at its most collectivizing. Mário composed a powerful, strange literary instrument, anchored deep in Brazilian realities and in the present in general, with few rivals in its ability to formulate the country's experience. In the present context of argument, what is striking is its diversity of tone, mirroring a society with little differentiation, where – with a little exaggeration – the schoolmaster, the revolutionary in letters and *mores*, and the guardian of national culture are one and the same person, whose prose unites all the different tones and moves easily between them, with the dedicated purpose of counter-balancing society's immobility and the general lack of representative institutions. That said, the outward aspect of this style that aspired to be functional could not be more personal or less transferable, and this suggests that its great ambition may be unrepeatable. Today, Mário's prose reads as an extraordinary feat of individual expression, associated, as it happened, with a desire to perfect the nation.

Seen in such contexts, *The Diary of 'Helena Morley'* emerges as an extremely interesting representative of a substantial trend in Brazilian literature. Its special note is owing to a certain ease of aesthetic fit, something in the manner of *Memoirs of a Militia Sergeant*, which does not row against the current but, for all that, is not trivial, and does not reek of ideological justifications. Contrastingly, I have suggested that sympathetic views of the country, even in authors of great distinction, depend on the exclusion of obvious aspects of reality. In Helena Morley's prose, this does not happen, not because of her superior artistic skill but because the historical moment had done the filtering for her: Abolition had put an end to slave labour, and the involution of the regional economy barred untrammelled bourgeois progress, thereby opening a breach for progress of another kind, an internal shift and a new settlement, of whose humanity the book's beauty speaks, and whose existence it proves. For one moment the reciprocal regulation of paternalism and private property seemed able to overcome the fracture in Brazilian society. There is testimony in this precarious harmony, liable to break down at the first jolt of economic progress, when the usual social discord will reclaim its prerogatives.

III

6

An Enormous Minimalism

If the lyric mode classically inscribes the poet as individual, the Brazilian writer Francisco Alvim is, in Cacaso's nice phrase, 'the poet of the others': finding his own voice by ceding the right to speak to all the rest – to the extent of transforming this attentiveness towards them into a new poetic technique. There is, of course, an element of irony in this depiction of the writer as good Samaritan: such close concern for one's neighbours can also be, as Cacaso himself insists, a literary device for catching them in flagrante. For the 'others' here are not the abstract figures of philosophical discourse. We should think rather of the 'Brazilians just like me' of whom Mário de Andrade wrote in the 1920s, and of his eponymous hero Macunaíma, who was the 'little heart of the others'. Or of the atmosphere, saturated with familiarity, to which Drummond referred with cordial ambivalence when he wrote in 1930: 'At least we know everyone's rubbish around here'.[1]

---

1   Francisco ('Chico') Alvim (b. 1938), the author of *Elefante* (São Paulo, 2000), is a poet and diplomat. Cacaso (Antonio Carlos Ferreira de Brito; b. 1944–d. 1987) was a leading member of the oppositional 'marginal poetry' movement in Brazil in the 1970s; see his 'O poeta dos outros' in *Não quero prosa,* ed. Vilma Sant-Anna Arêas, Campinas, 1997, 308. For Mário de Andrade,see chs. 2 and 4 above, pp. 11 and 78 respectively; and for Carlos Drummond de Andrade (b. 1902– d. 1987), 'Explicação', in *Alguma poesia,* 1930, in *Poesia e prosa*, Rio de Janeiro, 1979, 98; and ch. 5 above, n. 8. [*Tr.*]

In other words, three-quarters of a century after the modernist movement began in Brazil, the investigations carried out by its leading figures into the peculiarities of national life – its speech, its rhythms, the interactions of its people and their unspoken pacts – re-emerge in Alvim's collection *Elefante*. Quite a few things have changed since the twenties, and the poet's historical and aesthetic feel for these shifts is one of his fine qualities. The essence of his approach can be conveyed in the four words that together constitute the title and entire text of this poem:

Want to see?

Listen[2]

This is the work's poetic; more complex than it seems, once its shifting grammatical coloration is taken into account. The ill-disciplined slippage (a very Brazilian habit) between third and second-person modes of address, from the polite *Quer?* to the more intimate *Escuta*; the informality of treatment; the Oswaldian modernism, its brevity not without a glint of humour – all jar with the universalist tone of the maxim.[3] In fact, without the colloquialism and grammatical licence, this poem would be an impersonal, lapidary lesson about the relation between desire, vision and the spoken word. But it is not timeless in this sense: the social and cultural particularities of its intonations pull it towards a specific world setting, just as they destabilize its meanings. The poem's equivocal placing within the collection also needs to be taken into account. It can be read either as the last of a series of verses dominated by lyrical feeling or as the first of another set marked by a critical-realist note and a shrewd sense of specifically Brazilian

---

2   Alvim, *Quer ver?* // Escuta. All subsequent citations of the poems in the original are given in this format.

3   For Oswald de Andrade, see further n.8 below and also ch. 5, 165. [*Ed.*]

absurdities. Fitted between these two, the 'Want to see?' of the title -question could as easily be an invitation to poetry or the mocking humour of someone well acquainted with the beast of which he speaks – and in whose belly he belongs. The same words might, on one reading, be those of any intelligent person who recommends the humility of listening; of a poet, learned and concise; or again, of an unillusioned Brazilian advising his interlocutor on what to expect. Importantly, this three-in-one is sustained within everyday speech, with no sense of the interiorized conflict of the Romantic ego, or of exceptional beings or situations. Its context is the complexity, the peculiarity of Brazil's daily life – in which, I think, lies the secret of the work. Its language and contexts are rigorously commonplace, but they pertain to a specific social formation that is itself at odds with the conventions of contemporary civilization.

The book's consistency of tone lies in its dramatization – through the multiple freedoms modernism establishes – of a central, enduring concept: that of Brazilian interrelations between norms and informality; a heterodoxy that can be seen either as a manufacturing defect or as a gift from the gods. Much has been written on the theme of informality; the point here is that its systematic transposition into the structure of these poems forms the watermark of Alvim's book. The dissonances corresponding to this mismatch can be detected in every aspect of national life. They can be collected as anecdotes that encode a historical condition; reduced to diagrams or modules with variabilized powers of explanation, or invented, constructed so as to explore the extremities of the concept. Alvim, who has a devilish ear for these things, has done some of all three. The variety of which he is capable runs from the apparently innocent –

Argument

But they all do[4]

---

4   Alvim, *Argumento* / / Mas se todos fazem

– to almost imperceptible touches that are not easy to pin down as instances of informality but nevertheless bring the notion to life. Thus, on the opposite page, for example, the elaborate constructions of a French functionary, highly articulate if somewhat ridiculous, throw into relief the stumbling steps of a local civil servant:

> I wanted to propose something along those lines
> but then I thought
> but oh my god
> then he said[5]

In analogous fashion, Alvim sets the clarity and integrity at work in Spanish expressions in contrast to the slipperiness (*malandragem*), or lack of finish, of local diction. Both are ways of configuring the external face of a specifically Brazilian literary existence through its contrasts with the tones and languages of other nations.

In a remarkable poem, 'Open', about the gaze as it wanders through the field of light – a plausible subject for philosophy – the movement is introduced by 'At times', which instantly de-universalizes it. This is followed by an assortment of passing colloquialisms that render the encounters with 'time' and 'eternity', which 'is not far', more like meeting with acquaintances on a street corner, somewhere everyone stops, with no particular destination in mind, simply asking, ' – place?' In other words, there is an inflection towards the specific, to a situation beyond anthropomorphism, that softens the rigorous abstraction. In the opening poem, 'Carnival', the paradoxical, devaluing transfiguration of water into desert might simply be explained by the protagonist's hangover as he sits watching the sea with a thirst no water can slake; which – once this premise has been guessed at – raises a

---

5 *Debate* // eu quis colocar esse tipo de coisa / mas então pensei / mas meu deus do céu / aí ele disse

smile at the final question: what is the reality of poetry? In 'Commentary' – where one does not know who is who and the phrases do not fit together – the secret of the discontinuity lies in fear, in the voids that install themselves in people's heads when they talk about the military dictatorship.

Not all these dissonances seem, at first glance, to resonate with the structural malformations of Brazil; it is in reading the work as a whole that a wider set of references begins to assert itself, giving the poems – the briefest, in particular – a broader field of allusion to which the reader gradually grows attuned. Thus, in *Football*

> There are balls he doesn't go after[6]

the wisdom, or complaint, applies not only to the player but to all those obliged to exercise a certain caution: the politician, the head of the family, the drug trafficker; women too, as the case may be. The subject may be sport, but no clear border separates the zone of risk that the player might run into from the terror deployed – in the past and in other pages of the book – by the Brazilian military regime. The discovery lies in the relationship between the fears, between the decisions about how to play them.

I

Once polarized by the same forces as the social totality, the poems can deploy new possibilities of allusion, equivalence and ellipsis that permit them an even greater degree of concision, to the point where humour ceases to be an objective. But if the wit at play within each poem is restricted to the absolute minimum appropriate to a form that is still akin to the *trouvaille*, or joke, the contrary is true of the space glimpsed beyond the frontiers of the text, which open directly onto historical reality. But are we dealing just with 'texts', when ellipsis

---

6 *Futebol* / / Tem bola em que ele não vai

plays so great a part? Rarefaction and raw experience are conjoined here, though their objects are dispersed. This is a poetry of summary indications, a join-up-the-dots: cerebral, hypothetical, now realist, now allegorical – like the 'Itineraries. Itineraries. Itineraries. Itineraries. Itineraries. Itineraries. Itineraries.' that Oswald de Andrade recommends in the 'Cannibal Manifesto'.[7]

In these poems – there are around a hundred of them here, in a collection of 128 – the appropriate reading is frankly activist, as free, informed and observant as possible, to complement the extreme ellipticism practised by the poet. It is for the reader, alert to indications of every sort, to imagine the situations in which the spoken words arise, to grasp how sharply one-sided they are and thus to enter into the material, putting the poems' perspectives into perspective – often ending by turning the original phrase, the starting point, inside out. Each poem, even when it is composed solely of a title and a single line, can be seen as an episode, a coordinate, within the life of the whole. In this sense, while on one plane the poet takes compression to the absolute limit, he compensates on another by offering the full breadth of the social-historical world, represented without resort to any of the continuities of plot and character or the epic and dramatic frameworks offered by literary tradition. The outdated or illusory aspects of individualism – and their crisis in nineteenth-century literature – are rendered explicit in the miniaturization of these 'poem-drafts': sexual jealousy, social resentment, class guilt, family feuds, fear of contagion, delusions of grandeur, the urge to pull a fast one, are all present here, utterly reduced, yet without any loss of proportion or subtlety. In other words, *Elefante* belongs to that special category of works in which the reciprocal testing of artistic forms and historical experience is being worked through.

---

7 'Roteiros. Roteiros. Roteiros. Roteiros. Roteiros. Roteiros. Roteiros.': Oswald de Andrade, 'Manifesto antropófago, *Do Pau-Brasil à antropofagia e às utopias*, 2nd ed., ed. Benedito Nunes, Rio de Janeiro 1978, 15.

The poems group themselves in a series of unexpected ways –
through simple contrasts, scathing mutual commentary or more
distant interreaction.

Park

It's nice
but it's very mixed[8]

gives expression to a typical middle or upper-class opinion: in
favour of social improvements but hostile to popular participation
– a key variant of the national form of progressivism, still bound to
its colonial origins. The implication, of course, is that an 'unmixed'
park would not admit the miscellaneous mass of the poor, black and
white unless they were employed in some sort of service role: child
minder, park keeper, someone taking old people or dogs for a walk.
The antiquated expression *misturado*, predating the media's pseudo-
integrated Brazil, may bring a smile; but anti-poor sentiments have
not disappeared and continue, with the necessary adjustments, to
fortify the fault lines of Brazilian society. Out of context, the
vignette could be read as nostalgia; documentary; pro-oligarchy or
against it. One of Alvim's sure hits – and one of his originalities – is
the way in which he integrates such a moment into the present
crisis:

Look

A black man speaking
with such clarity
and human sympathy[9]

---

8 *Parque* / / É bom / mas é muito misturado
9 *Olha* / / Um preto falando/ com toda clareza / e simpatia humana

In contrast to 'Park', this poem apparently records a victory over bigotry but is itself so prejudiced as to make one balk. The critical impact is subtler, and more devastating, when we realize that even such an appreciation of clear, sympathetic speech – objectively, an enlightened response, entraining a genuine recognition of the Other and with it, the possibility of his emancipation – has ceased now to carry any weight; so that this moment of deepest prejudice currently appears to be a lost opportunity for moving beyond it. In

But

She's quite clean[10]

the content of the poem consists in what it does not say, all that precedes the title: the encyclopaedia of objections that those with property raise against those without it, those obliged to labour for them – of whom the best that can be said is that they are not very dirty. The term loses nothing (a friend has pointed out) if the context is shifted from the drawing room to the red-light district. Again, in

Disposable

feel like throwing me away[11]

we do not know if the wish is the speaker's, or someone else's; perhaps both. In either case, we find an internalization of the same class attitudes.

Time has passed between the earlier 'very mixed' and the 'disposable' here. One was born with the end of slavery, while the other belongs to the age of mass consumer society. Nevertheless, the class

---

10   *Mas* // é limpinha
11   *Descartável* // vontade de me jogar fora

formations to which the two refer have remained almost constant: on one side, the distinguished and enlightened, the 'civilized' who give the orders; on the other, the multitude of the rightless. The reciprocal conditioning of the two sides, within the para-legal terms of authority and informality, is a central, enduring nexus of Brazil's historical experience. Alvim's ear for the variations within this equation allows him to bring together, in sure, surprising ways, spheres that never usually meet: anecdotes from Minas Gerais and the rural hinterland; gossip from the time of the dictatorship; drug deals; house-proud mothers working the streets; casual labour abroad; a car crash caused by jealous rage; the stresses of bureaucratic life; politics and corruption; the guilt-ridden sparring of marital break-ups; she loves me, she loves me not – all share some undercurrent of the *not right*, which this work aims to know. In the great tradition of Machado de Assis, the poet is aware of the internal connexions between the opposite poles of Brazilian society, and refuses their stereotypical obsessions. Those without rights are capable of a special kind of courtesy as well as the truculence learnt from those above; while the civilized resort quite naturally to the double-dealing ways of small-time crooks, without imagining that these could impinge on their lofty moments of love, reflection or barbarity.

2

In describing Alvim as the 'poet of the others', Cacaso wanted to stress the non-bourgeois generosity of the impulse that takes an educated artist across the barrier separating the approved from the rejected or despised to seek the awareness expressed in words and situations there. Alvim himself, as a writer, certainly breathes an exceptional aura of humanity that derives from this approach. But such a stance in itself does not abolish social divisions; indeed, far from erasing them, the effect of the poet's attentive sympathy is rather to expose these fractures. There are, perhaps, no other works in Brazilian poetry in which the brutal subtleties of class have such presence. Ironically, by lending his voice to others, this disinterested, brotherly artist gives free rein to all the species of degradations produced by this system of conflicting interests. In 'Tradesman, Manicurist, Decorator', for example – the gestures of aspirational melodrama already played out in the title – more or less tolerable ways of earning a living get ranked to produce a result somewhere between the democratic and the seigneurial-sardonic. In a darker tone but still linked to the discoveries of listening, there are the rumours connecting land deals, the presidential succession and the torture of political prisoners – hinted at in passing, the sentences interrupted – in 'Commentary'. Alvim looks for poetry, and for his country, in unwonted places, normally frequented only by the tabloid press or those at home in squalor.

The voices that speak through the poet are not those of anyone in particular; but nor do they belong to everyone. Anonymous yet typical, neither individualized nor universalized, their utterances have the polyvalence of everyday use combined with a structural fit into the collective processes of Brazilian life that conveys its patterns and enacts its saliences. The poet ensures that we often do not know who is speaking, whom they are addressing, whose viewpoint provides the title – itself no neutral frame but a player within the overall field of uncertainties. This precise yet undetermined structure, demanding a set of diverse readings, allows systemic inequalities to speak for themselves – their asymmetries functioning as an immense, automatic subject, shaping destinies and teaching us how small we are before it. Is the point of view so-and-so's, or someone else's? The words might serve for either, but the effect is completely different when the roles are reversed. Is Cristiano the one who recalls the car crash, the idiotic slamming on of brakes that causes it, or is it – with a slight change of intonation in the last line – Darlene? We know nothing of these figures save their names and the social differences these suggest – a refined young man; a young woman who sounds like an actress – which may not correspond with reality, may be no more than prejudice. We are given no more objective evidence than this possibly non-existent opposition, of no importance in itself but in which the internalization of social power structures becomes tangible.

Alvim's poems contain a special sort of evidence from which the writer – in keeping with one of the radical promises of the avant-garde – has practically disappeared. The material itself, pre-forged within daily life, is crucial to this achievement, as is the expository technique, the pared-down, interrogative form learned from Oswald. Underpinning the poems, and informing both the scope and accuracy of the project, lies a profound critical understanding of Brazilian social relations, their covert correspondences and their deviations from modern norms viewed as if from a distance, yet always as 'ours'. This is an aesthetic approach that refuses to individualize either the poems' characters or the poet's persona; for Alvim – with certain exceptions, as we shall see – does not write from the basis of a personal mythology. The complexity he seeks lies in the public domain, accessible to all, as the radical modernist João Cabral had hoped, in contrast to the musty attics of private life.[12] The same refusal is at work at the level of language, whose basic unit is not the line of verse or written word but the spoken phrase, culled from the lived relations of 'a problem country'. The consequences of this – apparently anti-lyrical – engagement with second-hand experience as a point of departure are decisive.

Alvim's previous collection, *O corpo fora*, took Baudelaire's famous phrase from *Fusées* as its epigraph: 'Immense profundity of thought in commonplace turns of phrase, holes burrowed by generations of ants'.[13] What is expressed in everyday speech is an actual social system at work, through which – thanks to the invention of

---

12　For a brief description of João Cabral de Melo Neto (b. 1920–d.1999), see ch. 5, n. 52. [*Ed.*]

13　Francisco Alvim, *Poesias reunidas: 1968–1988*, São Paulo, 1988, 9.

this literary architecture – we can recognize and examine ourselves, for better or for worse. In part, the hard currency of this sort of talk is extrinsic to the artistic process, impossible to improve upon. The product of collective use, often popular or semi-popular, everyday speech has a tried-and-tested quality quite different from that of individual creations. To note these intricacies is always to do more than merely understand the poet. Modern poetry's desire 'to be' rather than 'to communicate' finds an unforeseen realization here. As immediate responses to contemporary social situations, these utterances just are, with the simplicity of behaviour sanctioned by practice. They have a dense, objective existence that challenges the reader from an unexpected direction, their contingency dependent on other factors than poetic whim. Not that the poet's ear has been limited to passive recording. These phrases have been finely tuned, scoured clean of superfluity, redundancy, cliché or generalizations: in other words, of conventional literary features. Alvim's work is to distil their experiential content and render them commensurable, as parts of the same system. The process is not dictated by poetic tradition but by a sense for the most effective means of representing this regime of generalized social ambiguity, through what he describes as the

> irony
> of polymorphous voices
> sibylline
> unsettled in the ear
> of language[14]

The line divisions – into something other than verses – also serve to expose and confuse the logic of the action, to make it polycentric. Something similar occurs with punctuation, where the organizing

---

14 *Escolho* // ironia / das polimorfas vozes / sibilinas / transtornadas no ouvido / da língua

role given to capital letters in some of the poems dispenses with the need for full stops; the opportunities for confusion that this creates are, again, fully exploited.

3

The work's most striking technical move – borrowed from modernist fiction – is the discontinuity of perspectives within the poems, which lack any stable point of view, even in their titles. These changes are effected with astonishing dexterity. Although tiny, the field for manoeuvre is regulated by the largest social forces, so that the inversions of viewpoint acquire a didactic dimension, providing distances and revelations. There is something Brechtian here, though without Brecht's political certainties. The minimalism, inspired by attitude and gesture as well as social and historical insight, also has a demonstrative aim, parallel to Brecht's. We have to hear to see. The paring down of speech, scenes, sequences and digressions, far from impoverishing the poems, gives greater force to the play of connexions, while the proliferation of virtual relationships within these miniatures intensifies the logic of the situations. The aim here is quite overt and provides a set of tasks for literary investigation far removed from the art-for-art's-sake approach of much experimentalism. The economy of minimal forms results in an almost modular reduction and an extreme concentration of the social relations within them – thereby gaining a force to which the brevity of the formulations should not blind us:

She

Hit her
Hit[15]

---

15   *Ela* / / Soca ela / Soca. On its own, *ela* can mean both 'she' and 'her'. [*Ed.*]

Depending on who is speaking and who listening, 'she' is ordering someone to be hit or is being hit herself – unless the poet is getting orders from the woman. Or is it he who is demanding she be hit? The precarious grammar – taken as an indicator of class – could explain the vehemence of the request, but the opposite is also possible, revealing that the tenuous commitment to grammatical correctness on the part of our educated elite can be shaken at the first jolt.[16] In sum, the systematic changes of focus work in tandem with the social investigation and serve it as a means of analysis and exploration, in close contact with the actual material relations.

> *You think I'm stupid*
>
> You're the boss
> and you let him act the way he does?
> He'd better pay
> what he owes you[17]

Here, too, the voice that speaks in the body of the poem might not be the same one as in the title; which in turn could be either introduction or conclusion. The provocateur – a woman? a hanger-on? – is in the right, from the money point of view. The listener, who is well aware that reason and legal right offer no guarantee in this instance – but what are the other powers in play? – has the bitter satisfaction, linked to the presence of third parties, of giving a title to this scene, getting the last word but without changing its essential parameters. Action and joke come in the dialogue, but the substance to be

---

16   An attentive observer lists the 'colonial linguistic regime' among the general conditions of Brazilian literature. Reflection on the aesthetic and class consequences of this regime, which did not disappear with decolonization, has hardly begun. Luciana Stegagno Picchio, *La letteratura brasiliana*, Florence, 1972, 27–8.

17   Alvim, *E eu é que sou burro* / / Você é o dono / e deixa fazer o que ele faz? / O que ele te deve / vai ter que pagar

deciphered lies in the relations of power in the background, which are neither named nor even touched by the poem's sarcasm. Since the title comes before the poem, not after, and is thought by the person who speaks the text, another, less interesting, reading is possible.

4

Given the current concretist–cabralist conjuncture in Brazilian poetry, it is worth noting how Alvim, at the formal level, takes his own path. He too is looking for the gains to be had from reduction and combination but without paying tribute to asceticism and geometry and, above all, without abandoning the world. Again, as in Brecht, a high degree of subtlety combines with a type of robust reflection that we do not normally recognize as a literary category. With no loss to the multiplicity of perspectives, there is a preference here for a lively, unaffected use of language, a stress on pragmatic fluidity and accuracy of vision: this is an avant-garde aesthetic opposed to deference, displays of authority and the grand abstractions of the bourgeois social order, to whose rigidity and falseness, here and now, it objects. It is a refusal that has its sights set on the posturings and façades of both individual and institutional dignity:

> So get off your high horse
> and say what you really think[18]

This is another point of contact with Brazilian 'informality', which relativizes everything, even the law, in the permanent, personalized game of accommodation to power that permits the breaching of all formal rules and with them – when taken to the limit – the

---

18 *Em família* // Então bota de lado essa cerimônia / e diga logo o que você pensa

state's guarantee of rights. The dizzying revaluations involved in these movements, in which the illicit goes unpunished and critical reaction and regression are confused, is a feature of many of the greatest moments in Brazilian literature.[19] There is a possible affinity between situations in which bourgeois categories only half hold sway and the de-conventionalizing tendency of modern art: one that is problematic in every sense. In this light, we can look at the various deals made in Alvim's work, none of them within the law:

Business

We'll sort it out later[20]

Once this stance – expressed aesthetically in the tone of this ubiquitous refrain, has been taken, bourgeois legality is out of the question. The economic transaction, when it happens, will not be encoded in a contract and will not create any formal equivalence between the subjects or provide any self-standing guarantees. In other words, the imbalance of power between the parties will not be suspended by the egalitarian fictions of the law. Legal rights must always take other incidental factors into account, making each case sui generis. When a sense of human sympathy makes itself felt, it does not come from respect for norms but from informal gestures that infringe the rules and seem to constitute a community inseparable from some kind of connivance. 'Business' acquires its full weight when read in conjunction with the poems already quoted – 'Go on, get off your high horse / and say what you really think', 'There are balls he doesn't go after', 'But they all do' and others – which allow the reader to sense their common framework and give a different form to the whole; one in which the rule of force always plays a role.

---

19   See Candido, 'Dialectic of Malandroism', 97–103.
20   Alvim, *Negócio* // Depois a gente acerta

Saddles

I tried it
He didn't resist[21]

The language is equestrian, the audience a family member or similar and the probable victim is a menial or a relative, in no position to object.

5

The subject matter raises another set of questions. Is this the poet's preferred choice of theme? Is it an involuntary diagnosis, the result of his effort to be mimetically precise and faithful to the language as spoken? Let us say that the rule of not abiding by the rules is a paradox that condenses the moral and intellectual condition of a peripheral country where today's canonical forms, those of the countries at the centre, cannot be put into practice in their entirety – which does not stop them being obligatory as mirror and yardstick. Clearly, there is a negative sign, a deficiency, inherent in this condition – complemented by the positive sign of the other, situated in different latitudes. The problem country may be presented as a form of exoticism; at its most serious, as an excrescence. But at another level, the logic of the situation produces not only an inferiority complex but a mutual contempt. From the Brazilian viewpoint, the rule of law can look questionable and outlandish, if not hypocritical and domineering, with its lack of spontaneity, lamentable impersonality, unreal abstraction, ridiculous presumption and so on. These clashing views, each with enough reason on its side to undermine the other, open up critical perspectives:

---

21   *Selas //* Experimentei / Não reagiu

Hospitality

> If your country's
> that great
> why don't you go home?[22]

Underlined by the clear irony of the title, here is the resentful rudeness of the hosts, citizens of a rich country, who cannot forgive the homesick immigrant and demand his social conformity as well as his labour. Central to the poem but left to the reader's imagination are the marvels that the poor devil has extolled in relaxed, informal Brazil, the country that he has fled from and to which he has no desire to return. If, on the contrary, the speaker is Brazilian, the sense of the words changes but not the coordinates within which they operate. The poem highlights the complementarity of the resentments or alienations in the peripheral and core countries, the joint system they create and the truths they tell about each other.

There are no good grounds for recommending informality: its foundations lie in social fracture, in the precarious integration of the poor and their lack of rights – which does not stop them taking advantage of informal practices for their own ends. But with this basic proviso, there is no reason to ignore the freedoms and polemical scope inherent in this quasi-state of nature, especially in comparison to the stiffness and artificiality of the bourgeois regulation of life. Alert to both considerations, and independent enough not to close his eyes to either of them, Alvim has much to teach in this respect. His de-idealized and debased world, structurally second class, nevertheless breathes a peculiar kind of poetry, linked to the advantages of naturalness that follow the relativization of law and the suspension of the sacrifices necessary to sustain the 'formal' brand of superiority. Yet how are we to assess the force of such despised, outcast material?

---

22 *Hospitalidade* / / Se seu país é assim / tão bom / por que não volta?

Let me tell you

A little pest of a pain
It starts I lose my stride
Hurts here and hurts there
Silly nuisance[23]

The discomfort – one that has no scientific name and elicits no remedy from the pharmaceutical industry – clearly falls on the peripheral side of the equation. There is no way to get rid of the pain, which does not kill and has no definite cure but does not for that reason cease to exist. This does not make it more 'natural' than pneumonia, say, which can be treated with antibiotics and figures in medical statistics, but connects it to other inescapable aspects of life that science and medicine have not been able to reach yet, or relegate without comment to a secondary order or sweep under the carpet. From this point of view, the arbitrary, capricious little pain is a radical presence, representing an unavoidable memory, a backhanded victory over modern presumption.

The pain's 'naturalness' is ambiguous, drawing now from nature itself, now from an out-of-joint social order; above all from the interchange between the two. The intimate relationship between the sufferer and the pain; its personification; the diminutives and irritated adjectives applied to it; the anecdotal form; the colloquial grumble of the title and the unceremonious way the pain comes and goes and changes place – all are thoroughly familiar. The pain and its victim conform to the ideal pattern of Brazilian informality, pressuring and being pressured, seeking some ad hoc compromise on the margins of medical progress. This in turn domesticates the unavoidable meeting place between human creature and physical suffering, giving it the stamp of naturalness and, with that, a certain

---

23   *Te contar* / / Dorzinha enjoada / Ela começa perco a graça / Dói aí e dói aqui / Dorzinha chata

metaphysical dignity, despite the fact that the object itself hardly exists. The conversation is inconsequential, but its horizon is the way things are, the inexorable flow of time and the *terra incognita* ahead of us: truths that are taboo in modern life and which subtly come to seem like forms of knowledge proper to Brazil. In

> *And now?*

> We were there yesterday
> He's much cheerier
> He's had a lot of pain[24]

the perplexity of the title comes after the relief which, contrary to what one might expect, has only worsened (or prolonged?) the problem. The outstanding quality of a poem so devoid of emphasis, so far advanced in its avoidance of any kind of conventionality, can be hard to grasp. The almost spatial simplicity of the positioning of the terms of the impasse, each one temporally specific, is a striking moment of materialist awareness.

Assimilated into the world of informality, with which it shares its diminished status, this complaint acquires a national coloration. As the title 'And now?' informs us, this is a case of patience being put to the test. The sense of physical existence reflects a form of sociability: the pain there is no getting away from takes on the features of someone you know, a member of the extended family. But the same theme can also recur in an explicitly social version:

> *Irani, tell Gilson to go away*

> I told him to
> but he won't[25]

---

24 *E agora?* / / Ontem estivemos lá / Está mais animado / Teve muita dor
25 *Irani, manda Gilson embora* / / Eu mando / mas ele não vai

This drama presupposes property, but in a precarious (antiquated?) version, not independent of the rule of force. The girl with the indigenous name – she could be a daughter, a poor relation, an employee or a dependant – gives the command as a sign of obedience. As for Gilson, there is no way of knowing why he disobeys. It might be cousin love, the doglike fidelity of an employee or a tenant, or the despair of someone with nowhere to go. His insubordination is silent but obstinate and disarming. The inconvenience of this refusal to move, from a bourgeois perspective, is obvious; its logic imposes a different parameter on freedom, so long as the forces in play are not too unequal and paternalism does not swap its amiable face for that of the unrestricted modern property owner.

In the intimate struggle with the ailment in 'Let me tell you', a give and take with no fixed rules, the sufferer brings to bear all his resources of will, patience, adaptability and humour at a certain comforting distance from universalized forms of right and wrong. There is a parallel with Gilson, who doesn't want to go, or with the business deal which 'we'll sort out later', or again, in domestic warfare: 'The more you say it / the more I'll do it'.[26] It is as if, below the equator of law, science, grammar, progress and all the other modern imperatives, there opens up another civilization, more malleable and less abstract, governed by relationships between people (including the arbitrary use of power and force). Its anachronistic satisfactions seem to be lacking in the life spent within the constraints of reified civil norms. This non-official, non-model civilization, something of a disgrace but with a utopian potential in its contrasts, is the non-bourgeois dimension of the reproduction of bourgeois society in Brazil: inferior but necessary, with its own wisdom and even, for some, a certain superiority. Its many aspects, from the sympathetic to the horrendous, are the substance and problem that Brazilian historical experience has to offer.

---

26 *Briga* [Row] / / Quanto mais você fala / mais eu faço

Informality changes aspect depending on whether it is in the service of one class or another. When it helps people find their way through the privations of a post-colonial poverty that provides neither civil rights nor paid work but is sanctified by the preposterous formalisms of law, it has a popular connotation, even in its way a civilizing role. Its sharp eye for the damage caused by bourgeois abstractions is an element of humanity and reason, linked sometimes to a certain unmistakable charm in Brazilian speech, behaviour and literature. Thus, for instance, the case of a cunning Portuguese ex-market stallholder, who 'brought up a niece / who gave him grandchildren'.[27] But it also often works as an ideological alibi for those on top, allowing them to feel easier about riding roughshod over those below. In tune with the times, the stress of Alvim's book lies on this second form.

Factotum

Nothing worse
than owing someone a favour
Look Virgílio
you don't owe me a thing
only your leg and[28]

The opening words underline the humiliation of debt, sufficient to sour one's whole existence. In reply, whether to ease the situation or aggravate it, the boss tells his dependant that he owes him nothing – just 'your leg and'. What is not said – with the sordid taste this brings – is left to the imagination of the reader, who can choose between the disgraces specific to this universe (but avoidable by

---

27 *Vizinho* / / criou uma sobrinha / que lhe deu netos
28 *Factótum* / / Pior coisa / é dever um favor a alguém / Olha Virgílio / a mim você não deve nada não / só sua perna e

intervention from above): jail, mutilation, death, a dishonoured daughter and much more. The note of perverse paternalism is stronger still in the iniquitous calculation, reeking of the plantation store, that imposes itself when we think about the title. After a lifetime of service, the factotum is still indebted while his protector owes him nothing, least of all any sense of obligation. It is a version of the double bind between dependants and property owners, in which the dependants' debt lies not in money but in unending personal obligation, whereas that of the owners is a question of convenience and calculation. Moving between two worlds, they can come and go at their leisure, swapping the roles of faithful protector and objective, carefree individual. In both cases, informality gives to those on top the impress of a pleasant civility, disguising the social chasm.

There is another variant of this theme in the poems linked to Brasília, power, the time of the dictatorship and of fear. Here the dimensions of bureaucracy and state expand the malign side of informality, producing the paradox of an anonymous personalization, while reducing the country to an underworld. Stripping off its old rural and patriarchal disguise, informality now oppresses everyone, even its beneficiaries.

Archive

it can't be for memories[29]

Why not? The backdrop here is the political police, who make the very concept of an archive frightening and the notion of memory futile. The phrase could be the black humour of a potential victim or the words of a torture expert.

---

29   *Arquivo* / / não pode ser de lembranças

Jangle

> Sometimes there's news
> of a less agreeable sort
> and your ears jangle[30]

What news? As in 'Factotum' and 'But', what is left silent is the most important part. The jittery speaker does not dare go into it but sticks to euphemisms and limits his political commentary to his nervous reflexes, assimilated to the irritation caused by an ill-tuned radio. In 'Shadow',

> that black edifice
> in the yellow shadow, immense
> astounds the whole city
>
> Not you[31]

With terrible deliberation, the speaker, or poet, is excluded from the ranks of the frightened, thus levelling at himself the grave accusation of being one of those who know (but know what?) and, for the same reason, owe. This is the current stage of evolution of the dependency, above all of the educated, upon power. Once again, all reference to social terror lies in silence. In sum, these are figures from a constellation that is both familiar and enigmatic, in which the pores of the state are intimately associated with the trade-offs of paternalism, marital rows, corrupt business deals, the habits of disease, liberties with the law and grammatical carelessness.

---

30 *Chiado* // Às vezes corre notícia / dessas menos agradáveis / e o ouvido chia
31 *Sombra* // Aquele edifício negro / na sombra amarela, imensa / assombra toda a cidade // A ti, não

6

If they are harder to pin down, the qualities of *Elefante* as a whole are at least as substantial as those of the individual poems. Some of these features are intentional constructions; others, which are unplanned by-products of the work, can be equally suggestive. Alvim is a master not only of reductions and shifting configurations but also of selection, which here plays a structural role similar to the choice of episodes in a realist novel. The process seems to go something like this. After panning for suggestive trivia and reducing them to their active nuclei, the poet will select a few, create a vacuum around them and leave them alone on the page, in order to note how they interreact with each other and what insights and correspondences they generate. The point of departure is arbitrary and contingent, but the procedure is disciplined by the systematic objective of putting one's ear to the country.

The sequence of the poems is plotted with the purposeful precision of montage, though it also draws on the skills of the stage director, pamphleteer and social analyst. The surprising thing is that these operations – their critical, demonstrative spirit much closer to thought than to spoken language – manage to succeed in this long-distance harmonization of the words without distorting their natural qualities. It takes an ear closely attuned to a certain tone to resolve the discord between current speech and constructivist limpidity, receptive passivity and conceptual energy, the immediate 'given' and the allegorical device. The reductions of modernism play a role here, too, as does its radicalism – though this is now a second-half version: not the explosive project for a more transparent, habitable world but the identification of the actual global order through attentive listening that recognizes the little we have been reduced to, in an implosion of identity that is itself a sign of the times.

Informality serves not only as a principle of selection but also one of rejection, laden with structural consequences. Intimations of duty in speech or actions are relativized or pushed to the margins, since here they would sound a discordant note. Observed with rigour, this decision to be unrigorous imposes its socio-historical stamp on everything. Yet the resonances of the inner imperative do not disappear: excluded as subject matter, they return in the severe objectivity of artistic composition, hovering over the book like a troublesome ghost, fully alive only in another hemisphere. That said, the whole has no separate, self-sufficient existence. The majority of the things, terms and ideas of which it is composed – the *modernized* part, to be precise – have no shape of their own; or better, have the shape of the world from which they differ. The discrepancy is the result of functional differences, which give rise to a kind of abstract local colour. Dissimilar and correlative, the social universes of centre and periphery are interwoven. Nonetheless, any awkwardness here would be no less noticeable and artistically fatal than it would be in prose works as distinctive and removed from the dominant usage as, say, *Macunaíma* or *Grande sertão: veredas* – works that are an inventive halfway house between dialect and idiolect, based on local, grammatical and orthographic peculiarities. It is as if, unbeknown to itself, modernized Brazil were developing an irregularity, a kind of regionalism, in the present context of a world presumed to be homogeneous. This differentiation demands a literary discipline of enormous subtlety.

The aim of the ironies is to measure up to the disappointments brought on by the actual course of events. The figurative task and clear-eyed conclusions of nineteenth-century realism act as a base-line of lucidity, although here they are extremely condensed, and far removed from the internal dynamism they formerly nourished – notably in the years prior to 1964, during the radical phase of developmentalist populism. The mini-episodes aspire to a certain loose representativeness, conveying something of capital and provinces, Brazil and Europe, mansion and slave quarters, educated and colloquial speech, plenty and destitution, rural patriarchy and urban anonymity, decorum and danger, all against an elided background of unsolved social problems. Once this order of oppositions is accepted, other poems find their place: the discordant informality in one resonating with its neighbouring variants to give the whole not only a common scale but also the material breadth and dimensions of a historical formation, a literary universe. What is new in *Elefante* comes not so much from the glaring social contrasts – these are well known – but from a certain modification of the inter-connexions between them, which seem to have been abandoned by an integrating, transforming tension. The present has expanded not only in space and time but in the social order, which now includes elements to which it was until recently opposed, or which it believed it had overcome. Some of the dicta in these poems go back to the end of slavery, others to the Old Republic – between the fall of the Brazilian Empire in 1889 and the 1930 revolution – and many more to modernized Brazil, including the leaden years of the dictatorship and the subsequent period of political liberalization ('the time of lean cattle / when the country had been redemocratized', as an ex-state governor explains in 'Ancient History').[32] Yet, notwithstanding the time-specific aspect such dicta present, as they take their places in historical order, the emphasis is on what remains constant, giving rise to the counter-intuitive feeling – the realization? – that change has made no difference. The past has not passed, and it no longer helps, as before, to invent a future that remains hidden from view. The persistence of the present marks it as different; but more in the sense of being defective than original, or backward, or on the road to recovery. Above all, the present leads one to see in the past premonitory signs of the current impasse, again refuting the appearance of progress.

In analogous fashion, the interplay between informality and norm has lost the temporal axis once linked to the promises of modernization. Informality has not been defeated, nor does bourgeois normality seem to lie ahead; indeed, it could be said that the

32 *História antiga* // Na época das vacas magras / redemocratizado o país

norm is *passé*, while informality has taken hold for the foreseeable future. It is worth pointing out that the static background to this dynamic is a silent relative to the scandalous discoveries of Tropicalism, which gave shape to the aesthetic consequences of the counter-revolution of 1964 and subsequent conservative modernization.[33] The typical image of the time, presented above all in theatre, film, popular music and the graphic arts, was an allegory of the Brazilian absurd, understood either as the ultra-modern reproduction of social backwardness or an incomprehensible penchant for recidivism. It was a formula for dramatizing the incongruous and de-polarized coexistence of elements of the patriarchal–personalized world, outdated, ridiculous and flourishing as never before, with international patterns of modernity, themselves equally open to question. This was a picturesque, strident, shameful and true juxtaposition, with no future in view, saying in its own fashion that the hypothesis of a historical reshaping on a different level had disappeared. The parallel between the artistic methods of tropicalism and *Elefante* and their respective historical moments merits reflection.

In a hostile review that appeared soon after *Elefante* was published, one commentator drew attention to the connexion between Alvim's poetry and a strand of critical thinking on Brazil, indebted to modernism and with links to the aesthetic and theoretical work of politicized university groups.[34] The observation is correct, but the objection is surprising. Is it inappropriate for poetry to reflect upon its country?

---

33   The heyday of the Tropicalist movement came between the coup of 1964 and the accession of Emilio Garrastazu Médici in 1969; its most famous proponent was the popular singer and composer Caetano Veloso (b. 1942), whose lyrics often juxtaposed modern and traditional aspects of Brazil in deliberately jarring ways. For an account of *Tropicalismo*, see Roberto Schwarz, 'Culture and Politics in Brazil, 1964–1969', in *Misplaced Ideas: Essays on Brazilian Culture*, London, 1992; and 'Political Iridescence: The Changing Hues of Caetano Veloso', *New Left Review* 75, May–June 2012. [*Tr.*]

34   Paulo Franchetti, O poema-cocteil e a inteligência fatigada, *O Estado de São Paulo*, Caderno 2, 5 November 2000.

Does the poet's proximity to political and social debate reduce the scope of what he writes? Is the attempt to give meaning to the world of the modernists, in changed circumstances, a failing in itself? Of course, it would be possible to consider the poet's 'intimate feeling for his time and for his country', recommended by Machado de Assis, and certainly present in *Elefante*, as no more than a nostalgic myth. There would be some truth in this if the nation really had ceased to exist, which is not entirely evident; but even this would not detract from the historic desire that it should exist. Besides, there is no reason why the weakening of the national pulse should not serve as material for reflection and poetry in its turn.

7

There is, however, another side to the book, composed of properly lyrical poems, to which nothing of what I have said is applicable; at least, not directly. Here, the mythology and language are personal, the intention expressive, the transfiguring power of imagination operates to a high degree and the subject is 'first' not 'second' nature: light and shade, water, sand and wind, animals and landscapes, rather than the system of our social constraints. A literal translation of 'Elephant' can give only the faintest sense of what is at play in this work:

> The air of your flesh, dark air
> darkens stone and wind.
> Enormity courses within your body
> the air of crushed skies. The firmament,
> a blaze of pilasters,
> is not outside – it is collapsing inside.
> On the shield there reverberates the dull brightness
> of the swollen battering ram
> with which you enrage distance and time.

Your smooth, dancer's tread
ennobles the cold, feminine
bellies.

When you turn everything sings.
Everything does not know.[35]

These are difficult poems, of great beauty, requiring a second
round of commentary that will have to wait for another occasion.
For the moment, a few preliminary observations: Everything
depends on understanding the reasons that would lead the poet to
combine such discrepant imaginary forms. Is he saying that,
removed from the shared ground and realist anecdotes of
Brazilian life, his lyricism begins to spin off kilter? Or that the
atmosphere of contemporary reality is necessary to the integrity
of his poetry? Or again, that this highly transfigured first nature
should be seen as a character within the other universe, with
which it forms a unity? If this is so, what is the connexion between
these two spheres, of such differing tonalities? What do they say
about each other? As a suggestion, we could ask what relations
might exist between the degraded social world and the visions of
the elephant, the rhinoceros, the sea: giants whose darkness
contains light, whose imposing, unified mass does good and
whose onslaught seems more likely to fertilize and repair than to
destroy. The intense moral suffering that dominates the book's
final poems may be seen as part of the same world as that of the
first poems: in this case as its truth. Here, the lyrical side of the
book occupies a sphere of revelation, analogous to the

---

35   Alvim, *Elefante* // O ar de tua carne, ar escuro / anoitece pedra e vento. /
Corre o enorme dentro de teu corpo / o ar externo / de céus atropelados. O
firmamento, / incêndio de pilastras, / não está fora – rui por dentro. / Reverbera
no escudo o brilho baço / do túrgido aríete / com que distância e tempo enfureces.
// Teu pisar macio, dançarino, / enobrece os ventres frios, / femininos. // A
tua volta tudo canta. / Tudo desconhece.

adventures of the central characters within the realist novel, to which correspond the constraints that operate on the secondary characters, even when neither know anything of them. That does not mean the anti-lyrical poems are secondary – quite the contrary. Still, the distance between the cosmic feeling and the interplay of interests is telling, and relates to history rather than to nature. The collection ends :

In a churchyard

Clouds go by
The gaze does not perceive the screech of the stars[36]

The formal operations through which Alvim works are incisive. By means of purification, juxtaposition, cutting and pasting, analytical dissection, a whole repertoire of intensely Brazilian scenes and phrases is mapped out against unforeseen coordinates. Instead of the lines and stanzas that would correspond to poetic traditions, we have a feel for living language and its written presentation; or, better, an ear for the objective ironies of everyday speech, pared to the bone – which is, in the end, no more or less than the aesthetic refinement of historical consciousness.

What is taking place is the de-conventionalization of form, its liberation from confinement, the removal of its esoteric element and its replacement by an open, amphibious state, in which the poetic process and the real order of things are truly joined to each other. There is no desire to renounce form and its true value, or to abandon refinement. Quite the contrary, the impulse is one of actualization, of bringing up to date. Opened up by local, national or cosmopolitan perspectives that can bear a negative or positive sign, depending on the angle and moment, phrases from common speech take on a dizzying resonance that dispenses with metaphor, that is itself

---

36 *Num adro* / / Nuvens passam / O olhar não percebe o barulho dos astros

metaphor and poetry. Pop art and the ready-made are obvious referents, though from a different context. Here, however, the objects randomly selected for our contemplation do not derive from industrial civilization, but specifically from the workings of a peripheral society, captured as such, as a modern focus of perplexity. As Oswald said, 'Poetry exists in facts.'[37]

But if Alvim is the contemporary poet who has most deeply assimilated the lessons of the Brazilian modernists, it is within completely changed horizons. It is enough to recall the dazzled fascination with which that earlier generation discovered our social and cultural peculiarities, embraced them and longed to transform them into historical solutions – '*so* Brazil'. These social forces persist in *Elefante* and compose a system; they yield a few fine moments of playful magic, but, in essence they constitute our hard political and moral inheritance. As Alvim himself has said, it is a question of Oswald revised in the light of Drummond – or of the problem that lay hidden within the Brazilian picturesque.

---

37   Oswald de Andrade, 'Manifesto da Poesia Pau-Brasil', in *Do Pau-Brasil à antropofagia e às utopias*, 5.

7

City of God

The 'City of God' – there is no irony in the name – is a slum of some 200,000 inhabitants on the western edge of Rio de Janeiro. It is famous for the unending shoot-outs between drug gangs and police – an uncontrollable, escalating war, emblematic in various ways of wider social developments in Brazil. Some years ago, a remarkable novel depicting the life of the place appeared. Its author, Paulo Lins, was born in 1958 in Estácio, a black district of Rio, close to the docks; after the disastrous floods of 1966, he was re-housed with his family in the City of God. This development scheme – a product of bungled planning by Carlos Lacerda, the notoriously reactionary governor of the time – was still quite new. Lins went to school there, and carried on living in the favela while he studied at the university. He knew the local gangsters – delinquents he had grown up with – and they came to trust him as someone who could mediate with the community on their behalf.

The most reflective and artistic circles in the favelas were alert to the subterranean cultural ferment against the military dictatorship in Brazil. By the seventies, discussions about popular music had become a locus of opposition, a form of political debate. On a much smaller scale, something similar occurred with poetry, where a subculture of casual colloquialism and mimeographed leaflets, passed from hand to hand, operated as an antidote to official censorship and conventional publishing. Some of these circulated in the City of God. In the early eighties, the anthropologist Alba Zaluar, arriving to make a field study of the new criminality, provided another opening and source of intellectual energy. Lins became her research assistant, responsible for interviews. It was through the course of this investigation that he acquired the formal discipline and range of empirical knowledge that would make his novel a work of quite another cultural order. *Cidade de Deus* appeared in 1997.[1] The explosive nature of its themes, the scope and difficulty of its ambition and its unprecedented form of internal narration marked it out immediately as a major event – a work pushing back the frontier of literary possibilities in Brazil.

I

The novel traces the world of what Lins calls the *neo-favela*, underlining the transformation of the older slum world under the pressure of the narco-traffic wars and the parallel developments in police violence and corruption. The quasi-encyclopaedic scale of the recreation of this process – the book is 550 pages long – is reminiscent of the great gangster movies; but the story opens, subtly enough, with a relaxed scene of popular life. Young Barbantinho is sharing a joint with a friend and daydreaming of a future as an ultra-fit lifeguard on the beach; not one of those lazy loafers who let the sea carry people away – he'd make sure he took every chance to keep fit, even running back home from the beach after work: 'Need to keep at it, feed well, swim as much as possible'. Illicit activities coexist, calmly and guiltlessly, with altruistic impulses, modest ambitions, punctuality and respect; keeping up with the latest health fads while trusting in the protective powers of

---

1   In English, *City of God*, trans. Alison Entrekin, London 2006. Translated material cited here is by John Gledson. [*Ed.*]

Yemanjá;[2] emulating the good example of his father and brother – also lifeguards. A degree of hesitation is introduced in the following pages, as this hopeful, conformist outlook is cast in doubt by poverty and unemployment – and by the first corpses, floating down the river. Quite another facet of popular life is about to predominate; but the contrast between the two, potentially surfacing at any moment, has a structural function, as if to suggest a historical perspective.

It is when the gangsters erupt on to the scene with the first armed robbery that the novel picks up the mesmerizing rhythm that will drive it to the end. Any serious reading of *Cidade de Deus* depends on taking the measure of this relentless dynamism. The figures in the action-packed foreground are lit up, as in a thriller. Revolvers in hand, the Tenderness Trio – Duck, Nail Clippers and Long Hair – tear across the playground into Loura Square to emerge 'opposite the Penguin Bar where the truck loaded with cylinders of domestic gas is parked'. The driver tries to conceal his takings, but they order him – 'the worker' – to the ground, then kick him in the face. Does the class description make their violence more reprehensible, or does it collude in jeering at the sucker who had tried to fool them? Impossible to tell. The ambivalence of the vocabulary reflects an instability of viewpoint, embedded in the action – a kind of con artist's to-and-fro between order and disorder (to adopt, for our times, the terminology of Antonio Candido's 'Dialectic of Roguery'[3]). Besides, the robbers themselves now hand out the cylinders of gas to the frightened bystanders, who had been trying to slip away from the scene but who now, instantaneously, carry the whole consignment away.

All is as clear as it is complex. Choreographic exactitude fuses with a blurring of good and evil. Both cops and gangsters,

---

2   Yemanjá is a goddess of Yoruba origin.
3   See Candido, in *On Literature and Society*, trans. and ed. Howard S. Becker, Princeton, 1995, where the essay is translated with the title 'Dialectic of Malandroism'. See ch. 2, n. 2 above, for a discussion of this choice.

exchanging fire, put 'half a face round the edge of the corner' – *meia cara na quina da esquina*. The internal rhyme and acute visualization suggest not only art as a concentration of life but life as a process inspired by TV series that are watched by criminals and police alike. In the escapes and chases that follow, the favela is a series of crumbling walls, backyards and alleyways, where one character, setting off round the block to surprise a second from behind, comes face to face with a third he didn't want to meet. The tension and danger, the vivid settings – seemingly made for such encounters – create a certain empathy, but any sense of adventure is undercut by the sheer brutality of what goes on. In the end, one is left with a kind of stunned comprehension.

Less palpable is a quasi-standardization of sequences, a sinister monotony in their very variation. First come the drugs, or some other diversion. Then the boys set off for a hold-up, maybe with killings; for a rape, or some other sexual revenge; to knock out rivals from another gang, or from their own. Going out for a good time – to play football on the beach or to stir it at some party – always runs into complications and the same brutal outcome: one of the book's most disillusioning themes. Finally, after the violence, escape – on foot, by bus, in a stolen car or taxi; and then holing up, till the necessary twenty-four hours have passed. Shut up in some room, the *bichos-soltos* – animals on the loose – knock back milk or do more drugs to chill out and get some sleep.

For all the constant repetition, there is a sense of crescendo – although nobody knows where it is leading: and here the novel confronts us with the inescapable nature of our times. The overall rhythm of the book depends not so much on points of inflexion in individual lives – although there is no shortage of these – as on escalations that take on a collective meaning. For example: an attack on a cheap hotel disintegrates into slaughter while, on the same night, a man revenges himself on his mistress, hacking to bits the white baby to which she has just given birth; on another corner, a worker mutilates his rival with a scythe. There is no link between these crimes, but the next day, the City of God emerges from anonymity, hitting the front pages as one of Rio de Janeiro's most violent zones. In their own eyes and those of the city, the gangsters' importance has grown. The hotel attack – which had only degenerated into a bloodbath because the boys were so nervous – becomes a newsworthy event, an elevation of the hoodlums' authority and that of the terror they inspire. A new mechanism of perversely inflating integration has been set in place: the most inhuman acts acquire positive value once they are reported by the media – which, in turn, become a kind of ally in the struggle to break the barriers of social exclusion. ' "Gangsters got to be famous to get respect," Long Hair told Little Black'.

In another instance, the leader of the gang, Little Joe, is badly disturbed by a friend's injuries. He strikes out at random, murmurs incomprehensible prayers, wants meat bought for a barbecue and readies his gang for war with heavy doses of cocaine. The next day, they set out for the kill, eyes bulging and teeth on edge. But their craziness has an unexpected logic: its victims are the owners of corner drug joints – *bocas de fumo*, or 'smoking mouths'. Revenge is Little Joe's pretext to move up from robber to local drug boss. Now, his concern is to impose order within the terror, so as not to deter customers from outside. Just as, on the night of the hotel attack, their blunders pushed disorganized robbers onto a higher level of integration, so here a random outburst of personal rage triggers the unification of local power and business. The immense disproportion between immediate cause and necessary outcome in the novel is one of those conjunctures in which the inexorable weight of contemporary history makes itself felt.

Such haphazard episodes slowly distil into a periodization, shared by the internal order of the fiction and Brazilian reality: from individual robbery to organized gang; from improvised assaults to regular drug trafficking; from simple revolvers to specialist weapons (at the height of gang warfare, Little Joe tries to buy ex-Falklands rifles); from seizing odd chances to the control and management of a territory. In successive waves, the violence grows and the age of the assailants drops. It soon comes to seem logical that seventeen-year-old gang leaders should dispatch ten- or twelve-year-olds – freer from vigilance than the older boys – to shoot down the eighteen-year-old owner of another *boca de fumo*. With tears in their eyes, the children accomplish their mission, to earn the status of *sujeito homem* – real men – and the esteem of the rest of the gang.

What are the frontiers of this dynamic? The action takes place within the closed world of the City of God, with only a few forays outside – mainly to prisons, following characters' destinies. Events are portrayed on a grand scale, but the space in which they unfold is far more limited than the social premises on which they rest. The higher spheres of drug and arms trafficking, and the military and political corruption that protect them, do not appear; their local agents, if not gangsters themselves, are scarcely any different from them. The real estate speculators and public administration that ensure the favela's segregation from the rest of the city barely figure either, save for odd glimpses – though these are quite enough to suggest that they too are all the same.

This limited compass functions as a strength in literary terms, dramatizing the blindness and segmentation of the social process. On their own patch – that of the excluded – the gang leaders are powerful figures, men with brains and hard experience who can withstand the highest levels of nervous tension. Yet they are still poor devils, dying like flies, far from the opulence the drug trade generates elsewhere. This dizzying oscillation in our perception of their stature gives literary form to an overall social fracture, repro- duced within the criminal world. Dead on the ground, the cunning, violent lord of life and death is a gap-toothed youngster, under- nourished and illiterate, often barefoot and in shorts, invariably dark skinned in colour: the point on which all injustices of Brazilian society converge. Crime may form a world apart, with a spell that lends itself to aestheticization, but it does not dwell outside the city that we share. It is this that prevents aesthetic distancing, that forces us to a committed reading – if only out of fear. This is a literary situation with properties all its own.

Locked into the action, the narrative viewpoint captures its instantaneous options, logic and dead ends. Pressures of danger, of necessity, bear down on the characters with the immediacy of breaking news. The result is a kind of irremediable reality and an absurd, stress-induced form of objectivity that cuts the ground away from any moral judgement. Yet *Cidade de Deus* refuses the exoticism and sadism of commercial gangster fiction. The closure of the horizon here is a calamity, although its implications are left for the reader to assess. It becomes immediately comprehensible, for example, why young children should start out by mugging pregnant women and the elderly. It is perfectly rational to beat up the disabled and steal what they've got. It is quite understandable why prostitutes should pull knives when they can't find clients; why gangsters live on their nerves; why so-and-so 'has never had sexual relations with a woman of her own free will'; why the best get-away vehicle after a crime is a bus – 'a black who takes a taxi is either a gangster, or at death's door'. The subject matter could be grist for sensationalism and black humour; it is treated in quite another spirit here.

The tight focus gives no respite from this murderous sequence of events. As maximum tension becomes routine, the trivialization of death pushes us far beyond any thrill of suspense towards a disabused, all-encompassing standpoint, only one degree removed from mere statistics; a point of view focused rather on the decisive, supra-individual parameters of class. We need to be intimate with horror yet still able to see it from a distance – if possible, an enlightened one: this is our situation today.

2

As in nineteenth-century naturalism, *Cidade de Deus* owes something of its boldness of range and conception to an association with
social inquiry. Under a different historical constellation, the findings of a vast and highly relevant research project, Zaluar's 'Crime
and Criminality in Rio de Janeiro', have been fictionalized from the
perspective of the objects of study – and (without promoting any
political illusions) with a corresponding activation of a different
class point of view. This is in itself a significant move. In addition,
the reordering of materials produces a distinctive tone and vigour,
powerfully at variance with 'well-wrought prose'. The systematiz-
ing, pioneering force that lends the book's cartography its specific
weight is closely related to its origins both in scientific work and in
a team. On the final page, as happens in film credits, the author
thanks two of his companions for their historical and linguistic
research. Artistic energies of this sort have no place in the comfortable conception of creative imagination cultivated by most
contemporary writers.

If the methods of interviewer and researcher contribute to the
artist's schematization, they also stamp his material with literary
unevennesses which themselves have wider implications. The
worker, the con artist, the hoodlum, the dropout, the go-between
are no longer defined within stable, separate roles. They are
elements – some, legacies from the past – of a new structure, still in
formation, that is to be investigated and understood. It is within this
totality that precise yet mutable new distinctions and relations begin
to distil, bestowing on the fictionalization its fine-textured relevance. The subjective testimony of the field notes sets up an
immediate complexity. There is the boy who would rather listen to
gangsters' talk than pray in the Assembly of God with his father,
and the *bicho-solto* who is so in love with a pretty black girl that he
dreams of becoming a manual worker. 'Slaving on a building site
– never', says another; then he turns believer and starts work for a

big construction company, his faith helping to keep at bay 'his feelings of revolt against the segregation he had to suffer for being
black, half-toothless and semi-literate'. The relational world set up
by the play of these positions stands at the intersection of the logic
of everyday life, imaginative literature and society's systematic
effort to know itself.

Another aspect of this composite art finds form in the intervals
between the action, in passages that explore the present or recapitulate the past. Such explanatory gestures owe their origins to
naturalist narrative, but here they assume a quite different register.
Unadorned field data, evoking the harsh efficiency of the scientific
report, combines with the sensationalist tone of the popular press –
mined for factual documentation and ideological raw material – and
the brutal terminology, at once obtuse and bureaucratic, of the
police. This miscellaneous discourse, with its charge of degraded
and alienated modernity, has played a real part in the universe of its
victims. Social policy has long worked on, if not improved, the
terrain on which they are abandoned. The playground – the
'Leisure' – the gangsters tear across was undoubtedly the contribution of some town planner. In Lins's work, the overriding
gravitational force of the drug trade in the neo-favela serves to
deflate a whole complex of explanations, once scientific and now
bien pensant: the alcoholism of the father, the prostitution of the
mother, the disintegration of the family and so forth. In the circumstances, such reasoning takes on an outdated, unreal look, even
though soaks and whores are everywhere. A set of naturalist sociological causalities is integrated, as one ideology among others,
within a discursive web that has no final word; and that operates, in
turn, as an element in a wider mystery, formed by the huge business
of crime, with its amorphous boundaries, and by the laws of motion
of contemporary society – of whose effective shape such explanations have nothing to report.

The vivid transcription of popular speech – lively and concise,
almost to the point of minimalism – offers a contrast to this, up to

a point; yet it can also seem, through its very brutality and repetition, its purest and simplest expression. But the most daring strand in the language of the novel is its quite unexpected – perhaps risky – insistence on poetry. The verbal resources of samba are combined with a delinquent, concretist wordplay – the book takes its epigraph from the work of Paulo Leminski – opening a seam of popular potentialities.[4] *'Poesia, minha tia'*, begins Lins's own eulogy to poetry, with a rough caress (*tia* is aunt, but here it is rather my baby, my old lady, my whore) that defies translation:

> *Poesia, minha tia*, blaze against what they say is – bullet-blast the phonemes of the prose. Speak the word that swells beyond its bounds, that talks, acts, happens; staggers from the shot. From a toothless mouth, a gaping cavity: our alleyway plans, our deadly choices. The sand shifts on the ocean floor.
>
> Absence of the sun darkens even the jungle. Iced strawberry-crush melts the hand. The word distils in the mind, takes soul as it's released from lips to ear – but sometimes, sound-magic cannot leap to the mouth. It's swallowed dry, choked in the stomach by black beans and rice; defecated instead of spoken.
>
> Speech fails. Bullet speaks.

The deliberate and insolent importance of the lyrical note in Lins's world, in the face of the crushing weight of misery that conditions it, is a distinctive gesture: a movement of refusal, difficult to imagine in a less heterodox author. It is tempting to wonder about the connexion between this improbable lyricism and the strength of mind required to change the class viewpoint of a social enquiry, from scientific object to subject of the action.

---

4   Paulo Leminski (b. 1944–d. 1989). Born in the southern state of Paraná, Leminski used the stylistic devices of concretism to create an irreverent popular poetry. [*Tr.*]

'All is true', announced Balzac, at the beginning of a novel full of the wildest flights of imagination.[5] Lins, too, is concerned not to deny the part of fiction in his work but to sharpen its powers of prospection and demystification. Faced with the task of giving novelistic form to his vast subject matter, he has availed himself of every support, from *Angústia*[6] and *Crime and Punishment* to cinematic super-productions. If his universe is adjacent to the sensationalist and commercial imaginings of our period, it is quite opposite in spirit: anti-Manichean, anti-providentialist and anti-stereotypical. Its structuring themes are the miring of all intentions – Mané Galinha, the gangster as sympathetic avenger, ends up as bad as his enemies – and the general dissolution of meaning within energies that become ungraspable. Which is to say: we are in the valid ambit of modern art, where there are no cheap consolations. So when, in epic scenes of collective action, interrupted and resumed to heighten suspense, police and gangsters head for a final, Hollywood-style showdown, nothing is resolved. Death always comes but before the projected climax, from adventitious hands, for half-forgotten reasons, with no bearing on the act at stake. Salgueirinho, the best-hearted con artist in the City of God, is run down by a reversing car. The worst crook of all catches a bullet in the stomach – a meaningless death that does nothing to restore justice, to re-establish a balance in the world.

Behind this methodical discarding of conventions can be traced another, more subtle transition between stages of transgression, no less desolating. When Salgueirinho dies, he is mourned by the samba schools and by his girlfriends, companions and disciples; and with him disappears the wisdom that people should only rob outsiders and not fight senselessly among themselves; that there are pickings enough for all. When Big Head – the hated police chief

---

5   Honore de Balzac, *Le père Goriot*, 1835. [*Tr.*]
6   Graciliano Ramos, *Angústia*, Rio de Janeiro, 2011, originally published 1936; translated into English as *Anguish*, trans. Lewis C. Kaplan, New York, 1946.

– dies, the favela is shaken up again, in a different way. But when the new-style gangsters die, the authentic sons of the neo-favela, nothing happens. The earlier forms of marginality were more sympathetic, perhaps, and less antisocial. In the months leading up to Carnival, the *malandros*, thieves and prostitutes would rob full steam ahead to get funds for their local samba school. The crimes were no less grave but they could be said to be outweighed by a larger objective, of bringing good times to the city – as if there had been a certain homeostasis within the older inequality that made it bearable, up to a point; and that the narco-traffic wars have destroyed. One of the book's most impressive achievements is to show how the liveliness of popular life and the splendour of the Rio landscape itself tend to disappear, as if in a nightmare, under the exigencies of their reign.

It has been said, in a perceptive phrase, that present-day society is creating more and more 'monetary subjects with no cash'.[7] Their world is our own. Far from representing anything backward, they are the product of progress – which, naturally, they qualify. Deep inside, the reader is at one with them – and with their regressive fantasy of simply seizing the glittering goods on display.

---

7 Robert Kurz, *Der Kollaps der Modernisierung: Vom Zusammenbruch des Kasernensozialismus zur Krise der Weltökonomie*, Frankfurt 1991, 225.

8

Brecht's Relevance — Highs and Lows

No one's to blame for crises!
Over us, changeless and inscrutable, rule
The laws of economics.
And natural catastrophes recur
In dreadful cycles.

— Bertolt Brecht, *Saint Joan of the Stockyards*

How relevant is Brecht today? Put another way: how severely has
the closure of capitalist horizons affected the unique combination of
political convictions, aesthetic theses and literary methods that
defines the texture of his art? The foregrounding of artistic artifice
was a general method of the avant-garde, of course, a part of its
determination to tear away the sanctifying veil of aesthetic form by
attacking reverential attitudes, de-automatizing the audience's
attention, dulled by habit, or highlighting the material aspect of the
artist's work, to align it with other forms of production. All of these
elements existed in the Brechtian method, yet there they also underwent a change of purpose through being directly inscribed within
the turn from capitalism to communism. The link between provoc-
ative experimentalism and the struggle for the political
transformation of society conferred on Brecht's work a peculiar
type of relevance, not to mention authority. For the same reasons,

it would become more vulnerable than that of others to the denial that history inflicted on its expectations. In exploring the complex ways in which different aspects of his project have resonated with specific historical and social experiences, I want to begin by playing devil's advocate – explaining the grounds for thinking that Brecht today has no relevance whatsoever.[1]

Although he considered himself the creator and theoretician of a new theatre, Brecht insisted on the antiquity of anti-illusionist drama. It had been practised by the Chinese and Japanese and by Elizabethans and Spaniards of the Golden Age, not to mention the medieval mystery plays and the didacticism of Jesuit priests. His representational techniques became modern in a strong sense only when they were taken up again within the horizons opened up by the revolutionary movements, around the time of the First World War. In those circumstances, several societies – perhaps more accurately, several cities – began to develop a political theatre.[2] Brecht would describe its public as 'an assembly of world transformers': proletarian in character, critical in spirit and equipped not only with a well-formulated dissatisfaction but with subversively practical proposals.[3] If it is not a retrospective illusion, this audience, tailor-made for political theatre, existed during a brief period, in a few places, attached to special conditions. It was the result of the junction between the 'free theatres'

---

1   This essay is adapted from 'Altos e baixos da atualidade de Brecht', which was first presented as a talk following a public reading of *Saint Joan of the Stockyards* by the Companhia do Latão in São Paulo in 1998 and then published in Roberto Schwarz, *Seqüências brasileiras*, São Paulo, 1999. For a full translation of the original by Emilio Sauri, see the online journal *Mediations*, 23, 1, Fall 2007. [*Ed.*]

2   Commenting on the conditions of existence of a real political theatre, Brecht notes with sardonic parsimony: 'After World War One, there was theatre in four countries: the first had endured a complete social cataclysm; the second, half of a cataclysm; the third, one quarter; the last, one eighth – The third was Czechoslovakia, and the fourth the United States, after the great crisis.' Needless to say, the first had been Russia, and the second Germany. See Bertolt Brecht, *Arbeitsjournal*, vol. 1, Frankfurt, 1974, 315.

3   Brecht, *Arbeitsjournal*, vol. 1, 270.

– an important experiment, affiliated with literary naturalism, in which the voluntary contribution of its members removed business considerations from the scene – and the historical advance of autonomous workers organizations; within its limits, the alliance would produce a 'popular appropriation of the means of cultural production'.[4] By the 1930s, however, with the imposition of Soviet national interests on the workers movement, the picture had changed. The critical dimension of Brechtian estrangement no longer had the winds of history in its favour, especially in the socialist camp; it became an exercise in style, or in nostalgia.

Brecht's trademark, of course, was 'narrative' theatre. As against conventional 'dramatic' staging, in which the actor identifies herself with her role and tries to live it in the flesh, here she would consider the role from a distance, as if narrating it from the outside, in the third person. Anti-illusionist staging would lay bare the methods of theatricalization: the audience would become aware of the constructed quality of the figures on the stage and, by extension, that of the reality they imitate and interpret. In underlining the pretence involved in theatrical action, the extent to which it is a *made* thing, Brecht wanted to demonstrate that actions of everyday life also have a representational aspect: the roles played there could be different too, for social processes were mutable. This was in contrast to the 'Aristotelian' theatre which, through catharsis, helped men and women to discover an equilibrium in the face of the eternal and immutable nature of human affairs.

I

Brecht summarizes these themes in the 1930 prologue to *The Exception and the Rule*, where the author-narrator addresses the students for whom the play is intended:

---

4   Iná Camargo Costa, *Sinta o drama*, Petrópolis, 1998, 19–26; Anatol Rosenfeld, *Teatro alemão*, São Paulo, 1968, 120–3.

We are about to tell you
The story of a journey. An exploiter
And two of the exploited are the travellers.
Examine carefully the behaviour of these people:
Find it surprising though not unusual
Inexplicable though normal
Incomprehensible though it is the rule.
Consider even the most insignificant, seemingly simple
Action with distrust. Ask yourselves whether it is necessary
Especially if it is usual.
We ask you expressly to discover
That what happens all the time is not natural.
For to say that something is natural
In such times of bloody confusion
Of ordained disorder, of systematic arbitrariness
Of inhuman humanity, is to
Regard it as unchangeable.[5]

We are asked, in such times as these, to be distrustful, to find normal behaviour surprising, even incomprehensible; to discover that what happens as a rule is not natural, therefore unchangeable. The didactic attitude and prosaic verse play an essential role in Brecht's literary technique: he sought out cold forms of enthusiasm and emphasis in order to respond effectively, as an artist, to the circumstances of class antagonism. The proximity to catechism is, of course, a risk.

Yet, as the words themselves suggest, the form of domination that owes its strength to custom and apparent naturalness is of a premodern type. The struggle of doubt against obscurantism was a classic figure of bourgeois emancipation, whose adversary was feudal authority and its religious guarantee. Clearly, Brecht's

---

5   Brecht, 'The Exception and the Rule', in *The Measures Taken and Other Lehrstücke*, eds. Ralph Manhcim and John Willett, New York, 2001.

anti-obscurantism no longer belongs to that period, though it does not disengage itself from it completely. It is as if something of feudal naturalness and prestige had been passed on to capital, and something of the resigned fatalism of the serf subsisted in the working class, so that the fight against the immobility of yesterday's powers remained on the agenda. As for today's capitalist system, whose foundation has not for some time been the veneration of old customs, it is obvious that the shift from naïveté to each-for-himself shrewdness will not be enough to overcome it. Let us say that in denaturalizing submission and in historicizing what had been eternity, the Brechtian theatrical gesture invoked a space of freedom in which the world figured as transformable *in the abstract*. Once the oppressed made out the strange in the familiar, the irrational in the everyday and the anomalous in the rule, an acceptable and comprehensive reorganization of society was close at hand. This is the context in which to understand the muted pomp of the estrangement effect and its revolutionary aspiration.

In much of Europe, the First World War had already swept away the superstition of order and authority that was, in principle, the target of denaturalizing criticism. The following years witnessed other equally 'unnatural' cataclysms. The list is well known: the Russian Revolution, hyper-inflation, the crisis of 1929, mass unemployment and the rise of Nazism. The summary of the contemporary world in the Prologue of *The Exception and the Rule* depicts a new scene: a time of bloody confusion, ordained disorder, systematic arbitrariness, inhuman humanity. In order for this state of things not to be considered immutable, the schoolmaster-actor asks the children to doubt the habitual, the familiar. There is, surely, a certain maladjustment between the synopsis of the period and the advice regarding it, which reflects an objective insufficiency. Counselling against the credulous acceptance of bloody confusion would seem superfluous. Can it really be true that a society on the road to fascism would seem *natural*? Or that the obstacle that keeps the exploited in their place resides in the illusion of naturalness?

Schematically, the Brechtian transformation of theatre – conceived in the 1920s – presupposed the imminent overcoming of capitalism or, on a parallel track, its cross-dressing as fascism. Directed against this last possibility, anti-illusionist methods preached an anti-kitsch mental sobriety capable of exposing impostures. As for capitalism, the estranging stance threw into relief its obsolete irrationality, which the workers would go on to overcome. Today it hardly needs to be said that the historical experience created in the name of communism moved worlds away from initial intentions and came off worst in its confrontation with the capitalist order. There are different explanations for the defeat; but whatever they may be, it was difficult to imagine that a better society might be gestating within the field of 'actually existing socialism'. Thus, the place on the leading edge of history that Brecht's method presumed found itself without support in the real course of things, transforming clear-sighted critical superiority into an illusion.

Capitalism's absurd and devastating character still imposes itself as a fact, but is now historically shackled to another: the revelation of the regressive dynamics of the societies that broke with the bourgeois model. This does not make that model insuperable; but it demonstrates that to stand outside it is not enough, in itself, to create another, better order. Against what the Left supposed, the passage from criticism to overcoming revealed itself to be neither automatic nor obvious. In these circumstances, the didactic component of Brechtian estrangement was left without anything to teach, at least directly; and so changed its meaning. A staging adequate to what we have painfully learned has to take that difficult horizon into account.

2

It was only after his death in 1956 that Brecht's worldwide consecration began. His work entered the cultural life of São Paulo in the second half of the 1950s, initially as part of the modernizing militancy of the professional theatre companies who were then bringing to the stage the renowned authors of the period: Tennessee Williams, Arthur Miller, Jean-Paul Sartre and others. It was only natural that Brecht's turn would come, announced by a growing European glory. His assimilation was more difficult, however. The problems ranged from the elementary – understanding what the 'estrangement effect' could be – to the inevitable clash with established interests. The professionalization of the São Paulo stage had also brought a bourgeois aggrandizement of theatre life. At the first nights of the Teatro Brasileiro de Comédia, one breathed class distinction reminiscent of the Cultura Artística concerts where internationally renowned musicians were presented in an atmosphere of cultivated leisure and fur coats. Meanwhile, the tempo of national life was stamping the notion of progress with a different content, as the radicalization of developmentalist populism began to gain momentum – a process that would lead to a pre-revolutionary questioning of the country's intolerable class structure before the military dénouement of 1964.

Living culture veered to the left. The new theatre generation aligned itself with the rapidly politicizing student movement and sought to make contact with the organized working class, the peasant struggle and popular music. The propensities and talents called for in this new situation were those of agitprop: political intelligence, formal inventiveness, organizational agility, a disposition towards confrontation, as well as the irreverent use of consecrated culture and the capacity to deal on an equal footing with the resources of high art and popular tradition. This was the stew of militant culture in which Brecht's artistic and ideological rigour, his systematic engagement with the revolution – more guessed at than known, partly due to language difficulties – would come to life. The usefulness of the Brechtian spirit for the Third World Left is easy to understand. The linking of language and literature to a programme of collective experimentation of all sorts – artistic, political, philosophical, scientific or organizational – along with the rejection of socialist realism, responded to real reformative impulses. The wide spectrum of Brechtian experimentation changed the quality of experimentalism itself, freeing literary modernism from mere scribbling. That said, his reception also occasioned certain incongruities, since the 1920s were not the 1960s, nor was Germany Brazil.

The bare language of class interests and contradictions that marks the sui generis sharpness of Brechtian writing has no equivalent within the Brazilian imaginary, informed as the latter is by relations of personal dependency and sallies of roguery. The understanding of life that is distilled in our popular speech has a specific critical meaning, distinct from that of Berliner proletarian slang. But the principal maladjustment was bound up with the idea of estrangement itself. This required opening up a space between the individual and his social functions, making the class logic of the system accessible to critical consciousness. Now, the nationalist dimension of developmentalism required, on the contrary, a large dose of that mystifying identification which Brechtian estrangement undid. The compromise solution developed by Teatro de Arena during this period became famous: at centre stage, a popular nationalist hero, with whom the actor and public strongly identified; surrounding him, anti-heroes of the dominant class, to which Brechtian recourses to disidentification and analysis, with their corresponding coolheadedness, lent a brilliance and truth which, by an irony of art, the other role, the one which should have served as a model, finally lacked.

It occurred to no one to follow Brecht's teachings to the letter, but they nevertheless functioned as a kind of challenge, coming from more demanding regions of aesthetic and political reflection. The prospects that the new type of political theatre opened to song – and vice versa – give an idea of the leap that was made. In Germany, Brechtian song was a product of the most advanced theatrical experimentation: its melodies were composed by avant-garde musicians, its lyrics were the work of a great poet; their conjunction marked a high point in the questioning of the bourgeois order. These elements were not found in Brazil, except, perhaps, the last. Yet the theatre's involvement with popular music brought about tremendous changes for both of them. The theatre joined its language, which was restricted in its circulation, to another of immense popularity, which had a very different productive process and class origin; while song was now directed not to consumers but to the country's radical counter-elites, in the name of freedom. The peculiar representativity of singer-songwriters like Caetano Veloso and Chico Buarque, or, in another sphere, the filmmaker Glauber Rocha, owed something to the radiation of that moment, when the processes of popular art, aesthetic experimentalism and political theatre came together as a historical force.

In 1964, the rightist military coup truncated the great democratic process to which the new theatre had sought to respond. The suppression of the workers and peasants movement was brutal, but for a while it proved possible for students and the intelligentsia to dodge the censors. Thus, the Left still managed to make its presence felt, though now in a socially confined environment ruled by the box office. The onstage triumph of the Left, after it had been beaten in the street, took Brechtian experimentation in unforeseen directions. For example, the use of narrative procedures, originally conceived as a means of fostering critical distance, was at times transformed by Augusto Boal and Glauber Rocha into its opposite: a vehicle for national emotions 'of epic proportions' to offset the political defeat. In 1968, the dictatorship extended the repression that it had hitherto reserved for the popular movement to the field of culture and the middle-class opposition. Critical intellectual life was robbed of any public dimension. However, to prohibit is not to refute, and in that sense Brechtian inspiration, like discussion on the Left in general, went offstage but did not lose its raison d être. On the contrary, its repression was living testimony of its relevance.

3

The surprise would come much later, in the course of the 1980s, when democratization opened up a space in which to resume previous positions – but these no longer convinced anyone. Due to the dictatorship, the political debate had remained in the freezer while the world and the country changed. Whatever literary criticism may say to the contrary, artistic methods have presuppositions that are not themselves artistic: the beginning of the end of communism, as well as new features of capitalism, affected the credibility of Brecht's theatrical technique. We were entering the world of today. In the early 1960s, when an actor said that the injustice of class was not a natural misfortune, like rain, and that it could therefore be contested, the effect of revelation, even galvanization, was incredible. It became even stronger if, on the contrary – through blindness or collusion – the character declared that injustice is, indeed, a natural misfortune, and therefore to fight against it is pointless. It was as if our rejection of the hypnotic force of conformism had its own mesmerizing power: once we understood that injustice was social, the difficulty seemed to have been overcome and the transformation of the world was within reach. That ease, not to say credulity, now seemed disconcerting.

The Brazilian military coup, in defence of 'tradition, family and property', had confirmed a classic political division of labour: the Left wanted to change society, while the Right clung to the past; something like this had been the horizon of the twentieth-century avant-gardes. But when the long-drawn-out democratization process permitted public aesthetic and critical communication once more, it became evident that the years of the dictatorship had not exactly been conservative. The 'economic miracle' had brought not just a leap in manufacturing and its internationalization but a liberalization of sexual mores, a normalization of drug use, the partial – and precarious – incorporation of the poor into mass consumerism and the desacralizing commercialization of culture. The Left's certainty that it was the party of historical progress while its adversary would be traditionalist, lost its footing in reality.

If capital's victory in Brazil during the 1980s was less complete than in the countries of the core, it was due to the political and cultural weight of a new independent trade unionism, the base of the Partido dos Trabalhadores, among the forces fighting for democratization. For a while, the antagonism between capital and organized labour appeared to command the Brazilian stage in the classic manner – until here, too, trade unionism lost the initiative, beaten by the supremacy that globalization conferred on capital. The attacks by globalization's 'progressive' proxies on the 'conservatism' of organized working-class layers expressed a new set of forces, with its concomitant system of illusions. Innovation resided with money. The questioning of capital was no longer only the business of workers, it seemed, but was prompted by its own contradictions, which, now unchecked, soon acquired the characteristics of a natural catastrophe. By comparison, the Brechtian denaturalization of social inequality seemed quite mild.

Meanwhile, commercial culture had appropriated the most sensational aesthetic discoveries of the avant-garde, Brechtian drama included, for its own purposes. The estrangement effect, conceived as a way of stimulating criticism and liberating social choice, changed its meaning against a background of generalized consumerism – helping to promote a new cleaning product, for example. The Brechtian focus on the material infrastructure of ideology – on the didactic inclusion of the wings on centre stage – had become a standard feature of TV newscasts, functioning as a prop for the authority of capital rather than a critique. The cameras and cameramen filming other cameras that filmed the studio, the giant logo and the anchormen all lent weight and immutability to the industrial-commercial apparatus which stood behind the highly partisan account of the world that we would shortly be given. The very materialism of Brechtian self-referentiality now seemed open to apologetic uses. Having once been a call to emancipation, the insistence on the social and non-natural character of the mechanisms that condition us had taken on — perhaps due in part to a matter of scale — a dissuasive function. What more could the materialist desire, if there are commodities for all to choose from? That objection lies behind Brecht's transformation into a classic — as a brilliant writer from another era.

4

In his essay on committed literature, Adorno at one point observes that, in Brecht's theatre, the primacy of doctrine acts like an element of the art itself. Didacticism, in this case, is a formal principle: while it smashed the bell jar of the aesthetic sphere, the militant relationship with the spectator would also function as a law of composition. The truth of the plays would thus lie, not in the lessons passed on, the theorems on class conflict, but rather in the objective dynamic of the whole. The essay, which understands Brecht's political-aesthetic positions and criticizes them, places greater emphasis on the work than on the theory; or rather, it sees the role of the latter inside the former.[6] It also helps to open our eyes to the formal elegance of his writing, obscured by the salience of political questions: the dissonant mixture of brutalism and intellectual perceptiveness, for example; or of a heavyweight materialism and a delicacy of procedure and reasoning that verges on abstract variation and the arabesque. In endlessly contradictory ways, these unexpected combinations suggest oblique and wavering correspondences with class relations. Thus formal immanence, disrespected on one level, in vanguardist fashion, re-establishes itself elsewhere, with a more ample compass and without conventional guarantee, through the immeasurable care taken with the composition. This care is

---

6 Theodor Adorno, 'Commitment', in Adorno et al., *Aesthetics and Politics*, London 1977; also on Brecht's position, see Adorno, *Aesthetic Theory*, Minneapolis 1997, 247.

subordinated to the political rejection of artistic insipidness – or vice versa? – in a manner that the stage production will have to shape. It is on this basis, however, that fresh grounds for Brecht's relevance may present themselves.

Take *Saint Joan of the Stockyards*, that extraordinary epic of Chicago meat kings, cattle breeders, stockyard workers, canning-factory owners and black-straw-hatted soldiers of the Salvation Army. It is a great work; yet it has features that are now hard to accept. Contrary to what Brecht intended, the language of the Communist leader is not very compelling compared to that of the other characters. It is true that he understands the essentials: he explains the mechanisms of capitalist exploitation and speculation; he knows that workers are strong only when they act collectively, and that the general strike is part of that logic: 'With things in this pass, we've got to realize that nothing can help us but the use of force'.[7] His hard and objective reasons are advantageously counterposed to the grandiloquence of the factory owners. Even so, his words do not resonate at the level they seem to promise. In spite of saying *what is*, the lines are grey and bureaucratic, an exception within the drama. It is as if the truth – or certainties – of the Communist position were unable to give off the light that the artistic composition expected of them.

Saint Joan was written before Stalinism had taken root on the Left. The Brechtian attempt to find poetry in partisan language – anonymous, authorized – expressed a historical sentiment and a wager: the outlawed militants, with their discipline and self-abnegation, would be among the key figures in the fight for the new age of freedom. Today, the question of the proximity of this sentiment to Stalinist absolutism is unavoidable – for example, in the stark panegyric to the heroism, or sacrifice, of professional revolutionaries presented in the exchange between two onlookers after the crushing of the general strike:

---

7   Brecht, *Saint Joan of the Stockyards*, trans. Ralph Manheim, London, 1969, scene 9*e*. Translation modified in some instances.

FIRST MAN: Who are those people?

SECOND MAN: None of them
Thought only of himself.
Never resting, they ran themselves ragged
For the sake of other people's bread.

FIRST MAN: Why never resting?

SECOND MAN: The unjust man walks the streets openly,
The just man hides.

FIRST MAN: What will become of them?

SECOND MAN: Although they
Work for little pay and are useful to many
Not one of them lives out his natural life span
Eats his bread, dies with a full belly and
Is buried with honours. All
End before their time. They are
Struck down, trampled, and buried in shame.

FIRST MAN: Why do we never hear about them?

SECOND MAN: When you read in the papers that some criminals
Have been shot or
Thrown in jail, it's them.

FIRST MAN: Will it always be like this?

SECOND MAN: No.[8]

Informed by the century that has passed, and the Soviet-nationalist appropriation of class struggle, it is no longer possible simply to welcome these 'just men' as the messengers of a new era. These strong activist figures have acquired an ambiguous air. And what if, on the contrary, they are the temporarily reprieved victims of the state's political police? The interrogation of these hallucinatory ambiguities, and of the expressive deficit that goes with them, is perhaps the greatest challenge facing any responsible staging of the play.

---

8   Ibid., scene 11*a*.

In everything it says regarding the nature of capital, on the other hand, the timeliness of *Saint Joan* could hardly be greater. Though it has been a matter of faith that the crash of 1929 will never repeat itself, the wailing of 'small speculators' crushed by bigger ones or the misery of workers left unemployed by 'competition' in the play could be taken from today's headlines. This is not the result of mere contingency. Written between 1929 and 1931, *Saint Joan* was in part the product of Brecht's intensive study of the workings of the capitalist economies in the late 1920s – reading Marx, but much else besides, including Ida Tarbell's *The History of the Standard Oil Company* and Gustavus Myers's *Great American Fortunes*. His aim was to grasp the real movements of contemporary society and transpose them to the theatre. Fredric Jameson aptly notes a Balzacian aspect in the work of the playwright, well-versed in all sorts of trade secrets: the processes of class conflict, the subtleties of money, the mechanisms of the stock exchange, the ruses of fascist rhetoric, the calculations of organized mendicancy.[9] To bring this realism, in Lukács's sense, onto the stage involved, among other innovations, the substitution of collective for individual axes in the composition of the drama. Around these, the narrative arranges itself according to the cycle of capitalist crisis, with stages of prosperity, overproduction, unemployment, crash and fresh accumulation.

But *Saint Joan*'s singular stature depends, in an equally important way, on the decisive resonance that the capitalist cycle finds in canonical cultural forms, which themselves served as the highest legitimations of the bourgeois order. The experience of the First World War and the Russian Revolution famously signified the ideological disqualification of the previous period. For many critics, anything that smacked of idealism, patriotic pabulum, the authority

---

9   Fredric Jameson, *Brecht and Method*, London and New York, 1998, 13, 154–5.

of national classics or the remnants of feudal life acquired a grotesque or odious tonality. Yet it is possible to distinguish different aspects of the materialist response. The millions of dead soldiers and the starving populations threw into relief an alliance between economic interests – colonial expansion, the arms industry – and cultural and nationalist indoctrination that made war possible; a class alliance. But at the same time, the catastrophe showed that everything is an illusion except personal economic survival, thus reproducing bourgeois individualism at a new level. In either case, the ideological corpus of pre-war civilization underwent a radical demoralization, be it in the name of the suffering masses – the Left's version – or in the name of raw economic interest: capital's new realism, which a prior bourgeois culture had politely hidden. *Saint Joan* incorporated both meanings but without accepting their 'reductionist' corollary – that is, the rejection of canonical culture tout court.

Rather than make a tabula rasa of the past, Brecht's tactic was to assemble a strategic anthology of the tradition's greatest texts, to which the language of *Saint Joan*'s protagonists systematically alludes. He did not abandon consecrated culture altogether. Instead, he presented the vicissitudes of class conflict and the calculations of the canned-goods cartel – his new material – in verses imitative of Schiller, Hölderlin, the final scenes of Goethe's *Faust II*, expressionist poetry or Greek tragedy, the latter perceived as German, honoris causa. The most celebrated resources of bourgeois culture shared the stage with economic crisis. To emphasize the affront, Brecht shows us the latter in the satirical and bloody setting of the meat-packing industry, where slaughter, financial reasoning and hunger naturally coexist. The novelty was not in the artistic contrast between the modern world and the classical tradition; the comical gulf between the Homeric hero and the fat-bellied capitalist was a commonplace of the nineteenth century. Similarly, there was nothing new in modernist writers endowing contemporary episodes with a semblance of the mythical in the attempt to provide them, even if ironically, with generality or archetypal dignity, or else to accentuate their sordidness: Gide, Proust, Thomas Mann, Kafka, Eliot, Joyce. In Brecht's work, which belongs to the same years, more or less, that distance between illustrious models and the tone of the present assumes its own distinctive shape. The cold yet mocking concatenation of the rawest economic interest and the loftiest philosophical and lyrical idealism of the German classical tradition, under the sign of capitalist crisis, gives birth to a Frankenstein monster. Even today, the fierceness of that caricature sends a chill down the spine.

Take, for example, the ingenious variations with which the canned-meat magnates formulate their distress — caused by unfulfilled contracts — in the majestic terms of 'Hyperion's Song of Destiny'. In his great lyric, Hölderlin contrasts a realm of the gods, where blessed spirits tread soft earth, peaceful as sleeping infants, while their eyes 'look out in still / Eternal clearness' to the lot of men:

> But we are given
>   No place to rest;
>   Suffering humans
>   Falter and tumble
>   Blindly from one
>   Hour to the next,
>   Like water from crag
>   To crag, hurled down
>   Year after year into the Unknown.

Here there is a Promethean tone in the nobility attributed to the 'Unknown', to suffering and dissatisfaction, in contrast to the serene plenitude of the divine. In *Saint Joan*, the first allusion to 'Hyperion' comes in the form of a warning from the other Salvation Army soldiers, when Joan decides to find out 'who's to blame' for the desperate lot of the stockyard workers:

In that case, Joan, your future looks black to us.
Don't get involved in earthly strife.
It will engulf you.
Your purity won't last, and soon
Your bit of warmth will perish in
The all-pervading cold.
Goodness departs from those who leave
The comforting hearth fire.
Striving downward step by step
In search of an answer never to be found
You will vanish in the muck!
For muck is what gets heaped upon those who
Ask incautious questions.[10]

In place of Hyperion's fall, we have the deliberate descent of Joan, who wants to find out about the misery that reigns down there, in the 'Unknown': a heroic descent and, in that sense, an ascension, though this is not the view of the Black Straw Hats, who are afraid that Joan will be engulfed by 'muck' and 'earthly strife' – suggesting an affinity between the Unknown and the poorer classes – or that the muck will be used (by whom?) to shut her up. The schema reappears in the language of the meat king, Cridle, who takes the lockout as an opportunity to buy some meat-processing machines that 'save a pretty penny in wages':

New contraption. Pretty fancy.
The pig rides up on a conveyor belt
Of wire netting to the topmost floor
And there the butchering begins. The pig
Plunges almost unaided, landing on
The knives. Not bad, eh? See, the pig
Butchers itself, converts itself to sausage.

---

10 Brecht, *Saint Joan*, scene 3.

> From floor to floor descending, first forsaken by
> Its hide, to be fashioned into leather
> Then parting with its bristles, used for brushes
> And lastly casting off its bones — which give us bone meal —
> It's forced by gravity into the can
> That's waiting down below. Not bad, eh?[11]

Here, the process is seen from the viewpoint of the gods — the industrial capitalists — who precipitate the fall of the mortal towards the Unknown: the waiting can of meat. The victim's fate is frighteningly close to that of the locked-out stockyard workers.

Convinced of the injustice suffered by the workers, Joan goes to join them in the stockyards, where the Communists are trying to organize a general strike, while the Army is using machine guns to clear the area. Assailed by hunger, fear and a horror of violence, Joan decides that her place is not there. Taking a didactic distance from herself, she describes her position:

> For three days Joan was seen
> In Packingtown, in the swamp
> Of the stockyards, going down
> Lower and lower, hoping to transfigure the muck
> And be a light to the poorest of the poor.
> For three days striding downward
> She weakened on the third day and in the end was
> Swallowed by the swamp. Say:
> 'It was too cold.'[12]

The descent has a Christian undertone and a salvational purpose, yet the pressure of misery — or the power of those above — prevails. At first glance, to be 'swallowed by the swamp' might mean to

---

11   Ibid., scene 3.
12   Ibid., scene 9.

lose oneself among the exploited, in their anonymous mass. At second glance, bearing in mind that Joan is speaking of having to leave the workers, it might suggest a return to her former petty privileges. Meanwhile, the meat king Mauler, Cridle's partner, has signed big contracts with the owners of the packing plants while quietly buying up all the available livestock. To fulfil their contracts, the meat packers are obliged to buy the carcasses from Mauler, whose agent raises the price higher and higher, finally causing the collapse of the meat-packing industry and the livestock market:

> Like water hurled from crag to crag, the prices
> Fell from quotation to quotation, plumbing
> Unfathomable depths. They stopped at thirty.

Here, it is the commodity price that plunges from the heights into the unknown of a stock-market crash. With the general strike crushed, however, the economy begins to function once again, on Mauler's terms: with fewer employees and higher meat prices – for the system can only be preserved, he explains, 'by taking extreme measures'. Helped by a large donation from Mauler, the Black Straw Hats prepare the soup and fling open the Mission doors to snare the redundant workers. In this case, the descent into the Unknown ends in unemployment, charity and religion:

> Here we stand! There, they're coming down. They are coming down!
> Misery drives them in our direction like herded animals!
> Look, they must descend!
> Look, they are descending, they're descending!
> Here they can't escape. For here we stand!
> Welcome! Welcome! Welcome! Welcome down to where we are![13]

---

13   Ibid., scene 10.

What lies behind these compositional sarcasms? We find ourselves on the terrain of the political cartoons of the Weimar period or Grosz's paintings – capitalists with thick necks, pig snouts, impeccable frock coats and bullet-proof cynicism crossing those mutilated by war, malnourished proletarians and starving dogs, all crowned by clichés of official humanism in an atmosphere of everyone-for-himself. Within the unfolding theatrical plot, however, these same stereotypes enter a dynamic of another order. Even as the Black Straw Hats and stockyard owners are singing their hosannas – 'Greatness to the great!' – loudspeakers begin to announce terrible news:

POUND CRASHES! BANK OF ENGLAND CLOSES FOR FIRST TIME IN 300 YEARS! EIGHT MILLION UNEMPLOYED IN USA! FIVE YEAR PLAN A SUCCESS! BRAZIL POURS A YEAR'S COFFEE HARVEST INTO THE OCEAN! SIX MILLION UNEMPLOYED IN GERMANY! THREE THOUSAND BANKS COLLAPSE IN USA! EXCHANGES AND BANKS CLOSED DOWN BY GOVERNMENT IN GERMANY! BATTLE BETWEEN POLICE AND UNEMPLOYED OUTSIDE FORD FACTORY IN DETROIT!

At the news, those not engaged in declamations start screaming abuse at one another:

'You slaughtered too much livestock, you rotten butchers!' 'You should have raised more stock, you lousy stockbreeders!' 'You crazy money-grubbers, you should have employed more labour and handed out more pay-cheques! Who else will eat our meat?' 'It's the middle-man that makes meat expensive!' 'It's the grain racket that raises livestock prices!' – 'The guilt is yours, and yours alone!' 'You should have been in jail years ago!'[14]

---

14   Ibid., scene 12.

Brecht's aim was not to moralize – which he thought useless – but to sharpen critical intelligence. The coupling of lyrical-philosophical pastiche to the brutalities of economic competition offers a technique of great scope. It avoids segregating proletarian experience even while it gives expression to the divergence – to be overcome – between cultural excellence and the standpoint of the working class. Against any sentimentalization of working-class culture, Brecht considered that only by transcending its insularity could the perspective of the exploited attain its full scope and get the better of its antagonist. On the same grounds, he rejected the notion that portrayals of the workers should be confined to their immediate environment and to a naturalist register. He sought, on the contrary, to place that life within the entirety of contemporary culture. In *Saint Joan*, the realities of work and unemployment, hunger and cold, organized struggle and military massacre are presented in direct and decisive reciprocity with the strategies of capital, with aesthetic conventions and economic theories, with the propertied classes' sense of themselves, with the lessons of morality and of religion, with the new means of production – causing an extraordinary amplification of the present, to which these antagonistic mirrorings lend an unparalleled literary and polemical quality.

The modern situation of labour is projected and examined by re-evaluating, on the play's own terms, the lyricism of the Romantics, the sobriety of Greek tragic discourse and the Christian commitment to poverty. The social recalibration of these aesthetic forms produces fundamentally new meanings, as when the Romantics' cult of simplicity, in the form of the *Lied*, is brought into relation with the plight of the homeless caught in the middle of a snowstorm. The verses of the song, written on a drop curtain, serve as a mute finale to the episode in which the machine guns triumph over the strikers:

> The snow's blowing this way
> So who would want to stay?
> The same as stayed before
> The stony soil and the very poor.[15]

These allusions to the most celebrated forms of German literature create a sort of lyrical topology: the sublime aspirations; the tragic downfalls; the Romantic idolization of summits and gorges, the divine ether composed of light, purity, immateriality and transcendence. In order for the parody to do its damage, these quasi-religious schemas need only be brought into focus alongside the capitalist exploitation of labour, to become the structural – and completely plausible – correlative of the contempt for what lies below, in the dark, in disorder, hungry and hard-working. Having drawn the parallel between the mountainous landscape of lyrical ascension and the social topography of capitalism, equally vertiginous, there is no way to stop the process of reciprocal contamination. The mountaineering of the poetic soul can be translated into the vernacular of free enterprise, with its inexhaustible greed, superprofits, bankruptcies and fraud; heights and depths can reverse their meanings.

5

But how much in this satire remains actual? The initial scandal of materialist criticism was its affirmation that capital, which is a class relation, was the secret of bourgeois society and the key to its laws, state, morality and culture. Far from promoting the human universality that they proclaimed, these spheres were systemically involved with economic exploitation – but an exploitation whose days would be numbered, once the exploited recognized it as a mere fact of class, without divine or natural guarantee. The virtuosity

---

15   Ibid., scene 9*g*.

with which Brecht makes us laugh at capital, presented in the very act of clothing itself as something else, more universal and less objectionable, belongs to the same epoch.

Today, the picture has changed. Economic determinism has switched sides and functions as an explicit ideology of the dominant classes, a justification for social inequality. 'The rules of the global economy are like the law of gravity', Bill Clinton famously announced. Naked profit-seeking, once a matter of shame, has become a public banner. If 'ideal' reasons had previously concealed material interests, understood to be particularist and so indefensible on generalist grounds, economic arguments – no less particularist – now serve to legitimate or undermine the rest. Governments will allocate funds for the arts on the basis of their benefits to tourism, or design educational reforms with an eye to gains in productivity. Proof of seriousness is now shown by subordination to the profit motive, whose anti-social tenor was once denounced as a dirty secret of class. The reversal imposed itself in jolts, but the process was arguably completed in the 1990s, when the necessities of capital became, to all intents and purposes, the equivalent of reason. What becomes of the relevance of *Saint Joan* in these circumstances? Does demystification, fixated on the hidden place of the economy in the order of things, become an empty gesture?

For an avant-garde writer of the Left to resort to the clichés of idealism as if they were a living force of the present would already have been strange when *Saint Joan* was written. Why restore to life what the Great War had buried? The Brechtian resurrection was naturally unique, emphasizing, to the utmost, the damage that the tradition had suffered, to the point of transforming it into a deformed and ridiculous figure – nonetheless endowed with reality. In the last scene of the play, poor Joan is canonized against her will and promoted as the patron saint of capital in its new phase, bathed in roseate light and accompanied by Goethean verses. This impudent and cynical proto-Hollywood kitsch provided a critical version of the falsifications with which Nazism was beginning to construct its grandiose idea of the national past and of itself. From another perspective, there was a commitment to making class conflict and canonical literature commensurable, so as to undo the conservative unctuousness that accompanied the latter and, therefore, return it to life.

In its own way, that cheek in dealing with bourgeois civilization's most prestigious ideas marked the threshold of a new era. The obsolete protocol of the idealist tradition is complementary, in this case, to the superlative cunning of the men of capital, who on the subject of demystification – if the term suggests the precedence of money over all else – represent the vanguard of the process. That said, the historical threshold of *Saint Joan* is another, more contemporary one. Since it nurtures and deepens the crisis, the capitalists' extraordinary cleverness changes meaning, in turn becoming obsolete and pernicious. What is on the stage, under the sign of crisis, is the transformation of the cunning of capital into reflexes that are counterproductive, almost antediluvian. The conjunction of gambling on the stock exchange and mass panic in face of the ups and downs of the economy suggests a loss of judgement on a species-wide scale.

In Brecht's structure, that negative progression – idealism overcome by cunning, which is revealed as blindness – is complemented by a positive movement: becoming unsustainable, the crisis foments the proletarian revolution, capable of transcending the impasse. Today there seems more to be gained from the play's configuration of that impasse, and of its deepening, than from its positing of the revolutionary exit, limited to the determination to win, or perhaps even die, so that other workers will win later on. Let us say that there is a lack of specific substance in the vision of 'overcoming' – a lack which, however, neither undoes nor attenuates the irrationalities to which it responds; irrationalities which, in the absence of a tangible alternative, take the shape (to borrow an expression from Benjamin) of permanent catastrophe: a metaphor for the historical present. It is this that we retain from Brecht's great play, at least until further notice.

Index